The Revelation of Jesus Christ

The Revelation of Jesus Christ

A Journey through the Apocalypse Guided by Its Purpose, Function, and Goal

Benjamin Gum

SOUL PURPOSE PUBLISHING
Books & Music

Copyright © 2020 Benjamin Gum
All rights reserved.
ISBN 978-1-7344962-7-7

Soul Purpose Publishing
Shawnee, KS

Unless otherwise noted, all Scripture quotations are taken from the Christian Standard Bible®, copyright © 2017 by Holman Bible Publishers. Used by permission. Christian Standard Bible® and CSB® are federally registered trademarks of Holman Bible Publishers.

Contents

ACKNOWLEDGEMENTS	IX
DEDICATION	XI
INTRODUCTION	1
LESSON 1: PREP WORK	**5**
The Interpreters	*5*
The Writer	*7*
The Date and Situation	*7*
The Genre	*9*
The Purpose	*12*
Interpretive Commitments	*12*
Reflection	*14*
LESSON 2: THE PURPOSE, FUNCTION, AND GOAL (CH.1, VV.1-3)	**15**
The Revelation of Jesus Christ	*15*
To His Servants	*16*
The PFG	*18*
Imminence	*20*
Reflection	*21*
LESSON 3: THE ONE BEING REVEALED (CH.1, VV.4-20)	**23**
The Main Character	*23*
The Witness	*24*
The Son of Man	*26*
The Temporal Template	*27*
Reflection	*28*
LESSON 4: TO THE SEVEN CHURCHES (CHS.2-3)	**29**
The Setting	*29*
Imminence for Them	*30*
Examining the Formula	*31*
Reflection	*41*
LESSON 5: THE ONE ON THE THRONE, THE SCROLL, THE LAMB, AND THE NEW SONG (CHS.4-5)	**43**
After this…	*43*
The One on the Throne	*44*
The Scroll	*47*
The Lamb	*48*
The New Song	*50*
Reflection	*52*

LESSON 6: THE FIRST SIX SEALS (CH.6) 53

    The Four Horsemen 54

    Lord, How Long? 55

    Who Is Able to Stand? 57

    Reflection 58

LESSON 7: THE SEALED AND THE SEVENTH SEAL (CH.7-CH.8, V.5) 59

    The Sealed 59

    The Vast Multitude 63

    Out of the Great Tribulation 65

    The Seventh Seal 67

    Reflection 69

LESSON 8: THE FIRST SIX TRUMPETS (CH.8, V.6 - CH.9) 71

    Succession or Recapitulation? 71

    About Trumpets 72

    The First Four Trumpets and the Thirds 73

    The Fifth Trumpet (The First Woe) 76

    The Sixth Trumpet (The Second Woe) 78

    Point of No Return? 80

    Reflection 81

LESSON 9: THE MYSTERY OF GOD, THE LITTLE SCROLL, THE TWO WITNESSES, AND THE SEVENTH TRUMPET (CHS.10-11) 83

    Opening discussion 83

    The Mighty Angel and the Mystery of God 83

    The Little Scroll 85

    The Two Witnesses 87

    The Functions of Testimony 91

    The Seventh Trumpet 92

    Reflection 94

LESSON 10: THE WOMAN, THE CHILD, AND THE DRAGON (CH.12) 95

    A Gospel Flashback 95

    A Gospel Short Story 95

    The Interpretation 96

    The War, the Banishment and the Proclamation 99

    The Persecution and Provision 101

    Reflection 103

LESSON 11: THE TWO BEASTS (CH.13) 105

    Opening Discussion 105

    The Beastly Proxies 106

Great Escape or Great Privilege? 116
Reflection 116

LESSON 12: THE LAMB, THE REDEEMED, AND THE HARVEST OF WRATH (CH.14) 119

The Lamb and the Redeemed 119
Three Proclamations 121
The Harvest 128
Reflection 130

LESSON 13: THE SONG, THE TEMPLE, AND THE BOWLS (CHS.15-16) 131

The Song of Moses and of the Lamb 131
The Heavenly Temple 135
The Seven Bowls 138

LESSON 14: THE PROSTITUTE AND THE BEAST (CH.17) 147

The Prostitute 147
The Beast 156
One Purpose 158
Reflection 160

LESSON 15: THE JUDGMENT OF BABYLON, EARTHLY LAMENTS, AND HEAVENLY PRAISE (CH.18 – CH.19, V.10). 161

The Initial Decree from Heaven 161
The Calling out of God's People 163
The Earthly Laments 166
The Final Decree 170
The Hallelujah Chorus 172
The Marriage Feast 175
Reflection 177

LESSON 16: VICTORY, THE MILLENNIUM, AND THE WHITE THRONE JUDGMENT (CH.19, V.11 – CH.20) 179

Victory over the Beast 179
The Millennium 184
Victory over Satan 191
The Problem of Why 192
Interpreting according to the PFG 194
The White Throne Judgment and the Second Death 195
Reflection 197

LESSON 17: THE NEW HEAVEN, THE NEW EARTH, AND THE NEW JERUSALEM (CH.21 – CH.22, V.5) 199

The New Heaven and New Earth 199
The New Jerusalem 204

LESSON 18: TESTIMONY, BLESSING, WARNING, AND INVITATION (CH.22, VV.6-21) 219

Reaffirming the PFG 219

Testimony, Blessing and Warning *219*
Invitation from the Spirit and the Bride *222*
Fatalistic Determination, or Free Invitation? *222*
Testimony of Warning Against Loss of Blessing *223*
Conclusion *226*

ABOUT THE AUTHOR **229**

Acknowledgements

I thank God above all for revealing Jesus Christ to me through the whole of his Word by the illumination of his Spirit and through the witness of his Church. I am so grateful for the contributions of many pastor-teachers, professors and theologians, many of whom instructed me unbeknownst to them in their own times and settings. I am equally grateful for the discussions with our church's Journey group that enriched and helped shape the content of this workbook.

It is one thing to come to conclude you might be starting to get a bare grasp on any biblical text, let alone the intimidating Apocalypse! It is quite another to somehow become convinced others might benefit from your particular approach and treatment of that text. For the compelling nudges that lead to this project, I am so very grateful for God's direct prompting and especially his working through my precious wife, Dawna, to encourage me that others have and might continue to be built up in their most holy faith through this work.

Thanks to all who contributed in these ways, and all praise to the One who collaborates with his creatures from his own generosity and for our own good.

Dedication

To the God whose nature makes it inevitable that you would reveal yourself especially to the creatures you made in your own image:

> Blessing and honor and glory and power
> be to the one seated on the throne,
> and to the Lamb, forever and ever!

Introduction

The first comprehensive Revelation study under which I can remember sitting occurred when I was a pre-teen. It was delivered from the pulpit of the independent Baptist church that was my church home until my early twenties. I recall detailed charts with vivid colors, timelines and a strong emphasis on the RAPTURE. (It probably did have all caps.) I remember gematria calculations to figure out best candidates for the Antichrist, and historical calculations regarding the temporal situations of both advents of the Christ, the regathering of national Israel, the events triggering the Millennium, the Great Tribulation and the end of the age.

All this amazing specificity – especially about the future – really ignited my interest in further study. So, I spent a lot of time in the coming years digging in greater detail through these subjects of the eschaton (the end of this age). That ongoing study rather effortlessly and seamlessly extended forward in the same interpretive camp. As is usually (and appropriately) the case, formal training exposed me to other, much older, and until recently, more widely adopted ways of seeing the text of Revelation.

So, a few months ago I thought again about the material widely circulated about this last book of the Bible. I thought about the potential unintended consequences of some interpretive dogmas. Especially I thought about the phenomenon of a subculture of evangelicals who gobble up fictional book series' and movies and online presentations that conflate those detailed charts with today's headlines. I contemplated why God put the Apocalypse in the canon for us, and essentially asked, "Are we using this gift for its intended purpose?" It seemed to me that many times we are not.

I've drawn a few conclusions regarding contemporary (and even some ancient) attitudes about Revelation. First, we tend to be extreme rather than balanced. That is, many of us either immerse ourselves in this book or avoid it altogether. The popular trend today echoes my own early infatuation with secret knowledge and forecasting, and naturally tends toward immersion. On the other side, the avoiders may be those put off by the difficult genre, the controversies of failed predictions or the fatigue of navigating a multitude of interpretive camps.

The immersion/aversion extremes are positions common among church leaders and teachers too. Those who believe they have most of the details figured out are eager to teach the Revelation, while those who know how difficult it can be to handle skillfully are eager to avoid it. It is much easier and safer to stick to the rich doctrinal books like the epistles that teach Christians how to live in this dark age. Why step into the fray? Still, we pastor-teachers are generally committed to the conviction that we are to teach the *whole* counsel of God. Wouldn't that necessarily include the matters of the eschaton as discussed in the Revelation?

In addition to the immersion/aversion extremes I also notice extremes in level of detail for those who do tackle the book. Many go after the text as though John was commissioned to record the

The Revelation of Jesus Christ

minutiae of the key future events for the church and cosmos. They seem to operate under the high goal of determining exactly where we are on the timeline. Everything is literal, every detail is a temporal clue, every event a time marker counting down to the Christian's escape and the judgment of all adversaries. The pushback against this approach is not so much whether the details can be accurately *discerned* but whether they are the *focus*. However, others approach the text in the opposite way. They see broad strokes of good and evil, and do not bother with many details at all.

Your favorite satellite mapping app might provide a helpful analogy. If you want to see what your hometown looks like, you can open the app and start from, say, 40,000 feet. The view here is much like from an airplane. You can see everything, but you may not be sure whether you are even looking at the right area. So, you drop to 10,000 feet. Now, perhaps you can make out some landmarks you recognize. You can still take in the big picture, but you can get a better sense of what you are seeing. You try 2,000 feet and find you can make out a good deal of detail. Drop to the bird's eye view and you can recognize homes and cars and probably even people. Of course, you can go all the way to street view and see your own home (probably from 2 or 3 years ago), but at this level you cannot see anything more than a few houses away.

Many teachers of Revelation seem stuck near the ground level, trying to make sense of today's headlines but without accessing an elevated perspective that reveals the context of the whole town. Others may stay at 40,000 feet and avoid the disputes below, but they will struggle to find in the message of Revelation much practical application after ch.3 (although the end of the book is really nice too). One extreme divides Christians endlessly while the other barely needs to call itself Christian. As I have already mentioned, the zoomed-in level seems by far the most popular today. I pondered with concern the results of our interpretive approaches regarding this book. If we avoid Revelation, or if we look at it only idealistically, we will likely diminish our sense of urgency. It will be easier to focus on or blow off our Christianly duties of the moment, oblivious to the great cosmic struggle working toward a climax around and beyond us. But I am even more concerned about the impact of the other extreme.

Having grown up with decades of exposure to a more zoomed-in view, I realized that even with the best of intentions my brain was being trained with a thinking that was not quite biblical and that I now believe to be accidentally opposed to the clear purpose of Revelation. I am afraid we have been inadvertently teaching the next generation (of currently non-persecuted Christians, at least) that God will almost assuredly rescue them before things get bad. I'm concerned that we might be preparing our grandkids to buckle posthaste under the first hints of actual persecution. I'm convinced Revelation was given to the church as an inoculation against exactly that.

To leverage this gift, and to take advantage of Revelation's purpose as stated within the book itself, we must let Revelation tell *us* the proper zoom level. I'm convicted careful inspection of the text reveals a metric for setting a general elevation for our perspective. This still allows for us to zoom in and out for reflection but keeps us generally at a level that keeps the whole picture in view while

Introduction

still seeing enough detail to allow the book to accomplish in us its practical objectives. We'll discuss a little later how that all works, but I have become convinced that many studies fail to operate at the level the book itself prescribes for us.

So, I was prompted to take action. I concluded we must not avoid Revelation even while we are careful not to become too enamored with it, at least in asking of it what it is not meant to deliver. It is not, after all, The Revelation of All Details Contemporary Christians Would Like to Know. It is the Revelation of Jesus Christ. (We'll talk about that when we discuss the prologue.)

It is reasonable to expect that the details of God's plan will be clearest to those nearest the culmination of that plan. This is somewhat affirmed internally by Revelation's calls to wisdom (13:10; 17:9) connected with what is being revealed. Still, we should be wary of thinking we in the last couple centuries have figured out all the fine points that have been fuzzy for nearly two millennia. We are likely not more convinced than the original readers that this book is about our own time. If we are not more *convinced*, it may also be that we are not more *correct*.

I also concluded it must be crucial to understand what this text IS meant to deliver, so that we can stay anchored to that mooring. We'll tackle the purpose, function and goal of the book in the prologue. For a teaser here, let me point out that those calls for wisdom are connected to the call for endurance (13:10; 14:12). In fact, the book speaks a lot more about faithful perseverance than it does about wisdom. The wisdom that comes through the Revelation is not its goal but the means to that end. Christ calls his followers to be people who *conquer* (seven times, once to each church in chs.2-4). What mysteries are peeled back in this book are exposed for the purpose of – and to the degree necessary for – compelling the Christ-follower to go faithfully all the way to whatever personal end, knowing the end of all is secure in Christ. Convinced of that, I was personally challenged to initiate a careful, guarded and guided look at this book with a mind to let it accomplish God's same purposes in myself and others around me.

So, I decided to gather some friends and try very hard to tackle Revelation the way I am convinced it is intended to be heard and understood. In the first case, that meant walking through the book together with a Sunday adult class at the church where I am a staff pastor. Now, since the indications have been that that endeavor was uniquely fruitful, I have attempted to collect and refine that study in the form of this workbook.

Let me explicitly acknowledge that many brighter and more skillful people have faithfully and carefully exposited, taught and obeyed this text. I do not mean to imply that anyone reaching different conclusions or having a different focus is necessarily sloppy, errant, or worst of all, that they are heretical or devious. This study is not intended as an apologetic against any interpretive system per se, though I will try to expose some of the challenges for those systems as is appropriate. Rather, it aims to be a properly focused approach that gives honorable treatment to interpretive options as they come up but keeps as its guiding dogma the purpose, function and goal of the book as stated in the prologue.

The Revelation of Jesus Christ

I have already acknowledged my early and long history with the currently popular interpretive system, and so it has already gotten special attention by default. This work does NOT aim to deconstruct that system but will inherently de-emphasize certain dogmas found at the level where that and competing systems divide. In other words, if I have done this right, by the end of this study a Dispensationalist or Amillennialist may still be so (perhaps even *more* so!), but she will be less concerned whether she is so.

See if this joke helps. An Amillennialist, a Postmillennialist and three Premillennialists (if we are free to laugh at ourselves) walk into a bar for a Bible study on Revelation. (Better make that a coffee bar, just to be safe.) Just as the study concludes, Jesus comes back. Who got stuck with the tab?

That's not much of a joke, but it can make my point. In spite of all their different conclusions, none of these is stuck with the tab unless they completely missed the point of the Bible study and turned out to not have true faith. I believe if we study Revelation correctly, we'll care relatively little whether or where we fall into those tribal distinctions. What will come out of the meeting is a like-mindedness to encourage one another to persevere in following Christ all the way to the end, whether that's the end of the age for us personally or for the whole cosmos collectively.

So, our commitment is to stay tethered to what John gives us in the prologue as the purpose, function and goal (PFG) of the Revelation. We will commit to not missing the forest for the trees. When appropriate we will offer major various interpretive options, but we will strive to keep our primary focus zoomed to exactly one point. **The PFG sets our zoom and focus.** As it turns out, when we are focused this way, we will find that this is where we happen to find wide agreement among evangelicals and a high degree of clarity in the text.

Lesson 1: Prep Work

Sometimes car maintenance is a big deal, while many times it's not. However, even doing relatively minor work on an automobile can open someone up to big, even dangerous, problems. For example, as issues come up, I tend to be a DIY guy on routine things like brakes. I may take a wheel or two off to inspect my brakes and find I can go ten or twenty thousand more miles before service. Any certified mechanic knows that even though I have done no repairs and replaced no parts, I have created a new risk that I must mitigate. I have to put the wheels back on properly. If I forget to properly replace and torque all my lug nuts, I risk damage and possibly an accident, even injury or death.

It is for this very reason that mechanics are heavily ingrained with developing habits. *Do it the same way every time and you will minimize mistakes and avoid bad, even disastrous, outcomes.* It is similar for biblical interpreters. I don't just mean the academics, seminary profs and pastors. It is important for every one of us who wants to understand the Bible that we have a consistent, disciplined approach to the text, that we have good interpretive habits.

I emphasize this because it seems that many do well in this respect with other books of the Bible and then for some reason abandon some of those habits with Revelation. That may be more dangerous than forgetting to torque your lug nuts. People have done some strange things when their study of the Apocalypse went off its wheels! So, given what's at stake, let's walk through some good interpretive prep work.

Much of the prep work is external to the text, so this first lesson will largely focus on interpretive process, historical information and analysis that concludes with some discussion. The lessons that follow will be aimed at exposition and interpretation of, and then reflection upon, the biblical text itself. The primary consideration for breaking up the text is to keep a sense of the book's flow and stay tethered to the PFG. The secondary goal is to keep the chunks manageable to target one lesson of this workbook as suitable for a single (roughly one hour) study session. Of course, you should take on as much or as little as you need, depending on the settings and where the discussions lead. The prep work may prove challenging to cover in one session, but as it is so crucial to the study itself, I have kept it all in this first lesson and offset its length with only a few very pertinent discussion questions at the end.

Let's dig in!

The Interpreters

The first thing the interpreter does is look in the mirror to know himself. If we need the mechanic's disciplined routine, the first thing we surely need from that routine is seeing the nametag stitched onto the uniform and understanding what comes with it. Why is this important? We need to know what background, what preconceptions, what distractions we bring with us to this work of understanding Scripture.

We have to realize that we are not flat, disinterested data processors that take in biblical information and mechanically render accurate and practical outcomes. We are more like the algorithm-driven social media engines of our day. We tend toward *desired* outcomes. We skew the data. We come to the text – in this case the Revelation – already loaded with some ideas. Our starting point is us: we read *from* our own situation, our own background and our own ideas about everything and probably about this text.

We must not only recognize this but work as hard as possible to set these things aside. We are not *telling* God what he means but *asking* him what he means. This first task is impossible to perform completely but crucial to undertake wholeheartedly. We are attempting to strip away, to acknowledge and surrender to God's guiding Spirit, every possible influence that we bring to the task that would cause us to read IN to God's communication rather than to read OUT of it. Before the meaning of the text can be exposed (*exegesis* means *reading out*), our accumulated biases must be exposed.

We are limited and weak to shed these biases, but we must consciously search for them, admit them and submit them to God so that his Spirit might navigate us through them to the real meaning of the text. On one level this sounds mystical, but on a practical level it amounts to confessing, "I probably think I understand this way better than I really do. Lord, help me lose my own ideas about what this means, and truly hear you speak, understand you and obey you." In other words, *please join me in praying that God directs our understanding of his Word through his Spirit.*

What biases might we bring? For many, we have to loosen our mental grip on previous teaching on Revelation. In my case, that meant holding out open hands that held years of doctrine informed by a particular fundamentalist dogma. Perhaps your bias is similar, or maybe it is formed in the popular arena. Maybe most of what you already believe about the Revelation finds its source in a fictional book series or a movie. It may be that your only bias has been that position of aversion mentioned earlier, the conclusion that this book is inaccessible and so has no practical relevance to you. Whatever the case, *take inventory and relax your grip.*

We also must realize that we have a 21st century mindset heavily influenced by modernism and post-modernism. This means we may be inclined to think we can figure out every minute detail, including those attached to the many symbols of the Apocalypse. Or we may be convinced objective truth – like the meanings of *any* of these symbols – is impossibly out of reach.

We may well also have a misunderstanding about this last book of the biblical canon. We may think that God intends for us – or at least someone – to understand and recognize everything going on in the last days. It is, after all, an apocalypse, which means something previously hidden is being revealed. But what is being revealed in this book? It may not be what we've come to think. Is it the exact identity of the Beast, or the precise meaning of his mark? Probably not.

Once we have prayerfully committed to recognizing and setting aside our own biases, we have other prep work to do. Our first task has much to do with forgetting what we *think* we know. Now we seek to accumulate other things we *can* know, for these will be tools the Spirit uses to guide our interpretation.

The Writer

Some books of the Bible are anonymous. That means that although his original audience may have known who wrote it, the *writer* does not identify himself. In other books the writer does identify himself by name and or often with a title, e.g., *"Paul an apostle of Christ Jesus..."* or *"The elder..."* If the book is not anonymous, it is important that we try to accurately identify the writer and ascertain what we can about him, for we may reasonably conclude that the Holy Spirit meant his identification to be a help in understanding the meaning of his writing. Did this writer compose any other biblical writings? If so, his use of words, phrases, symbols, etc. in one place may help us understand them in others.

John the Apostle has traditionally and widely been held to be the John who identifies himself in the opening verse of Revelation. History tells us he outlived the other eleven disciples, most or all of whom were martyred (excepting Judas). John's longevity makes sense of God's appointing him to deliver the final words of Scripture. This disciple was part of Jesus' inner circle of three, perhaps his closest earthly friend. It seems most appropriate that he would be given the task of penning the Revelation of Jesus Christ.

Suggestions that our writer is another John, perhaps the elder of the Johannine epistles (supposing that John to be different from the apostle), find only a minority of adherents. These opinions are largely based in the linguistic differences between Revelation and other writings attributed to John the Apostle. However, these can be explained by the fact that Revelation is a different and very unique genre, and they are offset by themes that are common among John's writings.

I see no convincing evidence to overturn the long and widely held view that Revelation's John is the disciple *"whom Jesus loved,"* the one of the Twelve who also penned the Gospel of John. So, to the extent authorship impacts interpretation, this workbook operates with this understanding.

The Date and Situation

If John the Apostle is the writer, it is also appropriate to hold the prevailing view about *when* he wrote Revelation. Again, there is early and widespread consensus. It is that John wrote late, probably around the mid-90's during the reign of the Roman emperor Domitian. This is not only possible but probable, given the historical record that John was still living then and in exile on the Isle of Patmos, as stated in Rv 1:9.

Minority opinions about alternate dates place this writing just before AD 70. These opinions are usually closely tied to an interpretive commitment called Preterism that we will address more in a moment. The Preterist requires this earlier date because he sees the events of chs.5ff as having already played out, culminating largely with the destruction of Jerusalem in AD 70. This view has some significant problems, not the least of which is that many events in the book do not seem to be adequately fulfilled in the first century. For these reasons, this study presumes the traditional date in the 90's.

Dating the book is only the beginning of a bigger challenge to learn of John's setting. We want to put on John's skin. What is the view from his chair? What are the joys and stresses of his day? Even while John is living in exile, what is going on in his culture, his church? What sayings are his contemporary readers registering? These things add up to his *situation*. We need to know all we can about John's situation and that of his audience to understand his writing, so we draw from G.K. Beal here for some crucial information.

Persecution from Rome
"Though it was sporadic, there was an ongoing threat that Christians would be brought before Roman officials and asked to show their loyalty to the emperor by invoking the Roman gods "according to the [set] formula, offering sacrifices of wine and incense before the emperor's image and cursing Christ." For a polytheist to say "Caesar is Lord" was not problematic, but for a genuine Christian, doing so was a direct contradiction of the confession that "Jesus is Lord." Christians could respond to this situation in a number of ways. First, they could recant and deny their Christian faith, as Pliny records that some did. Secondly, they could openly confess Christ and suffer persecution, as Pliny also tells us happened. Thirdly, they could compromise, which is what some of the false teachers in the churches were encouraging (2:14–15, 20)."[1]

Pressure from Judaism
"According to Roman law, religions were considered illegal outside their country of origin, though this was not enforced unless there was overt social misbehavior associated with the practice of a religion. The only exception to this law was Judaism, the practice of which was allowed throughout the Empire. Christians were probably considered a sect of Judaism until 70 a.d., though they likely would not have been completely disassociated from Judaism in the minds of pagans in the years following 70. After that date Judaism made formal attempts to dissociate itself from Christianity, at least partly because Christians claimed that Jerusalem's destruction was punishment for the Jews' crucifixion of Jesus. Furthermore, Christianity was winning a significant portion of Gentile "godfearers" to its ranks, who formerly had associated themselves with synagogue worship. This likely increased Jewish animosity toward the church. The antipathy

---

[1] Beale, G. K. (1999). *The book of Revelation: a commentary on the Greek text* (pp.31-32). Grand Rapids, MI; Carlisle, Cumbria: W.B. Eerdmans; Paternoster Press.

would have been heightened, since Jews would have viewed Christianity as offering the godfearers a cut-rate Judaism whereby salvation could come without the obligation of keeping the Law."[2]

Trade Guilds and Patron Deities
"Apparently, a significant group among the Asia Minor churches did not think it a grave sin to show open expressions of loyalty to such trade guild deities. This was especially the case when they were expected to pay their "dues" to trade guilds by attending annual dinners held in honor of the guilds' patron deities. Homage to the emperor as divine was included along with worship of such local deities. For the culture in general these expressions of loyalty were part of being patriotic. After all, the patron gods of the guilds together with the imperial god of Rome were purportedly responsible for the social and economic blessings that the culture had enjoyed. Refusal to show gratefulness to these gods was bad citizenship. The likelihood that demands of emperor worship slowly but surely were increasing would have intensified this situation. There was probably no official, widespread demand to show loyalty to the imperial cult, but there is at least evidence that references to the emperor as god, especially in Domitian's reign, were used by both provincial Roman officials and local people who were trying to flatter the emperor in order to gain the favor of Rome."[3]

Summary
If we put all these things together, we get a good sense of the situation from which John writes. *His first century audience was surrounded by pressures to compromise or even abandon their faith.* Within the church communities were self-seeking false teachers and Judaizers who wanted to corrupt the gospel. Outside the church were pressures from Jews who rejected Christ as well as pagan authorities and a populace who were entrenched in polytheism. Christian faith, expressed publicly, could bring financial ruin, disassociation in the public square, imprisonment or even execution. John knew these pressures well, as he penned the book from the situation of his own exile for his expressed Christian faith. Knowing these details, especially the issues surrounding the trade guilds, will be very important as we try to understand John's message, first to his contemporaries and then to later readers like ourselves.

The Genre
Once we have an idea of the writer and his situation, we need to know what kind of work he is writing. Is it a friendly letter? Is it aimed at doctrinal instruction? Is it poetic? Understanding the *genre* – or genre *combination* – of this book is critical to understanding what God is telling us through John. This is especially important as we decide how deeply to dig into the details and how confident or measured to be about our conclusions. This seems to be where many interpreters have abandoned their otherwise good interpretive habits.

---

[2] Beale, G. K. (1999). *The book of Revelation: a commentary on the Greek text* (pp.30-31). Grand Rapids, MI; Carlisle, Cumbria: W.B. Eerdmans; Paternoster Press.
[3] Ibid.

The Revelation of Jesus Christ

Many notable pastors, authors, and theologians who are widely recognized for their careful and skillful treatments of biblical books and topics seem to me to modify their own methods when they tackle Revelation. When defending their highly literal interpretations of the book, some of them offer the classic mantra: "I take the text literally unless given some good reason to do otherwise." I think that's a sound commitment. I also think we do in fact *have* good reasons to not force literalism on much of what we read in Revelation.

The first reason has to do with the genre combination defined internally by the writer himself. In the first sentence – in fact the first word in the Greek – John defines this work as a revelation, or *apocalypse*. Two verses later he twice calls it a *prophecy*. Apocalyptic-prophetic is a blend of distinct but very similar biblical genres that has as a major feature its use of symbolism. Apocalyptic is characterized by use of symbols and the symbolic use of numbers. It also frequently resists temporal restraints, often finding fulfillment in the present or near future, the distant future and then an ultimate fulfillment. Prophecy is characterized as speaking the words of God, and by warnings and calls for repentance.

This means that from the outset we should read this book expecting to run into images and descriptions that are meant to point to non-literal – or bigger-than-literal – realities. That's exactly what we find. Yet somehow many interpreters who quickly agree John is not looking at a literal slaughtered lamb in ch.5 still want to a count a literal 144,000 ethnic Jews in ch.7. Even if the latter is a literal accounting, the genre demands that we ask this: What is the symbolic *function* of this number broken down by tribes?

This question will apply to a lot of important numbers in the book, especially the number seven. Even in John's Gospel he is fond of sevens (e.g., seven signs), and Revelation is full of them:

- Churches/lampstands (1:4,11,12,20; 2:1; 3:1)
- Angels/stars (1:20; 2:1; 3:1; 8:2,6; 15:1,6,7,8; 16:1; 17:1; 21:9)
- Spirits of God (1:4; 3:1; 4:5; 5:6)
- Seals (5:1,5; 6:1)
- Thunders (10:4)
- Trumpets (8:2,6)
- Bowls (15:7; 16:1; 17:1; 21:9)
- Heads/mountains/kings (12:3; 13:1; 17:3,7,9-11)

Many accounting options see seven sevens in the book. Sevens are so prevalent that many prefer to outline the book something like the following from Kevin DeYoung:

Prep Work

    Prologue: 1:1-8
- I. Seven letters: 1:9-3:22
- II. Seven seals: 4:1-8:5
- III. Seven trumpets: 8:6-11:19
- IV. Seven visions: 12:1-15:4
- V. Seven bowls: 15:5-16:21
- VI. Seven judgments: 17:1-19:10
- VII. Seven last things: 19:11-21:8
- VIII. The beautiful bride: 21:9-22:21

(DeYoung points out that eight is a biblical representation of new creation and suitable for the last part of the outline. That's a pretty cool argument, at the least!)

In addition to all these sevens, we also find threes, fours, tens, twelves and multiples that, while they may have literal expression as well, certainly carry clear symbolic meaning.

We should also expect to find material that seems to be set in the present or near future and other material that seems farther off and events that seem to find a climax or a final fulfillment. That's what we do find. We should also expect calls for repentance and reform. We find that too.

We also discover that while this book is a revelation, it still contains mystery. In fact, it directly declares so several times (1:20; 10:7; 17:5,7). This reminds us that we should not expect all details to be exhaustively exposed.

Genre in Revelation becomes even more complicated and more important than the implications of apocalyptic-prophetic. It is also a *letter* (epistle) that Jesus himself commands John to circulate among the churches (1:11). So, our interpretation is also influenced by epistolary concerns. Christ himself addresses problems in the churches and establishes themes that are continued throughout the book, themes that relate to all the churches then, and find application for all churches since.

So, Revelation is a rare blend, not quite like any other book in the Bible. Beale, whom we cited above, summarizes this way:

> "Therefore, the most preferable view is that Revelation is "a prophecy cast in an apocalyptic mold and written down in a letter form" in order to motivate the audience to change their behavior in the light of the transcendent reality of the book's message."[4]

---

[4] Beale, G. K. (1999). *The book of Revelation: a commentary on the Greek text* (p.39). Grand Rapids, MI; Carlisle, Cumbria: W.B. Eerdmans; Paternoster Press.

The Revelation of Jesus Christ

The Purpose

The next reason we should not get too stuck on literalism is because of the purpose of the book. This is a key corrective to a large number of studies out there, and that is why I have written so much about it already in the introduction. Even more than the genre blend, I think a strong tethering to the purpose of this book will generally keep us zoomed out to a higher level where the concerns and difficulties of understanding many specific details lose some of their gravitational pull.

God gave us a gift here, and we do not want to miss it. He told us explicitly, clearly, immediately, and throughout the book what his purpose was in giving this revelation to John for his churches. We find it in 1:1: *"...to show his servants what must soon take place."* Sadly, many interpreters hang their hats there and do not incorporate the clarification of v.3 into that guiding purpose statement. V.1 is the WHAT, but v.3 gives the WHY: *blessing*. In that verse we also get the HOW: through *hearing* and *keeping* the words of the prophecy. We'll go into more detail about the purpose, function and goal when we study the prologue of the book. Suffice it here to say that I am convinced that many have labored over Revelation trying to satisfy secondary or even tertiary concerns while largely unplugging from that stated primary purpose, function and goal.

Interpretive Commitments

The last part of prep work I want us approach most carefully. Picking back up on our self-examination as interpreters, it may be helpful to see whether we already feel like we fit into one of the major interpretive camps. I cannot stress enough that my goal in presenting the following information is neither to further entrench anyone in a particular camp nor to encourage them to abandon it. The goal is self-awareness.

That said, here are the major interpretive views on Revelation:

1. **Preterist**: Revelation is either A) a prophecy about the fall of Jerusalem in AD 70 (in which case Jerusalem = Babylon) or B) the fall of the Roman Empire in the 5th century (in which case Rome = Babylon).
2. **Historicist**: Revelation predicts major historical movements of Christianity – represented by the seven churches – most or all of which were future to the original audience and are mostly history for us today.
3. **Futurist**: Revelation is primarily a prophecy about the very end of the age, focused almost entirely or entirely on the last few years before Christ's return.
4. **Idealist**: Revelation is a non-historic and non-prophetic symbolic portrayal of good vs. evil.
5. **Mixed** or **Eclectic**: Most notable commentators opt for some blend of the above.

Here you may clearly see some of the characteristics of zooming in or out as discussed. You may also see some of the challenges faced by proponents of the first four views. If one takes the Apostle Paul literally in 2 Timothy 3:16, she may conclude that while Scripture is not written directly *to*

Prep Work

her it is all written *for* her. This would make it challenging to hold a strict version of any of the first three views, since they do not see Revelation as offering value to all generations of the church. Of course, many soften or blend these views for this very reason. It would be odd to read a letter from Paul as though it had application for today's Christian and then to cut Revelation out of your Bible as only relevant to the first century saints.

Likewise, on some Historicist or Futurist views, this letter that got circulated in the early centuries of the church would have been no revelation for them, since its meaning would be tied to the end of the age. Of course, the Idealist has to explain why there are in fact so many particulars in the book if they are unimportant. It seems a proper zoom really matters.

As you can imagine, most Christians who engage the book seriously take some kind of Mixed view. Still, I would argue that the teachers behind the popular materials flooding Christian media today function as mostly Futurists (seeing our time as the time being described near the end of the age), although I'm quite sure most of them would define their own views as Mixed.

There are a few more related terms and categories you may have heard that I think are worth listing here. These have to do especially with the latter chapters of Revelation where it discusses a millennium period where Christ reigns on earth before a final rebellion, judgment and the renovation of all creation.

Here are the major views on the Millennium:

1. **Amillennialism:** There is no literal millennium but only a symbolic one that depicts the struggle of the Church to spread the gospel until Christ's return.
2. **Premillennialism:**
    a. Historic: Believers and unbelievers go through the Tribulation, then Christ returns to establish his millennial reign before final rebellion, judgment and the final state.
    b. Dispensational: Christ returns for his Church and *then* unbelievers go through all or the last part of the Tribulation.
3. **Postmillennialism:** Christ comes *after* the millennium (whether a literal or figurative amount of time), a culmination in a glorious final state after the age where the Church triumphs.

Whew! That is a lot of important prep work! We aim to humbly approach the text asking God to speak clearly and give us ears to hear. We may find ourselves tucked neatly away in one or more of these interpretive camps, or we may feel completely free of them. There's a good chance we will come out thinking differently about this book than we do going in. I hope we do. Whatever the case, I will again encourage you to approach the text with an open mind and with a commitment to these good prep work habits we have now defined.

The Revelation of Jesus Christ

Reflection

Have you ever been through a study on Revelation? If so, what was it like?

In your experience, if Revelation comes up in a conversation, what topics are usually being discussed?

Which part of the prep work struck you as most important for you personally? How will it impact this study for you?

Lesson 2: The Purpose, Function, and Goal (Ch.1, Vv.1-3)

We have prayerfully prepared ourselves to hear God speak through the text of Revelation. Now, in this lesson we will focus on a small opening portion of the prologue. Like all Scripture, the first three verses of this text are living and powerful, and we will surely be reflecting on them millions of years from now and still find them invigorating.

For now, we probably have around an hour, so we want to make it count. We are only covering this small portion in this lesson because it sets the table for all our meals to follow. We must not only hear and understand as God reveals his purpose, function and goal (PFG) but we must also carry these with us into every portion that follows in this multi-course feast.

First, read the text (preferably aloud) and then we will work hard together to grasp it and carry it with us.

> **Revelation 1:1-3**
> **1** The revelation of Jesus Christ that God gave him to show his servants what must soon take place. He made it known by sending his angel to his servant John, **2** who testified to the word of God and to the testimony of Jesus Christ, whatever he saw. **3** Blessed is the one who reads aloud the words of this prophecy, and blessed are those who hear the words of this prophecy and keep what is written in it, because the time is near.

The Revelation of Jesus Christ

Immediately, we have grammatical options to consider. That this is a revelation *of* Jesus Christ can allow three meanings. First, Jesus Christ may be presented as *owner*. That sense means the revelation belongs *to* him. Second, Jesus may be the *witness*. In this case the revelation comes *through* him. Third, Christ may be the *object* of the revelation. Here, it is *about* him. Does John help us choose?

He does. In fact, he gives us good evidence that he means for us to take the Revelation of Jesus Christ according to *all* these options. He presents Jesus as the owner in v.1a, for it is something given to him by God. He also presents Christ as a witness to the revelation, for in vv.1b-2 he is offering this revelation as testimony, and in v.5a John does in fact call Jesus not only *a* witness but *the faithful witness*. Then it becomes clear as we read through the rest of the prologue in vv.5b-18 that Jesus Christ is in fact the object of this revelation. He is the one being revealed. So, we may confidently conclude that John intends for us to take Jesus Christ as the owner of, witness to and object of this revelation.

That this is a revelation *about* Jesus brings up an important question that will relate strongly to the PFG of the whole book: *In what sense is something new being revealed about Jesus?* Hasn't

The Revelation of Jesus Christ

Jesus already been revealed? Does this book tell us something new about Jesus? Is there something about the Christ we wouldn't see apart from this book's inclusion in the Bible? Take a moment for the following questions:

What do we know about Jesus from the OT? From the Gospels? How is he presented in the theology of the NT writers like Paul, Peter, James, John (excluding Revelation) and Jude?

The NT writers present an already/not yet perspective of salvation, the kingdom of God and – to our point here – of Christ's reign. The Gospels record Christ's humiliation. The books that follow show his work of redemption as complete, and they are largely written to explain gospel realities more fully and to call Christians to express them in holy living. The fact of Christ's now-exalted status is acknowledged, especially in texts like the Christ Hymn of Php 2:5-11. The writer of Hebrews makes it clear that God has exalted Christ to the highest kingly authority by subjecting everything to him (Heb 2:5-8b). Still, it is acknowledged, *"As it is, we do not yet SEE everything subjected to him"* (v.8c, emphasis mine). He goes on to clarify the distinction: we *do* see Jesus now crowned with glory and honor, but we do *not* yet see everything subjected to him.

I think what the writer of Hebrews is expressing here is the answer to our question above. The Revelation of Jesus Christ gives us a vision of Jesus that is laid out theologically in the rest of the NT but is revealed only here as the reality that comes upon the entire cosmos at the end of this age. What we glimpsed as the Gospel writers took us to the Mount of Transfiguration, we will now see unfold completely as the Father's will is done through the exalted Christ on earth as it is in heaven. Jesus will be revealed not only *propositionally* but *personally* as the exalted King of Kings, the Lamb of God who comes to judge those who reject him and vindicate those who trust in him. The world has known the humble Suffering Servant, but this book reveals the Lord of Lords.

We will actually see a lesser but also important and related revelation in this book. John's visions will repeatedly peel back the curtain to reveal that behind the evil darkness of this world's human systems is the satanic and demonic power that fuels and catalyzes them. But every time that dark power is revealed, it pales in comparison to the unquestionably omnipotent God who is revealed in the person of Jesus Christ. So, evil is exposed and dealt with. Jesus Christ is revealed and reigns forever!

To His Servants

Next, we must consider an interpretive necessity we might well have covered in the prep work. *Who is John's audience as he passes on this revelation from and about Christ?* As we said earlier, because this is Scripture, we know it is written *for* all believers from John's day forward, but we

The Purpose, Function, and Goal

also know it was written *to* an original audience in a particular situation. A survey of the book reveals its relevance for both the original audience and all audiences to follow:
- *"to...his servants"* (1:1)
- *"to the seven churches"* (1:4,11,20)
- *"to the angel of the church in..."* (2:1,8,12,18; 3:1,7,14)
- *"to the churches"* (2:7,11,17,23,29; 3:6,13,22)
- *"for the churches"* (22:16)

Take a moment to consider the following:

How do these references show the book's value for the ancient audience and all future audiences (including us)? How do they show its relevance for both specific situations and for broader applications?

The recipients of this revelation are called "servants" of Jesus Christ. This is a strong term in the Greek that might also be translated "slaves." This is not the first time John has recorded Jesus revealing something to his servants.

> **John 15:12–17**
> **12** "This is my command: Love one another as I have loved you. **13** No one has greater love than this: to lay down his life for his friends. **14** You are my friends if you do what I command you. **15** I do not call you servants anymore, because a servant doesn't know what his master is doing. I have called you friends, because I have made known to you everything I have heard from my Father. **16** You did not choose me, but I chose you. I appointed you to go and produce fruit and that your fruit should remain, so that whatever you ask the Father in my name, he will give you.
>
> **17** "This is what I command you: Love one another.

According to v.15, how does Jesus elevate the status of his servants? How does this passage inform our understanding of the servant status of the audience in Rv 1:1? According to v.16 here, what is the goal of Jesus' informing his servants about what he is doing?

The Revelation of Jesus Christ

The PFG

It is common practice in biblical commentaries to attempt to identify the purpose of the book being considered. This is an important guide to interpretation in every case, and it is most helpful where it is most clear. In our case, I think it is important to break out three unified, but distinct, ideas related to the purpose of Revelation. All three are apparent in the prologue of its first chapter, and the design of the book reveals that its writing is governed according to the logical flow they imply.

There is a clear purpose to the book, and it has a clear goal in mind, stated both early and throughout. The third element is the interpretive crux: *How does the book function to accomplish its goal according to the stated purpose?* We may hear the purpose and aim at the goal, but if we misunderstand *how* the book is supposed to work, our interpretation can easily go sideways, and we may find ourselves perplexed and derailed somewhere out in the field.

So, let's look into the prologue to understand not only the purpose of the book, but how it is intended to function to bring about its stated goal. We'll take each in turn according to logical order.

Purpose

Any time we are seeking to understand Scripture, we are wise to ask why God led the writer to say this or that. What is the writer's intention, and how does that suit God's purpose? Sometimes we are given a clear purpose statement, like John gives in his Gospel: *"...these are written so that you may believe that Jesus is the Messiah, the Son of God..."* A "so that" is really helpful for the interpreter.

Here, in Rv 1:1 the clue is the word "to." God gave this revelation to do what? *"...to show his servants what must soon take place."* This is a clear purpose statement for the book. This is a revealing, a showing, of something – more than that, Someone. The *"things that must soon take place"* will be a *"revelation of Jesus Christ."* This revelation comes to God's servants through the testimony of witnesses. Christ is the first and perfect Witness (vv.1-2), and he then passes testimony through his angel to and then through John.

How does the witness of this revelation continue today?

The Purpose, Function, and Goal

Function

If the purpose of the book is expressed in the revealing of *who* and *what*, then it also functions to bring about some kind of *end*. How, when, and where does it function, and what is that end? We find out if we keep reading.

Notice the activities mentioned in v.3, for these are the functions that bring the revelation or testimony to bear in the lives of the servants. The words are *read*, they are *heard*, and they are to be *kept*. It is suitable to focus on the last one, for it is the fulfilling function of the first two. Reading and hearing are to lead to keeping. These activities are mentioned throughout Revelation (1:3; 2:26; 3:3,10; 12:17; 14:12; 22:7,9,11).

Once again, John's Gospel is helpful, for from it we already understand what is meant by *keeping* the words of Jesus. In particular, as Jesus discusses keeping his words in close conjunction with the term "commands," he makes clear that one can *have* his commands only or one can go further by also *keeping* them (Jn 14:21). The context makes it clear. To keep the words of Jesus is to *obey* them. To keep words about Jesus is to *believe* them and to *hold fast* to him. Another key term in Revelation that expresses this idea of keeping is *endurance* (1:9; 2:2,3,19; 3:10). To keep Jesus' words is to *endure*.

So, the purpose of this book is to reveal Jesus Christ in and through coming events. Christ is revealed through reading and hearing, and ultimately through keeping – obeying his commands and clinging to him.

Goal

That word "keeping" begins to propel us toward the *goal* of this book, and that too is very clear. The book is intended to bring *blessing*. This goal is given immediately here, given at the end and throughout (1:3, 2x; 5:12,13; 7:12; 14:13; 16:15; 19:9; 20:6; 22:7,14).

Blessing is a key theme of the entire biblical canon. God blessed his original good creation in the first chapters of Genesis. Then, even after the Fall, God began to announce his plan to restore blessing to his creatures. Through the covenants of the OT and then in the New Covenant God promised to bring blessing to all people groups through one chosen Seed, Jesus Christ himself. So, the blessing of Revelation brings full circle the blessing of Genesis and all of Scripture.

How does one get the blessing intended by the book? By keeping what they read or hear. This is where many studies seem to drift off center. The blessing does not come through a super-informed cleverness to figure out every detail of God's plan for the end of this age. It comes the way it is stated here, through obeying and clinging to Jesus, the one who is being revealed in these events to come. We don't have to fully understand everything that John writes to receive the blessing. We don't even have to always know for sure to what level of detail he means to communicate, so long as we understand what his symbols are intended to tell us. The symbols are clear. The details don't have to be. In fact, *it seems that the details have been brilliantly crafted with deliberate ambiguity such that the symbols communicate effectively to every generation of the Church until Christ returns.* We have to see and cling to the exalted Lamb that is being revealed. We have to obey his commands and stay true to him. That is the goal.

Summary
This little chart summarizes the PFG. These ideas will govern our treatment of the text from here forward.
- **P=Revealing** (what/who) The book does not reveal minutiae but essentials: 1) God's sovereign authority expressed in Jesus Christ and over 2) satanic evil empowering and catalyzing mankind's evil in the world. It is the revealing OF Jesus Christ. It also reveals the powers (demonic and human) that oppose Christ because this exposes them as seemingly power*ful* but ultimately power*less*.
- **F=Keeping** (how/when/where) The revelation delivers truth and hope. Calls for wisdom are coupled with calls to endure in the situations of the persecuted Christians who are looking for Christ's return at any time.
- **G=Blessing** (why) Revelation is given to bring believers through faithfulness to their blessing in the Christ who is revealed.

Taken together, we could express the unified **PFG** as follows: This book is given **to reveal Jesus Christ so that his servants faithfully endure suffering in order to receive blessing**.

Imminence

As we get on board with the stated PFG of this revelation, there is one more key idea we need to acknowledge from this beginning portion of the prologue. The long-standing Doctrine of Imminence is a significant emphasis. We see it here in the terms "soon" (v.1) and "near" (v.3). These terms, along with "quickly" are in play throughout the book (1:1,3; 2:16; 3:11; 11:14; 22:6,7,10,12,20). They can be used to describe something *about to happen*, something that will *happen quickly*, or both.

We know from Paul's writings to the Thessalonians that first century Christians looked eagerly for Christ's return in their own time. We see in Revelation that they were justified in that belief. Every generation of the Church since has also been right to believe Jesus could return in their own day. Jesus himself taught this doctrine in his parables about servants either awaiting the return of their master or, in the case of wicked servants, acting as though he was not coming back anytime soon (Lk 12:35-48).

The Doctrine of Imminence is woven into the PFG of Revelation. The servants are being shown what is coming so they will pay attention and be faithful. If they will persevere in faithfulness, then they will be rewarded with blessing, just as Jesus described in Luke's Gospel. What will unfold in Revelation will be the ultimate expression of persecution and suffering but also the incomparable blessing of vindicated saints.

The Purpose, Function, and Goal

Reflection

Remembering that many of them were suffering persecution, how important was it to Jesus' servants to hear that this book was given to provide blessing?

How is an understanding of the terms "servants" and "keep" important for both the original audience and for us?

Do you think we give enough attention to the Doctrine of Imminence today? How so, or why not?

Lesson 3: The One Being Revealed (Ch.1, Vv.4-20)

Layers are being peeled back in this revelation. Much of what we perceive in this age is distorted. Our own fallenness distorts our sense of things, and we are deliberately misled by the propaganda of a great Deceiver. He has honed his spin craft for millennia and is able to convince many that he is a god, even convincing them he is able to do things only a god can do, like raising the dead. His propaganda machine is exposed in Revelation, but even in that he is only a wannabe, a bit player.

The Main Character

Revelation exposes the true main character and the source of all reality. Ultimate truth is on display, as from the first words of the prologue this book reveals the One who is the rightful center of all attention and glory. Like the opening says, this is the revelation of Jesus Christ.

Having established the prophetic/apocalyptic nature of this writing, John now greets all the churches in letter form. Even in his greeting, John begins to point the spotlight on Jesus:

> **Revelation 1:4-6**
> **4** John: To the seven churches in Asia. Grace and peace to you from the one who is, who was, and who is to come, and from the seven spirits before his throne, **5** and from Jesus Christ, the faithful witness, the firstborn from the dead and the ruler of the kings of the earth.
>
> To him who loves us and has set us free from our sins by his blood, **6** and made us a kingdom, priests to his God and Father—to him be glory and dominion forever and ever. Amen.

How does John identify the Trinity in this greeting and dedication, and why is this important?

What specific phrases are used to describe Jesus, and how are each significant?

Who is the "him" in v.6, and why is this important?

The Revelation of Jesus Christ

John goes on to lift the listener's eyes to the skies, and makes a bold prediction drawing from OT passages like Dan 7:13 and Zech 12:10:

> **7 Look, he is coming with the clouds,**
> and **every eye will see him,**
> **even those who pierced him.**
> **And all the tribes of the earth**
> **will mourn over him.**
> So it is to be. Amen.

Notice the language of "look" and "see" as it relates to this revelation of Jesus. Remember that sometimes John will record hearing one thing and then seeing something else.

Who does John say will see Jesus, and why is that a big deal?

Who will mourn over Jesus, and why?

God then speaks in v.8:

> 8 "I am the Alpha and the Omega," says the Lord God, "the one who is, who was, and who is to come, the Almighty."

Notice, there are no specific identifiers to make a distinction regarding Father, Son and Spirit. The one who calls himself *"first and last"* in Is 44:6 identifies himself as Yahweh, the King of Israel and its Redeemer as well as the LORD of Armies, the only God. The Jewish reader would hear v.8 here and think of Yahweh. Note that God adds the next phrase marking his eternality and omnipotence.

The Witness

Now, John picks back up:

The One Being Revealed

9 I, John, your brother and partner in the affliction, kingdom, and endurance that are in Jesus, was on the island called Patmos because of the word of God and the testimony of Jesus. **10** I was in the Spirit on the Lord's day, and I heard a loud voice behind me like a trumpet **11** saying, "Write on a scroll what you see and send it to the seven churches: Ephesus, Smyrna, Pergamum, Thyatira, Sardis, Philadelphia, and Laodicea."

How does John describe himself and his situation in v.9?

How does this tie even John himself into the challenge of endurance that is addressed by the PFG of this book: **to reveal Jesus Christ so that his servants faithfully endure suffering in order to receive blessing**?

What is the significance that John is "in the Spirit" when he is commanded to write?

The churches in v.11 were literal, historical churches, but given that a Jew like John understood seven to symbolize perfection or fullness, what is the significance that he is instructed to write to seven churches?

The language of "looking" and "seeing" provides an important connection to a key theme of this prologue and the whole book. John is a witness delivering firsthand testimony to what he sees (vv.1,7,11,12,13,17,18,20) and hears (vv.3,10). In this, John is a witness (vv.1,9) following after Jesus' own witness (vv.2,5,9).

How does it serve the PFG of the book to know it is the first-hand testimony of Jesus and John?

The Revelation of Jesus Christ

The Son of Man

Having recorded his charge to write, and having *heard* this voice like a trumpet, John now turns to look, and he describes whom he *sees*:

> **12** Then I turned to see whose voice it was that spoke to me. When I turned I saw seven golden lampstands, **13** and among the lampstands was one like the Son of Man, dressed in a robe and with a golden sash wrapped around his chest. **14** The hair of his head was white as wool—white as snow—and his eyes like a fiery flame. **15** His feet were like fine bronze as it is fired in a furnace, and his voice like the sound of cascading waters. **16** He had seven stars in his right hand; a sharp double-edged sword came from his mouth, and his face was shining like the sun at full strength.
>
> **17** When I saw him, I fell at his feet like a dead man. He laid his right hand on me and said, "Don't be afraid. I am the First and the Last, **18** and the Living One. I was dead, but look—I am alive forever and ever, and I hold the keys of death and Hades.

The lampstands and stars will be explained in v.20. First, let's dig into what is revealed about the one speaking to John.

While the speaker in v.8 identifies himself more broadly as "the Lord God," what are the clues in vv.12-18 that it is now Jesus the Son who uses the title of "the First and Last" that is parallel to "the Alpha and Omega"?

In fact, these terms about God's eternity are applied to Jesus throughout the book. He is *"Alpha and Omega"* (1:8; 21:6; 22:13); the *"First and Last"* (1:17; 2:8,19; 22:13) and *"the one who is"* (1:4,8; 4:8, 16:5). Similar titles, like *"the one who lives"* echo the designation even further.

What is communicated about Jesus through the above descriptions of his clothing, hair, eyes, feet, voice and face?

How are all these titles and the other descriptions for Jesus from ch.1 important to the book's PFG?

The One Being Revealed

The Temporal Template

It is widely agreed by commentators that v.19 establishes a sort of two-part outline for all the material that follows in the book:

19 Therefore write what you have seen, what is, and what will take place after this.

At first glance, this may look like three temporal distinctions – past, present and future – but the context clarifies the first category is what John just recorded in ch.1. What follows in chs.2-22 describes what is and what will take place after this.

Here we must be VERY careful, because many interpreters seem to forget that this is apocalyptic literature! We should NOT take Jesus in v.19 to necessarily mean that everything that follows is recorded in a chronological sequence. It IS true that the letters to the churches in chs.2-3 address the first century situation and the events of chs.4ff describe events that largely are *ultimately* future to that original audience. Still, it is dangerous and unjustified to draw hard temporal lines between the contents before and after that division between chs.4 and 5.

In fact, what Jesus says to the churches in chs.2-3 describes persecution by human and demonic evil that already found expression in their contemporary situation. The chapters that follow will continue to remind them of their own situation even as they point to an ultimate fulfillment. Even as the future events of chs.4ff unfold, they are not necessarily – many would say not *likely* – a long string of chronological events.

Remember, the whole book was given to resonate with those seven named churches of the original audience, the other churches of the day to whom it was circulated, and every believer who has read it since. We would naturally think of "what is" for the original audience to be history for us, but it is also appropriate to look for ourselves even in chs.2-3, and we will, for there are things in common between their situations and ours.

John's command in v.19 to write starts with "Therefore." What precedes this that gives John his reason for writing? How does this directly connect to the PFG?

The last verse of ch.1 is a hinge that connects the prologue to Jesus' direct communication to the churches of the first century. Jesus says he will dictate his message through John to his messengers:

The Revelation of Jesus Christ

20 The mystery of the seven stars you saw in my right hand and of the seven golden lampstands is this: The seven stars are the angels of the seven churches, and the seven lampstands are the seven churches.

Reflection

What did the prologue (ch.1) make clear to the original audience?

What does it say to us today?

How does ch.1 direct our focus going forward?

What did the PFG tell us is the <u>reason</u> that Jesus will now reveal "what is, and what will take place after this"?

Lesson 4: To the Seven Churches (Chs.2-3)

We've spent a lot of energy trying to faithfully understand the foundation that the prologue of ch.1 establishes for the message of this book. John has been commanded broadly to testify to this revelation, but now in chs.2-3 the mode of communication has become even more direct. The letters to the churches are given like dictation to an amanuensis (a secretary that writes down the dictation).

Before we begin to examine these seven messages all together, remember that this study takes the blended interpretive view. In terms of these two chapters this means that we understand these seven churches to be historical bodies of believers spread throughout Asia Minor in John's day. There is plenty of historical evidence to support that understanding. We also see that while these seven churches are directly addressed by Jesus in their own contexts, the other churches of that day were meant to hear these letters, contemplate the parallels to their own situations and then apply the timeless universal truths to themselves. Further, just as we do with Paul's letters to specific churches, we also look for parallels to our own situations today and apply the principles we discover.

So, as we read these direct communications to seven historical churches of the first century, we will first seek to understand what Jesus was saying to *them*. Then we will consider how Jesus means to speak to *us* through what he has said to them. It's much like the way a parent may praise or correct one child in front of his siblings. The parent expects the indirect audience – the other children – to hear and apply the encouragements or rebukes to their own lives.

Let's recap the historical setting for these churches. We'll revisit the Doctrine of Imminence. Then we'll consider the pattern these letters take on together as a sevenfold address to the Church collective and consider how these chapters apply to us today.

The Setting
First, remember John, the amanuensis penning this dictation, is himself immersed in the same struggle as his first century contemporaries. He is in exile on Patmos precisely because of his testimony for Jesus (1:9). He describes himself as being *"in the Spirit"* when he *hears* a powerfully authoritative voice *"like a trumpet"* (v.10). When he turns around, he *sees* the one who has commanded him to write. It is Jesus, whom John has already recorded in his Gospel as having *"authority over all people"* (Jn 17:2). That Jesus possesses the full authority of God is clear from the context of the prologue of Rv 1. Therefore, the command to write is powerful, and since this message is directly dictated to the churches it could not possibly carry more weight than it does.

Second, remember the struggle and challenge of being a Christian in the first century. Remember that Christians are being tested strongly by paganism, by legalistic Judaizers, by socio-economic pressures of polytheistic trade guilds and by the political stresses of being brought before civil authorities for offering worship to Christ alone. The pressures for many to compromise, to blend in or even to turn away from Christ are immense.

Imminence for Them

To those pressures, add disillusionment. We know from Paul's letter to the Thessalonians that many Christians in these first century churches had a high expectation of Christ's imminent return. Some had become convinced he might have already come back, and they had missed it. Others were wondering if they had misunderstood Jesus. It certainly felt like their struggle might simply go on for the rest of their lives, and they would easily be tempted to wonder if it was worth it.

To what we know from Paul, add John's own words from the end of his Gospel, where he had to correct a myth. Some had taken Jesus in Jn 21:22 to mean that he would return so soon that John would never die. John had to clarify that Jesus was simply using a hypothetical statement to refocus Peter on his own role in following him rather than to worry about what was ahead for John. Jesus was *not* promising that John would live until his second coming. Still, the rumor spread that John would escape death, seeing Christ's return in his lifetime.

Now, decades later, John is an old man in exile on Patmos. Still no Jesus. The struggle goes on, and many begin to doubt and flounder. Imagine how powerful it must have been to hear this letter read, to hear your church named and to be spoken to directly by Jesus! You've been wondering if he really would ever come back, if he was even there at all, and now he speaks to you, church by church. Remember the agony of the 400 years of prophetic silence between the OT era and that of the NT?

How powerful would it be to hear from Jesus after decades of persecution and struggle and anticipation?

So, given this backdrop, what does Jesus have to say to these first century Christians? Because the collective formula is so important to understand how these two chapters relate to the PFG, we will treat them together as a sevenfold whole. Rather than walk through each section of the text in linear sequence, we'll consider the elements of the pattern one by one.

First, if you have not already done so, please read all of chs.2-3, preferably out loud. Doing this will already begin to prick your ears to the pattern.

To the Seven Churches

Examining the Formula

In keeping with John's affinity for sevens, let's examine the collective formula according to seven parts that are either present in each church's address or notable precisely due to their omission.

1: Direct Addresses

All seven churches are addressed specifically, *"To the angel of the church in..."* and this would hold much meaning. As in the illustration given before, this is like a parent speaking up to grab the attention of each particular child by naming them directly. "The other kids had better be listening too, for their turn is coming, but right now I'm speaking to YOU."

What is meant by the "angels" of the churches is not clear. The Greek term means "messenger" and could refer either to angelic beings or to humans, likely primary elders who led each church. Whatever the case, it seems to refer to persons assigned direct oversight to specific churches.

Brief historical background is appropriate here, so we'll draw from commentator L. Morris:

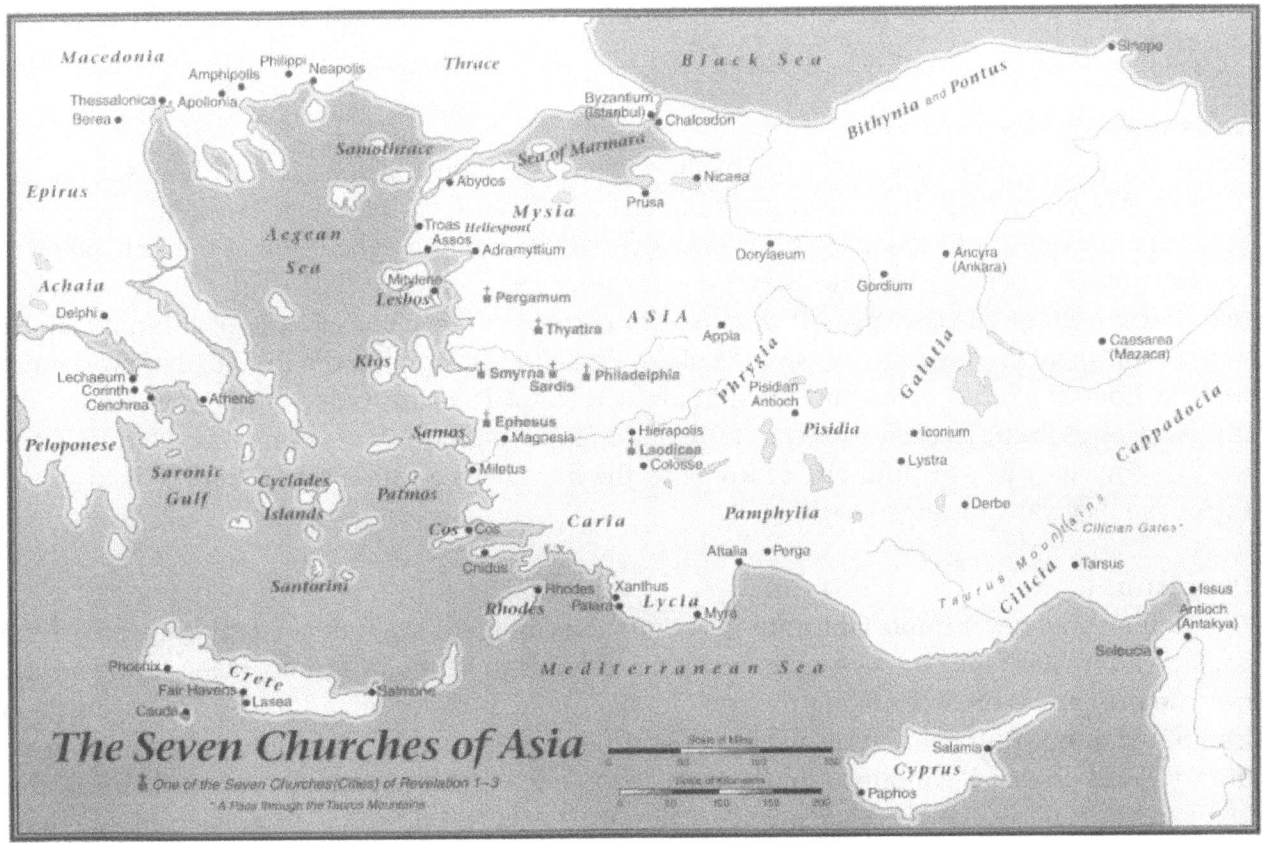

[5]

---

[5] Map image is from Dockery, David S., ed. *Holman Bible Handbook.* Nashville, TN: Holman Bible Publishers, 1992.

The Revelation of Jesus Christ

Ephesus

"Ephesus was the most important of the seven cities. Though Pergamum was apparently the official capital of the province of Asia, Ephesus was its greatest city. It was an assize town and a seat of proconsular government (Acts 19:38). When a proconsul took up his appointment he had to enter his province at Ephesus. Situated near the mouth of the river Cayster, it was a great commercial centre (despite problems posed by the silting up of its harbour which persisted so that the site is now several miles inland). Much of the trade of the East came to the Aegean via the port of Ephesus. The great road from the Euphrates terminated there, as did roads from the Cayster valley and the Maeander valley to the south.

Ephesus was an outstanding religious centre, the chief cult being that of Artemis (cf. Acts 19:24ff.). The city had the prized status of neōkoros (lit. 'temple-sweeper'!) in connection with the great temple which was one of the seven wonders of the world. But religion and magic were hopelessly intermingled, and magical arts were popular (cf. Acts 19:19). 'Ephesian letters' were charms widely supposed to cure sickness and to bring luck. Paul spent over two years in Ephesus establishing the church (Acts 19:8, 10), to which the important Epistle to the Ephesians was later sent. Timothy was there for a time (1 Tim. 1:3), and tradition says that John lived there in his old age."[6]

Smyrna

"Smyrna was one of the greatest cities of the region, and indeed disputed with Ephesus for the title 'First (city) of Asia'. It enjoyed great natural advantages, including an excellent harbour at the head of a well-protected gulf. It was thus the natural outlet for the trade of the rich valley of the Hermus and regions beyond. Smyrna was destroyed c. 580 BC, but c. 290 BC Lysimachus rebuilt it to a comprehensive plan. It was thus one of the very few planned cities of antiquity. Many writers comment on its beauty. It was one of the first cities to worship the Roman emperor and it won the honour of erecting a temple to him in the reign of Tiberius. Indeed there was a temple to the goddess of Rome as early as 195 BC (Tacitus, Ann. iv.56; Barclay says this was the first in the world). Smyrna was a faithful ally of Rome in the days before Rome was acknowledged in the region, so its loyalty meant something."[7]

Pergamum

"Pergamum was never important until it became the capital of the independent kingdom of the Attalids after Alexander the Great. Its last king willed it to Rome in 133 BC, when it apparently became the capital of the Roman province of Asia. About 15 miles inland, it did not have a good trading position. But, apart from its administrative importance, it was significant for its great library, said to have contained more than 200,000 parchment scrolls. Indeed, our word 'parchment' is derived from this name 'Pergamum'. It was an important religious centre. People came from all over the world to be healed by the god Asclepius, and Pergamum has been described as 'the Lourdes of the ancient world'. Zeus, Dionysos and Athene also had notable temples in the

---

[6] Morris, L. (1987). *Revelation: an introduction and commentary* (Vol. 20, pp. 63–64). Downers Grove, IL: InterVarsity Press.
[7] Ibid., p. 67.

To the Seven Churches

city. Pergamum was a centre of Caesar-worship, and it had a temple dedicated to Rome as early as 29 BC. It attained the coveted title neōkoros, 'temple-sweeper', before either Smyrna or Ephesus, and took its devotion to emperor worship seriously. In due course it added a second and a third temple in honour of the emperor. It was the principal centre of the imperial cult in this part of the world. But emperor-worship was not its sole religious activity. Behind the city was a great conical hill, the site of a multitude of heathen temples."[8]

Thyatira

"The longest of the seven letters is written to the church in the smallest and least important town! The values of God are not the values of men. Thyatira was situated between the Caicus and Hermus valleys. This was a good position for trading and the city appears to have been quite a commercial centre. There appear to have been a large number of trade guilds in Thyatira. In fact Sir William Ramsay says 'more trade-guilds are known in Thyatira than in any other Asian city. The inscriptions, though not specially numerous, mention the following: wool-workers, linen-workers, makers of outer garments, dyers, leather-workers, tanners, potters, bakers, slave-dealers and bronze-smiths.' Over in Philippi we read of Lydia that she came from this city and was a 'dealer in purple cloth' (Acts 16:14). The town was famous for its wool dyeing, which may well explain this lady's occupation."[9]

Sardis

"Situated at the junction of five roads, and commanding the Hermus valley, Sardis was an active commercial city and very wealthy. It had been the capital of Croesus who was proverbial for his riches. The city's easy wealth seems to have made for slackness. It was captured by Cyrus the Persian (549 BC) and by Antiochus (218 BC), both times because of its slackness. The city was built on a hill so steep that its defences seemed impregnable. On both occasions enemy troops scaled the precipice by night and found that the overconfident Sardians had set no guard. A great earthquake in AD 17 made a profound impression. But the city was soon rebuilt, partly owing to generous aid from the emperor Tiberius.

The most important religion at Sardis was the worship of Cybele. John does not mention anything like the persecutions at Smyrna and Pergamum or the heresies of the Nicolaitans. It may be that this church had not suffered disturbance from without and that its troubles stemmed from its comparatively sheltered existence. The temptation for the sheltered is always to take things easy, and they readily become slack. Like the churches at Pergamum and Thyatira this one has a mixed membership. But in those the faulty members are a minority. At Sardis they predominate. Only 'a few people' have not 'soiled their clothes'."[10]

---

[8] Morris, L. (1987). *Revelation: an introduction and commentary* (Vol. 20, pp. 69–70). Downers Grove, IL: InterVarsity Press.
[9] Ibid., p. 73.
[10] Ibid., p. 78).

The Revelation of Jesus Christ

Philadelphia
"Philadelphia was founded c.140 BC at the junction of the approaches to Mysia, Lydia and Phrygia. It was not unjustly called 'the gateway to the East'. Its founder, Attalus II Philadelphus of Pergamum, from whom the city derived its name, intended it to be a centre of missionary activity for the Hellenistic way of life. The city was prosperous, partly from its strategic situation, partly from the grape growing that flourished in the vicinity. It was a centre of worship of the god Dionysos, but contained also temples to many other gods. Volcanic activity caused hot springs in the vicinity, but also earthquakes from time to time. Philadelphia suffered from the earthquake of AD 17 and received imperial assistance for rebuilding. The church was evidently small (v. 8), but of good quality. Its enemies came from outside, not inside, for there is no mention of heresy or factiousness. It had a good deal in common with that at Smyrna. Both receive no blame, only praise. Both suffered from those who called themselves Jews and were not, both were persecuted it would seem by the Romans, both are assured that the opposition is satanic, and both are promised a crown."[11]

Laodicea
"Laodicea, at the junction of the valley of the Lycus and the Maeander and at the intersection of three important roads, commanded the approaches to Phrygia. It was one of the richest commercial centres in the world, so that we have here a picture of the church in an affluent society. Laodicea was noted for its banking and for its manufacture of clothing from the local black wool. It was an assize town and boasted a famous medical school.

An interesting feature of the city's religious life was a colony of over 7,000 adult male Jews. They had been granted the right to preserve their own customs. The Christian church had apparently been established by the preaching of Epaphras (Col. 1:7; 4:12–13). Paul wrote it a letter (Col. 4:16) which has been lost (unless, as some hold, it is our Ephesians). In John's day the condition of the church in this city had deteriorated sadly. This church receives the severest condemnation of all the seven to whom letters are sent."[12]

Faussett adds this: "Physicians used lukewarm water to cause vomiting. Cold and hot drinks were common at feasts, but never lukewarm. There were hot and cold springs near Laodicea."[13]

So, now that Jesus speaks directly to the church's specific messenger, what does he have to say?

2: Unique Authority
The next part of the formula is for all seven as well. Here Jesus identifies himself in ways that express his authority particular to each church's challenge. While it is difficult to know exactly what challenges each church faced, we begin to get clues based on the titles Jesus uses to approach

---

[11] Morris, L. (1987). *Revelation: an introduction and commentary* (Vol. 20, p. 80). Downers Grove, IL: InterVarsity Press.
[12] Ibid., pp. 83–84.
[13] Jamieson, R., Fausset, A. R., & Brown, D. (1997). *Commentary Critical and Explanatory on the Whole Bible* (Vol. 2, p. 562). Oak Harbor, WA: Logos Research Systems, Inc.

To the Seven Churches

the churches. Note also that all these descriptions are used of Christ elsewhere in the book, especially the prologue. So, from Jesus comes, *"Thus says..."*

- To Ephesus: *"the one who holds the seven stars in his right hand and who walks among the seven golden lampstands:"* (Cf. 1:16,20; 3:1)
- To Smyrna: *"the First and Last, the one who was dead and came to life:"* (Cf. 1:17-18; 22:13)
- To Pergamum: *"the one who has the sharp, double-edged sword:"* (Cf. 1:16; 2:16; 19:15,21)
- To Thyatira: *"the one whose eyes are like a fiery flame and whose feet are like fine bronze:"* (Cf. 1:14-15; 19:12)
- To Sardis: *"the one who has the seven spirits of God and the seven stars:"* (Cf. 1:4,16,20; 2:1; 4:5; 5:6)
- To Philadelphia: *"The Holy One, the true one, the one who has the key of David, who opens and no one will close, and who closes and no one opens:"* (Cf. Is 22:22; Rv 1:18; 3:8; 4:1; 5:2-5,9; 6:1,3,5,7,9,12; 8:1; 9:1-2; 10:2,8; 11:19; 15:5; 19:11; 20:1,3,12; 21:25; 22:16)
- To Laodicea: *"the Amen, the faithful and true witness, the originator of God's creation:"* (Cf. 1:2,5; 4:11; 19:11; 21:5)

3: Firsthand Knowledge

Once Jesus establishes his specific authority to speak into the situation, he tells each church, *"I know..."* This section is especially powerful. Whether Jesus is offering sympathetic understanding or a harsh rebuke, it is always jaw-dropping when God says, "I see you." The downside is far more terrifying than the same claim from Sauron in the Lord of the Rings fantasy. The upside is far more encouraging than any pep-talk by a popular conference speaker. Jesus, while still not *visible* to them until his return, is *with them*. Remember his promise in Mt 28:20? *"I am with you always until the end of the age."* Jesus is with his disciples even now. So, he tells the churches, *"I know..."* and his information is very specific to each church.

Notice that Jesus mentions *"your works"* in all but two of the addresses, those to Smyrna and Pergamum. To Smyrna, Jesus sounds more emotive, more sympathetic, as though they were really going through difficult persecution. He doesn't even rebuke this church, as we will see.

4: Commendations and the Exception

As Jesus has expressed his firsthand knowledge of each church's situation, now he expounds upon what he has been observing. He has something for which to commend all of the churches except for one, Laodicea.

The commendations cover a range of ways the churches have been faithful to some degree, especially in spiritual discernment and doctrinal faithfulness, but also for perseverance and godly deeds. The situations that make these things commendable are directly connected to those that are driving the PFG of the book. These believers are facing a variety of conditions that make fidelity and endurance especially difficult.

- To Ephesus:

  Revelation 2:2-3
  2 I know your works, your labor, and your endurance, and that you cannot tolerate evil people. You have tested those who call themselves apostles and are not, and you have found them to be liars. **3** I know that you have persevered and endured hardships for the sake of my name, and you have not grown weary.

- To Smyrna:

  9 I know your affliction and poverty, but you are rich. I know the slander of those who say they are Jews and are not, but are a synagogue of Satan.

- To Pergamum:

  13 I know where you live—where Satan's throne is. Yet you are holding on to my name and did not deny your faith in me, even in the days of Antipas, my faithful witness who was put to death among you, where Satan lives.

- To Thyatira:

  19 I know your works—your love, faithfulness, service, and endurance. I know that your last works are greater than the first.

- To Sardis, the commendation is hidden later in the message:

  Revelation 3:4
  4 But you have a few people in Sardis who have not defiled their clothes, and they will walk with me in white, because they are worthy.

- To Philadelphia:

  8 I know your works. Look, I have placed before you an open door that no one can close because you have but little power; yet you have kept my word and have not denied my name.

Laodicea is the one church for which Jesus offers no commendation. Their lack of commendable works seems tied to self-deception, where these believers see themselves utterly the opposite of how their sovereign Lord sees them. Especially notable is the mention of material wealth (possibly a sign of compromise in the marketplace).

5: Criticisms and the Exceptions
Jesus goes on. He is not only intimate with the challenges facing each church. He is not only aware of the degree to which they are or are not meeting those challenges. He is also qualified to judge their shortcomings: *"I have this against you..."* For most of the churches, Jesus has criticisms, some of them quite strong:

- To Ephesus: *"You have abandoned the love you had at first."*
- To Smyrna there is only acknowledgement of a challenging situation but no rebuke, as discussed earlier.
- To Pergamum: *"You have some there who hold to the teaching of Balaam... You have...those who hold to the teaching of the Nicolaitans."* The ancient is compared to the contemporary to describe a corrupt lifestyle lived in the name of so-called Christian "freedom."
- To Thyatira: *"You tolerate the woman Jezebel."* The context shows again a tolerance of immoral, idolatrous and rebellious behavior.
- To Sardis: *"... you are dead. I have not found your works complete... if you are not alert..."*
- Philadelphia is the other church not rebuked. Notice that they are to be spared testing because they already have been enduring.
- Laodicea: *"... you are neither cold nor hot. I am going to vomit you out of my mouth." "... you are...wretched, pitiful, poor, blind, and naked."* Especially notable is the ironic exclusion of the one they supposedly worshiped in their gatherings. This picture of Jesus locked out will be reversed in 22:15 when the ungodly will be excluded from the New Jerusalem.

Notice that *the criticisms are generally characterized by some form of compromise or failure to persevere faithfully*, as this relates directly to the PFG of the book.

6: Exhortations
Jesus is fully present in every specific situation of these churches. Even in his harshest rebukes he shows no willingness to abandon even those who are dramatically missing the mark of fidelity. He calls all to faithfulness, sometimes exhorting with comforting words and sometimes with strong charges.

- To Ephesus:

The Revelation of Jesus Christ

Revelation 2:5
5 Remember then how far you have fallen; repent, and do the works you did at first. Otherwise, I will come to you and remove your lampstand from its place, unless you repent.

- To Smyrna:

10 Don't be afraid of what you are about to suffer. Look, the devil is about to throw some of you into prison to test you, and you will experience affliction for ten days. Be faithful to the point of death, and I will give you the crown of life.

- To Pergamum:

16 So repent! Otherwise, I will come to you quickly and fight against them with the sword of my mouth.

- To Thyatira:

22 Look, I will throw her into a sickbed and those who commit adultery with her into great affliction. Unless they repent of her works, **23** I will strike her children dead. Then all the churches will know that I am the one who examines minds and hearts, and I will give to each of you according to your works. **24** I say to the rest of you in Thyatira, who do not hold this teaching, who haven't known "the so-called secrets of Satan"—as they say—I am not putting any other burden on you. **25** Only hold on to what you have until I come.

- To Sardis:

Revelation 3:2
2 Be alert and strengthen what remains, which is about to die, for I have not found your works complete before my God. **3** Remember, then, what you have received and heard; keep it, and repent. If you are not alert, I will come like a thief, and you have no idea at what hour I will come upon you.

- To Philadelphia:

9 Note this: I will make those from the synagogue of Satan, who claim to be Jews and are not, but are lying—I will make them come and bow down at your feet, and they will know that I have loved you. **10** Because you have kept my command to endure, I will also keep you from the hour of testing that is going to come on the whole world to test those who live on the earth. **11** I am coming soon. Hold on to what you have, so that no one takes your crown.

To the Seven Churches

- To Laodicea:

18 I advise you to buy from me gold refined in the fire so that you may be rich, white clothes so that you may be dressed and your shameful nakedness not be exposed, and ointment to spread on your eyes so that you may see. **19** As many as I love, I rebuke and discipline. So be zealous and repent.

Notice the theme of repentance for those churches that were falling away from fidelity. Notice again the call to endure.

7: Promises
So, after Jesus speaks with all authority to call his churches (back) to faithfulness, he then holds out the promise of reward for those who obey and endure. It is important to realize these promises are conditional, and so offered only to *"the one who conquers."* Either right before or after the statements of promise, there is one statement made to all seven churches: *"Let anyone who has ears to hear listen to what the Spirit says to the churches."* It is this statement that closes out the sevenfold address in the last verse of ch.3. If anyone will listen to and obey Jesus – *keep his word* – they will realize the promised blessing. See how this call ties to the PFG of the whole book?

Here are the promises offered to *"the one who conquers."* Notice that, as with the statements of authority, these promises are expressed in language that appears in other portions of the text of Revelation, particularly in the last chapters.

- Ephesus:

Revelation 2:7
7 "Let anyone who has ears to hear listen to what the Spirit says to the churches. To the one who conquers, I will give the right to eat from the tree of life, which is in the paradise of God."

- Smyrna:

11 "Let anyone who has ears to hear listen to what the Spirit says to the churches. The one who conquers will never be harmed by the second death."

- Pergamum:

17 "Let anyone who has ears to hear listen to what the Spirit says to the churches. To the one who conquers, I will give some of the hidden manna. I will also give him a white stone, and on the stone a new name is inscribed that no one knows except the one who receives it."

The Revelation of Jesus Christ

- Thyatira:

26 "The one who conquers and who keeps my works to the end: I will give him authority over the nations—

**27 and he will rule them with an iron scepter;
he will shatter them like pottery—**

28 just as I have received this from my Father. I will also give him the morning star."

- Sardis:

Revelation 3:5
5 "In the same way, the one who conquers will be dressed in white clothes, and I will never erase his name from the book of life but will acknowledge his name before my Father and before his angels."

- Philadelphia:

12 "The one who conquers I will make a pillar in the temple of my God, and he will never go out again. I will write on him the name of my God and the name of the city of my God—the new Jerusalem, which comes down out of heaven from my God—and my new name."

- Laodicea:

21 "To the one who conquers I will give the right to sit with me on my throne, just as I also conquered and sat down with my Father on his throne."

To the Seven Churches

Reflection

Remember these communications directly to the churches are given **to reveal Jesus Christ so that his servants faithfully endure suffering in order to receive blessing**.

What is being revealed about Jesus Christ and by Jesus Christ?

How is Jesus directly challenging his followers to endure faithfully?

What blessing is Jesus promising to those who are faithful?

How do chs.2-3 advance the PFG of Revelation for YOU?

Lesson 5: The One on the Throne, the Scroll, the Lamb, and the New Song (Chs.4-5)

The direct communications to each of the seven churches closed out with that repeated statement: *"Let anyone who has ears to hear listen to what the Spirit says to the churches."* Jesus, through his Spirit, speaks through John, his amanuensis. He speaks *to* the faithful – *"those who have ears to hear"* – and calls them to *be* faithful – *"listen."* That word *listen* is the same word used in 1:3, and the context makes clear that this is the kind of listening that is coupled with *heeding*. This ties directly to the PFG of the whole book. Only those who hear *and keep* the words of Jesus will come through to that goal of blessing that drives this revelation. Jesus just said seven different ways how he promised to bless those who would listen, those who would conquer by their obedience and faithfulness to him.

Remember that although Jesus addresses each church in particular, he is also addressing the Church collectively. This whole letter of Revelation, including that section of particular addresses in chs.2-3, was to be circulated among all of the local churches of that day. Further, it was recognized as holy Scripture to be circulated among the churches of every succeeding generation of this Church Age. So, the PFG of this Revelation has been in chs.2-3 voiced in very particular ways into local contemporary situations of the original audience, but it also carries timeless principled meaning into every situation of the churches to follow, including ours. Jesus has spoken into the very real earthly situations in which believers struggle. What is revealed next?

> **Revelation 4:1**
> **1** After this I looked, and there in heaven was an open door. The first voice that I had heard speaking to me like a trumpet said, "Come up here, and I will show you what must take place after this."

After this...
There is a distinct shift in the text where we see the break from ch.3 to ch.4. A repeated phrase comes up in the first verse of ch.4, and we have to be cautious. Several times in this book we will run into the marker *"after this."* We must be aware that even though it refers to a succession of events *for* John, it may or may not refer to a chronological succession in terms of the events being revealed *to* John.

In 4:1, we already have a distinction. The first *"after this"* simply means that something else is now being revealed to John following the messages given to the churches. The second *"after this"* from the speaker with the *"voice like a trumpet"* refers back to what he said in 1:19, that he would reveal through John to the churches events that were future to John's writing.

The Revelation of Jesus Christ

As we learned earlier, we must be careful because this is apocalyptic literature. Even though *"after this"* characterizes the material from 4:1ff as future to John's writing and the first century audience's reading/hearing, that does not mean that everything from ch.4 forward is laid out in strict chronology. We should be especially careful about this point when we run into other such markers going forward. These separate successive visions, but it may not be that the events within those visions are in temporal succession.

Who is speaking to John in this verse?

Why do you think he said these things must take place?

After the invitation is issued, there is another shift, this one in *location*. Jesus has spoken through his Spirit right into the particular earthly situations of the churches. He is *with them* just as he promised. Now, through John, he takes them *with him* into the domain of heaven.

The One on the Throne

> **2** Immediately I was in the Spirit, and there was a throne in heaven and someone was seated on it. **3** The one seated there had the appearance of jasper and carnelian stone. A rainbow that had the appearance of an emerald surrounded the throne.
>
> **4** Around the throne were twenty-four thrones, and on the thrones sat twenty-four elders dressed in white clothes, with golden crowns on their heads.
>
> **5** Flashes of lightning and rumblings and peals of thunder came from the throne. Seven fiery torches were burning before the throne, which are the seven spirits of God. **6** Something like a sea of glass, similar to crystal, was also before the throne.
>
> Four living creatures covered with eyes in front and in back were around the throne on each side. **7** The first living creature was like a lion; the second living creature was like an ox; the third living creature had a face like a man; and the fourth living creature was like a flying eagle. **8** Each of the four living creatures had six wings; they were covered with eyes around and inside. Day and night they never stop, saying,

The One on the Throne, the Scroll, The Lamb, and the Song

> Holy, holy, holy,
> Lord God, the Almighty,
> who was, who is, and who is to come.

9 Whenever the living creatures give glory, honor, and thanks to the one seated on the throne, the one who lives forever and ever, **10** the twenty-four elders fall down before the one seated on the throne and worship the one who lives forever and ever. They cast their crowns before the throne and say,

> **11** Our Lord and God,
> you are worthy to receive
> glory and honor and power,
> because you have created all things,
> and by your will
> they exist and were created.

John had already said in 1:10 that he was *"in the Spirit,"* so when he restates it here in 4:2 we understand it carries new significance. As stated above, John's state of being in the Spirit is now giving him access to the heavenly domain.

He continues to record his eyewitness account. There are symbolic representations everywhere, as we expected with this book's genre. We have many clues that John is consistently struggling with the insufficiency of human language to make his report. He resorts to similes and analogy, doing the best he can.

Still, there can be no doubt who is seated on the throne. He is the central figure of the heavenly scene. His throne is ultimate while the surrounding thrones symbolize only delegated rule and derived authority. The dazzling colors of the rainbow remind the reader of an ancient covenant (Gn 9:12-17). The lightning and thunder echo back to the terrifying scene at Mount Sinai when the law was given to Moses (Gn 19-20). The imagery of a "sea of glass" might symbolize the absolute power of the Creator to bring perfect calm and order out of chaos but as a barrier before the throne would especially emphasize God's royal purity and holiness. The surrounding presence of the seven spirits of God connects not only to the Spirit hovering over the waters in Genesis but also to the description in Revelation's prologue.

The *"one on the throne"* must be God. More specifically, it is the Creator and Ruler of all creation. In terms of the NT doctrine of the Trinity, it is the Eternal Father, the one Daniel described as the Ancient of Days:

The Revelation of Jesus Christ

> **Daniel 7:9**
> **9** "As I kept watching,
> thrones were set in place,
> and the Ancient of Days took his seat.
> His clothing was white like snow,
> and the hair of his head like whitest wool.
> His throne was flaming fire;
> its wheels were blazing fire.

John mentions thrones more times by far than any other NT writer, nearly in every chapter of this book. The Almighty God's throne is clearly the hub of all power and authority. Surrounding his throne are 24 other thrones, and seated upon them are elders, dressed in white and wearing crowns. Some believe these to be either angels or angelic representatives of humans. Others make the case that the robes – symbolizing the righteousness of Christ applied to the saints – are especially a clue to the humanity of these to whom rule is delegated. Are these two twelves, symbolizing the twelve tribes of Israel and twelve apostles?

Whichever of the options is correct, the importance of the symbolism seems clear. The Almighty is ultimate in his power and authority, but he chooses to rule through those whom he has created and given the privilege of the closest proximity to his presence.

John also reports seeing four living creatures right up against the area of the high throne. Four is symbolic of totality. Later John will write of four winds and four corners of the earth in this way. These creatures seem to represent the totality of God's creatures.

So, in these verses are represented the totality of created beings, from heavenly council to earthly creatures. And these all pour forth in unison a lofty proclamation. The living creatures incessantly give thanks as they pronounce God's holiness, his power and his eternity. When they do this, the elders fall down before the one ultimate throne and declare God as worthy of all glory, honor and power.

What is the reason the elders give to declare God's worthiness?

What is the reason given that all created things (including us) exist?

The One on the Throne, the Scroll, The Lamb, and the Song

What happens next is pivotal as we move forward in John's text, and that is why we will examine ch.5 together with ch.4. John has just been given a glimpse of the ongoing worship of the Almighty God. In terms of the Trinity, he has just observed the Father upon the throne along with the sevenfold manifestation of the Spirit. *Where is the Son?*

The first century audience would understand that Jesus had accomplished what the Father sent him to do. He had poured out his life in the once-for-all sacrifice for sins upon a Roman cross in a temporal, historical event. He had been vindicated in being raised from the dead, he had shown himself to his disciple-witnesses, and then he had ascended back to the Father. He was now (in the late first century) understood to be at the Father's right hand. This was taught by the NT theologians. Stephen, the first recorded martyr, had used his last breath to declare it to be so (Acts 7:56). They understood that even while Jesus was through his Spirit maintaining his promise of presence for the Church (starkly illustrated in chs.2-3!) he was also in a real sense present with the Father at his throne.

So, where is Jesus? As we move into ch.5, John's report builds the tension a little further before it resolves it.

The Scroll

> **Revelation 5:1-5**
> **1** Then I saw in the right hand of the one seated on the throne a scroll with writing on both sides, sealed with seven seals. **2** I also saw a mighty angel proclaiming with a loud voice, "Who is worthy to open the scroll and break its seals?" **3** But no one in heaven or on earth or under the earth was able to open the scroll or even to look in it. **4** I wept and wept because no one was found worthy to open the scroll or even to look in it. **5** Then one of the elders said to me, "Do not weep. Look, the Lion from the tribe of Judah, the Root of David, has conquered so that he is able to open the scroll and its seven seals."

The scroll is the next important symbol in this revelation. What it represents is expressed in various ways, but commentators generally agree that it has to do with the unfolding of God's will and plan for the cosmos.

The things of God are inherently inaccessible to his creatures unless he takes action. They only know what he reveals, and only when he reveals it. God revealed himself first of all in creating. We know that as *General Revelation*. The Apostle Paul argues in Rm 1 that all people are aware of God through his creative activity. God went further, as he revealed himself to mankind in the Garden of Eden. After man's rebellion there, God's presence and activity was veiled to mankind due to our sinful disposition. So, God began to reveal himself in *Special Revelation* by speaking to and through prophets. He gave us his *written* Word. Then, God sent his *incarnate* Word. As the writer of Hebrews puts it:

The Revelation of Jesus Christ

Hebrews 1:1–4
1 Long ago God spoke to our ancestors by the prophets at different times and in different ways. **2** In these last days, he has spoken to us by his Son. God has appointed him heir of all things and made the universe through him. **3** The Son is the radiance of God's glory and the exact expression of his nature, sustaining all things by his powerful word. After making purification for sins, he sat down at the right hand of the Majesty on high. **4** So he became superior to the angels, just as the name he inherited is more excellent than theirs.

This scroll in Rv 5 represents the unfolding of God's will and plan, but it seems to carry more specific meaning too. It unfolds the plan for the redemption of creation and the restoration of all things (Acts 3:21). It especially reveals vindication and judgment.

The scroll might make a first century Christian think of the scroll of a *legal will* that would trigger the endowment of an *inheritance*, like the one the NT writers described as ours in Christ (Eph 1:11-12; Col 3:24; Heb 9:15-17; Jas 2:5; 1 Pt 1:3-4 and esp. Rv 21:7). Only someone with authority could remove a wax seal from an official document. If the one who conquers is eagerly awaiting a heavenly inheritance, who has the authority to dispense it? That is the question expressed by the angel in 5:2 of our text: *"Who is worthy?"* Who has the power and authority to finish unfolding the will and plan of the Almighty God? Who can vindicate those who cling to him, and judge those who reject and fight against him? Who can open the seals and trigger both kinds of judgment, blessing and destruction?

It seems hopeless in v.3. The language of *"heaven," "earth"* and *"under the earth"* covers the whole cosmos. No one can even look into the scroll, let alone open it. Feel John's despair as he represents every frustrated and disillusioned Christian of his day and since, including our own. He weeps and weeps.

Then hear the voice of the elder. There IS one who is able. Who is he? *"The Lion from the tribe of Judah, the Root of David."* Hope begins to rise up, but there is still tension. Like the leprous man of Mt 8:1 acknowledged, it is clear that Jesus is *able*, but is he *willing*? The Lion has conquered, but will he open the seals so that his followers may conquer as well?

The Lamb
Here is one of those key moments in Revelation when John records something he *hears* (and holds a corresponding expectation) but then records *seeing* something that is not quite the same. We, along with John, have been waiting. The Father is on the throne, and the Spirit is everywhere around it. Where is the Son, the Lion who has conquered? At the height of the tension, what does John see?

The One on the Throne, the Scroll, The Lamb, and the Song

Revelation 5:6-7
6 Then I saw one like a slaughtered lamb standing in the midst of the throne and the four living creatures and among the elders. He had seven horns and seven eyes, which are the seven spirits of God sent into all the earth. **7** He went and took the scroll out of the right hand of the one seated on the throne.

We expect the Lion, but John sees *"one like a slaughtered lamb."* Let's process this turn of events together carefully, so we enjoy the fullness of this great depiction of our Savior.

What is the significance that this "one like a slaughtered lamb" stands "in the midst of the throne and the four living creatures and among the elders"?

How closely is this person connected to the Holy Spirit, and why is that important?

Since horns usually symbolize power and authority and eyes are symbols for knowledge and wisdom, what do the seven horns and eyes say about this lamb?

What do we understand about the lamb's power and authority that he can walk right up to the Almighty and take the scroll out of his right hand (the hand that represents power)?

In one sense the great redemptive plot arc has reached its zenith, and we only await the tying up of loose ends. But remember, the NT teaches us there is an already/not yet dynamic to the Church Age. As the writer of Hebrews puts it:

Hebrews 2:8–9 (CSB)
8 For in subjecting everything to him, he left nothing that is not subject to him. As it is, we do not yet see everything subjected to him. **9** But we do see Jesus—made lower than the angels for a short time so that by God's grace he might taste death for everyone—crowned with glory and honor because he suffered death.

The Revelation of Jesus Christ

Here, in Rv 5, we see Jesus *"crowned with glory and honor because he suffered death."* This suffering is, in fact, the reason that the Lamb is honored with a new song.

The New Song

Revelation 5:8-10
8 When he took the scroll, the four living creatures and the twenty-four elders fell down before the Lamb. Each one had a harp and golden bowls filled with incense, which are the prayers of the saints. **9** And they sang a new song:

> You are worthy to take the scroll
> and to open its seals,
> because you were slaughtered,
> and you purchased people
> for God by your blood
> from every tribe and language
> and people and nation.
> **10** You made them a kingdom
> and priests to our God,
> and they will reign on the earth.

Imagine what an encouragement is this glimpse into the heavenly reality that the Lamb is already crowned with glory! Still, the reason this glimpse – this peeling back to reveal the supernatural reality – the reason this is so needed is precisely because the Christians for whom John is recording this are experiencing the harsh struggle of this fallen world. They are still stuck in Heb 2:8b: *"As it is, we do not see everything subjected to him."* In their frustration they offer prayers to God (v.8), likely including prayers for vindication. So, Jesus, in his grace, is granting his people to see him as he truly is now, and as the cosmos will soon all see him to be.

God's plan will be unfolded. The Lamb has all authority and power to remove the seals. Saints will be vindicated in their Savior, and the wicked will perish in judgment. The prayer modeled by Jesus for his disciples will finally be answered. With the breaking of the seals, the will of the Father will be *"done on earth as it is in heaven."* So, it is no surprise the heavens erupt with praise for the Lamb.

The song expands:

The One on the Throne, the Scroll, The Lamb, and the Song

11 Then I looked and heard the voice of many angels around the throne, and also of the living creatures and of the elders. Their number was countless thousands, plus thousands of thousands. **12** They said with a loud voice,

> Worthy is the Lamb who was slaughtered
> to receive power and riches
> and wisdom and strength
> and honor and glory and blessing!

13 I heard every creature in heaven, on earth, under the earth, on the sea, and everything in them say,

> Blessing and honor and glory and power
> be to the one seated on the throne,
> and to the Lamb, forever and ever!

14 The four living creatures said, "Amen," and the elders fell down and worshiped.

If we compare the new song of 5:9-12 with the praise already offered to the one on the throne in 4:11, we find that each Person is declared to be worthy of all glory and honor. We already noticed that the Father is worthy of these because he created all things. We also understand that the Son too deserves worship as Creator (Jn 1:3; Col 1:15-16; Heb 1:2). We also see the Spirit's role in creation in Gn 1:2, so we see our Trinitarian God as worthy of all worship.

The new song parallels the language of worthiness, but for a new reason, because of God's redemptive work, another Trinitarian enterprise. The Father sent the Son (Jn 5:23,36-37,44,5; 8:16,18,42; 12:49; 14:24; 17:21,25; 20:21), who was empowered by the Spirit (Zech 4:6; Lk 4:14; Rm 1:3-4) and who humbled himself to the point of death on a cross (Php 2:6-8). Father and Son are seen together in the praise of v.13.

So, the new song of ch.5 expands the worship of the one on the throne to include the Lamb. It also expands the justification for worship to include the redemption of mankind. God is worthy of all worship because he is the Holy One, the Creator, and also because he is the Redeemer.

The worshiping body also expands. The living creatures and the elders are joined by many angels, until the heavens cannot contain the praise. Ultimately, every creature everywhere declares God's eternal worthiness, the one on the throne and the Lamb.

The Revelation of Jesus Christ

Reflection

How does the specificity of the song parts in ch.5 vary according to the groups making the declarations? How does this relate to your own personal reasons for praising God?

How can we reconcile the already/not yet dominion of Jesus with the fact that the praise of 5:13 is said to be offered by EVERY creature?

If apocalyptic tends to blur the timeline, what might that tell us about the timing of this universal praise to God?

Remember the PFG of this book is **<u>to reveal Jesus Christ so that his servants faithfully endure suffering in order to receive blessing</u>**. *How does the heavenly scene of chs.4-5 reveal Jesus? How does this function to encourage suffering Christians, and how does it point toward blessing?*

Lesson 6: The First Six Seals (Ch.6)

As we proceed through the rest of the Revelation, remember that there is a wide range of interpretive disagreement about the level of detail and the chronological order with which Jesus communicated through John for the sake of the Church. We will continue to discuss those options but also stay committed to the zoom level established by the PFG to make sure we do not lose sight of the core purpose of the Revelation, its goal and how it functions to fulfill that purpose and draw believers to that goal.

In his Gospel, John records that just before the cross Jesus told his disciples three truths that underpin this later Revelation. First, he said, *"I have called you friends, because I have made known to you everything I have heard from the Father"* (Jn 15:15). This echoes Amos 3:7 that *"the Lord does nothing without revealing his counsel to his servants the prophets."* Now in Revelation Jesus is revealing to the churches what he is going to do. Second, Jesus tells his disciples, *"If they persecuted me, they will also persecute you"* (Jn 15:20). Jesus is now revealing the complete measure of persecution that will be filled up in his followers. Third, Jesus commands them, *"Remain in me"* (15:4). If his disciples will remain in him by keeping his commands, they will have his own joy in themselves (v.11). What Jesus calls "joy" in John's gospel equates to the promised "blessing" in Revelation, and it depends upon the same thing: keeping Jesus' word, obeying his commands.

This book was given to reveal God's total authority and power at work through Jesus, who having humbled himself in ultimate suffering, is now the exalted Lord of all. He will exercise all authority in bringing God's judgment upon sin and vindication for himself and his followers. He is revealing his glory and power, and he is revealing how he will surely bring this age to an end so that his followers will be blessed by enduring faithfully as witnesses through persecution and suffering. This revelation works in the churches through revealing hidden powers and future events, through encouraging the weary and disillusioned, through exhorting and even rebuking those who are wavering or even sinning. The believers are called to repent, hold fast, to cling to and obey the word of the Lord so that they may receive the blessing.

As we come to ch.6, Jesus the Lamb is exercising his authority to bring all things to culmination. For the idolaters this means perfect justice carried out in destruction. For the faithful this means mercifully measured suffering down to the last brother or sister. The judgment of the world is carried out not only by supernatural calamity on a total cosmic scale but also through demonic and natural human agency. The complete reversal of God's original "very good" creative activity impacts all the cosmos and all creatures and culminates in complete clarity. The faithful – after enduring their suffering – are guaranteed of their eternal safety and vindication while the rebellious are perfectly aware that the *"day of their wrath has come!"* They are being judged by Father, Son, and Spirit, the One True God. The rhetorical question in 6:17 drives home the whole point of the book: *"Who is able to stand?"*

The Revelation of Jesus Christ

The answer is played out. Only those people clothed in righteousness and victory by union with Christ will stand. All those who reject him and persecute his faithful will fall in judgment. The cry from under the altar in 6:10 is for the fulfillment of this very reality, that the Lord carry out this judgment and vindication.

Let's examine the text now as the Lamb begins to open the seals:

The Four Horsemen

> **Revelation 6:1-8**
> **1** Then I saw the Lamb open one of the seven seals, and I heard one of the four living creatures say with a voice like thunder, "Come!" **2** I looked, and there was a white horse. Its rider held a bow; a crown was given to him, and he went out as a conqueror in order to conquer.
>
> **3** When he opened the second seal, I heard the second living creature say, "Come!" **4** Then another horse went out, a fiery red one, and its rider was allowed to take peace from the earth, so that people would slaughter one another. And a large sword was given to him.
>
> **5** When he opened the third seal, I heard the third living creature say, "Come!" And I looked, and there was a black horse. Its rider held a set of scales in his hand. **6** Then I heard something like a voice among the four living creatures say, "A quart of wheat for a denarius, and three quarts of barley for a denarius, but do not harm the oil and the wine."
>
> **7** When he opened the fourth seal, I heard the voice of the fourth living creature say, "Come!" **8** And I looked, and there was a pale green horse. Its rider was named Death, and Hades was following after him. They were given authority over a fourth of the earth, to kill by the sword, by famine, by plague, and by the wild animals of the earth.

You've probably heard of the Four Horsemen of the Apocalypse before, and this is the text that has inspired so much fascination. Let's examine what these characters together tell us about the contents of the first four seals, for they form a unity. There are four riders on four horses, each called forth by one of the four living creatures. Taken together, these seem to represent God's sovereign decree over the timing and totality of using natural human destructive forces – corruption, war, famine and pestilence – as his agents for judgment. Man's sin has for millennia wrought destruction to the earth, and in all its ways this destruction is brought to its full height.

The first horseman is intent on *conquest* and is given power (the crown that is *given* to him) toward that end. It seems he is characterized more by use of political leverage (the bow) than by actual warfare (the arrows are missing), but his aim is clear, and the whiteness of his horse likely

The First Six Seals

suggests victory in his efforts. It may also draw the biblical mind to think of deception, just as Satan and false teachers disguise themselves as those of the light (2 Cor 11:13-15).

The second horseman is where we find the implication of conquest clearly realized in the violence of *warfare*. If the first player is an instigator, the second represents the eruption of those forces being stirred up to slaughter. "Fiery" and "red" are common symbols for war and bloodshed. Think of the millions who have died in warfare in just the 20th century. This horseman represents the height of that kind of carnage.

When political strife leads to widespread warfare, the fallout has always included *economic strife*. The third rider represents this reality, though we notice there is some decree of restraint. That oil and wine are not harmed probably serves as a warning of more complete shortage to come. It may also attest to the fact that in such dire circumstances the rich still enjoy luxury while the poor do without basic needs.

All of the seals to this point seem to accumulate in the fourth. Man's thirst for conquest leads to war, and war leads to economic strife and famine. The sum of human wickedness is always *death*. The fourth rider is on a deathly looking horse, and Death is this rider's name. Hades, a term referring to the place of the dead, or the underworld, follows him like a demonic Tails trailing after a dark version of Sonic the Hedgehog. Just as the first rider was given a crown and the second was allowed to take peace, this duo is given authority. Every kind of natural havoc known to plague human history is dispensed, even including the attack of wild animals. It may even be that this last image of v.8 is meant to depict the beast-like nature of human depravity at its worst.

The cumulative effect of the Four Horseman is clear. It is dramatic but, thus far, limited. Death is business as usual in a fallen world, and it has been since the Fall. But here it is everywhere, to the tune of one fourth of the earth's populace.

Thus far ch.6 probably sounds like the daily news – for the first readers and for all of us since! How important is the revelation that this calamity is subject to heavenly decree, and that it is, at this point, still restrained?

Lord, How Long?

Revelation is full of OT imagery and language, drawing from the prior prophets whom God had begun to show glimpses of how his sovereign plan would play out. Evil will continue to surge and build until God's incredible patience and mercy are finally exhausted and the very last of his chosen ones have suffered for the sake of the Savior. How long before that point finally arrives?

The Revelation of Jesus Christ

> **9** When he opened the fifth seal, I saw under the altar the souls of those who had been slaughtered because of the word of God and the testimony they had given. **10** They cried out with a loud voice, "Lord, the one who is holy and true, how long until you judge those who live on the earth and avenge our blood?" **11** So they were each given a white robe, and they were told to rest a little while longer until the number would be completed of their fellow servants and their brothers and sisters, who were going to be killed just as they had been.

This group of souls certainly includes literal martyrs – those who have died specifically because of their witness to Jesus. Many commentators think the symbolic nature of this book allows or even suggests that this group actually enfolds *every* believer, since all who are true to Christ suffer in some way. Remember Paul's call in Rm 12:1 to offer ourselves as living sacrifices to God? Notice that these souls are under the heavenly altar, the place where sacrifices are made.

Regardless of the sacrifice, every believer can certainly identify with the cry of these disembodied souls, and that seems to be John's intent. Don't we all wonder, "How long are you going to put up with all this, Lord? And how long must WE?"

How is the cry answered? With white robes, the gift of already-present righteousness while awaiting not-yet-realized vindication. *"Rest."* It is not the final state of eternal rest, but it is rest, nonetheless. Assurance. This waiting won't go on forever but only *"until the number would be completed."* Others have to finish their race just as they have. This group is much like the *"cloud of witnesses"* in Heb 12:1, except that there they are cheering on the faithful, while here they are questioning how long until the last race is run.

Can you feel the frustration and the anticipation? The first century audience could. This is a normal experience for the Christ-follower, and it should probably give us pause if it is foreign to us.

How has the waiting been frustrating for YOU as a Christian?

What does this passage tell us about the patience of God? About his sovereign power and wisdom?

The First Six Seals

How important is the fellowship of suffering, that these fellow-sufferers are in v.11 referred to as "brothers and sisters"?

It seems that the question, *"How long?"* is answered not only with a call to patience in v.11, but then ultimately with the events of the sixth seal. Remember, since this is apocalyptic literature, we do not know if, or how much, time passes between these seals. It is probably best to understand the question as one that has been being voiced throughout the Church Age, and that is now being answered with the last two seals.

As judgment and vindication really begin to unfold, a new question arises:

Who Is Able to Stand?

> **12** Then I saw him open the sixth seal. A violent earthquake occurred; the sun turned black like sackcloth made of hair; the entire moon became like blood; **13** the stars of heaven fell to the earth as a fig tree drops its unripe figs when shaken by a high wind; **14** the sky was split apart like a scroll being rolled up; and every mountain and island was moved from its place.
>
> **15** Then the kings of the earth, the nobles, the generals, the rich, the powerful, and every slave and free person hid in the caves and among the rocks of the mountains. **16** And they said to the mountains and to the rocks, "Fall on us and hide us from the face of the one seated on the throne and from the wrath of the Lamb, **17** because the great day of their wrath has come! And who is able to stand?"

Remember, while we are in the middle of a heavenly vision (4:2), with the opening of the seals our attention has been pointed earthward. Notice now how the scale of events transcends this globe. From an earthquake to the sky's splitting apart to a blood-moon and falling stars, the calamity is clearly moving beyond the natural destructive activities of humans. God's almighty hand is finally moving in judgment for the whole cosmos to see. Such events were foretold by a number of biblical prophets, including Isaiah (13:10), Joel (2:10; 3:15) and, most notably, Jesus himself (Mt 24:29).

The above summary is not the interpretation of a studied theologian reflecting on ancient prophets, but it is that of all humanity before whom the events are unfolding. When the sixth seal is opened, everyone from kings to slaves realizes that this is God's doing. All that came before in these seals – that was normal, everyday human wickedness and violence at work. But this stuff – it seems everyone will realize – this is *God's* moving. More than that, John makes it clear that it is God's *judgment*. It is the pouring out of God's *wrath*.

The Revelation of Jesus Christ

People have for centuries ignored or explained God away, denying he even exists. One of the fastest-growing trends of our 21st century culture is secular materialism. Yet in the face of these cataclysmic events described by John, there are no atheists. It seems to be the *unbeliever* who seeks some hiding place from the *"face of the one seated on the throne and from the wrath of the Lamb."* (The believer has already found her shelter, cf. Rv 7:15.) The way John writes it, it is the *terrified* who ask the most important question of all human history: *"Who is able to stand?"* This same question was asked long before the first century by the psalmist, King David (Ps 24:3; 15:1). Now, even on the lips of the condemned, it is a powerful and probing question for the reader. It is that question that voices utter despair for the determined rebel but blissful peace for the humble recipient of a white robe. The answer means condemnation or vindication.

Reflection

Why is it important that the wrath being poured out is said specifically to be that both of the "one seated on the throne" AND "the Lamb"?

What do you think John intends to communicate by the totality of the calamity in vv.12-14 and the response to it in vv.15-17?

If you can understand the frustration of the question "Lord...how long?" then what is your answer to the question "Who can stand?"

Remember this revelation is given **to reveal Jesus Christ so that his servants faithfully endure suffering in order to receive blessing**. *How do these questions from the text help this book accomplish its PFG for you?*

Lesson 7: The Sealed and the Seventh Seal (Ch.7-Ch.8, V.5)

The first six seals carry two very weighty questions. The first, *"Lord, how long?"* begins to be answered in the sixth seal, which brings its own question. Once judgment begins to undo the entire cosmos, the question becomes, *"Who is able to stand?"*

That question comes from the mouths of the terrified, who are looking for any kind of shelter from the wrath of the one seated on the throne and from the Lamb. When the answer comes in ch.7, we get a picture of those who have already found shelter and security. Who is able to stand, and how are they able? We read on:

The Sealed

> **Revelation 7:1-8**
> **1** After this I saw four angels standing at the four corners of the earth, restraining the four winds of the earth so that no wind could blow on the earth or on the sea or on any tree. **2** Then I saw another angel rising up from the east, who had the seal of the living God. He cried out in a loud voice to the four angels who were allowed to harm the earth and the sea, **3** "Don't harm the earth or the sea or the trees until we seal the servants of our God on their foreheads." **4** And I heard the number of the sealed:
>
> 144,000 sealed from every tribe of the Israelites:
> **5** 12,000 sealed from the tribe of Judah,
> 12,000 from the tribe of Reuben,
> 12,000 from the tribe of Gad,
> **6** 12,000 from the tribe of Asher,
> 12,000 from the tribe of Naphtali,
> 12,000 from the tribe of Manasseh,
> **7** 12,000 from the tribe of Simeon,
> 12,000 from the tribe of Levi,
> 12,000 from the tribe of Issachar,
> **8** 12,000 from the tribe of Zebulun,
> 12,000 from the tribe of Joseph,
> 12,000 sealed from the tribe of Benjamin.

This *number* of the sealed is certainly symbolic. 144,000 is twelve times twelve multiplied by ten times ten times ten. This total is replete with the symbolism of completeness. As we said before, since this is apocalyptic literature, we *may* or *may not* conclude these numbers are literal, but we *must* understand them as symbolic. So, what we can know for sure is that John hears a number that is certainly meant to communicate a fullness or a totality *"from every tribe of the Israelites."*

The Revelation of Jesus Christ

There is a problem, though. Dan is left out and Manasseh (one of Joseph's two tribal heirs) is included, though he would have inherited through his father Joseph. Manasseh and Ephraim both became heirs in the apportioning of the promised land (Josh 14:4; 16:4), though Ephraim, like Dan, is not listed here. Why are these missing?

The answer may tie to the PFG. Dan was the first tribe to employ idol worship (Jdg 18:30; 1 Kgs 12:29-30), and Ephraim was also especially known for idolatry, so these perhaps were excluded here in Revelation as not being part of "true Israel." In terms of our PFG, then, perhaps these tribes are excluded as a warning, as representatives of those who do *not* keep the word of God, those who do *not* persevere to the end.

Is there significance in the order? Judah was not typically first in OT lists but is now associated with the Lion of the tribe (Rv 5:5) and takes priority. So, now the list is bookended by Judah (the new first tribe) and Benjamin (the last tribe).

Many note that this list takes the form of a military census, like those Israel used to record her readiness for war in the OT historical books (e.g., Nu 1:20-46; 2 Sam 24; 1 Chr 12:23-37; 21:1-2). There is accounting of the full amount of each tribe ready for war. However, if these tribes represent NT warriors, they are those that conquer ironically – like Jesus – through suffering.

The ones who are *"able to stand"* are those who are *sealed* with God's seal (v.2). First, this seal *associates* the sealed with God – they belong to him. Second, this seal *protects* those belonging to God. The restraining of winds symbolizes the restraining of destructive powers. The number four in *"four corners"* and *"four winds"* depicts the totality of the destructive forces, and the "earth," "sea" and "trees" refers to their earthly impact. There is good reason to think that these forces are to be understood as the four horsemen of the first four seals. God through his angel is decreeing security for his own. Security against what? Protection from what? The options are expressed by G.K. Beal:

> "Why God "seals" his servants is debated. The main alternatives are: (1) for protection from physical harm, (2) for protection from demons, and (3) for protection from losing their faith and hence their salvation. Ezekiel 9 is often correctly proposed as the best background for the divine sealing. There God commands an angel to put a mark on all genuine believers but instructs other angels to slay unfaithful Israelites. The mark on believers is to protect them from the coming wrath, which will be inflicted by the Babylonians and which unfaithful Israelites will suffer.[14] ...uppermost in John's mind is certainly not physical security but protection of the believers' faith and salvation from the

---

[14] Beale, G. K. (1999). <u>The book of Revelation: a commentary on the Greek text</u> (p. 409). Grand Rapids, MI; Carlisle, Cumbria: W.B. Eerdmans; Paternoster Press.

The Sealed and the Seventh Seal

various sufferings and persecutions that are inflicted on them..."[15] "... The sealing enables them to respond in faith to the trials through which they pass..."[16]

Others point out that it was not uncommon for a soldier or guild member of the first century to receive a mark or "seal" as a religious devotee to a particular deity. This mark was usually placed on the forehead because it was "most conspicuous" and "most noble." Remember, many in John's original audience had been part of these trade guilds and were acquainted with such seals.

How might the "seal" of ch.7 relate to the "mark" of ch.13 (vv.16 & 17; cf. 14:9,11; 16:2; 19:20; 20:4)?

It is important to realize that the sealing protects God's own from his wrath but not necessarily from every kind of suffering. In fact, the immediate context of the fifth seal indicates that those souls have been slaughtered for the name of Christ. Even if that group is taken to represent all believers, many of whom suffer to a lesser degree, their sealing cannot mean absolute protection from persecution but protection from God's wrath. In fact, the expectation from that fifth seal is that a certain number is yet appointed to experience a martyr's death. Still, even these will be harmed only temporarily but not ultimately. As Paul put it to the Corinthians:

> **2 Corinthians 4:7-9; 16-18**
> **7** Now we have this treasure in clay jars, so that this extraordinary power may be from God and not from us. **8** We are afflicted in every way but not crushed; we are perplexed but not in despair; **9** we are persecuted but not abandoned; we are struck down but not destroyed.
>
> **16** Therefore we do not give up. Even though our outer person is being destroyed, our inner person is being renewed day by day. **17** For our momentary light affliction is producing for us an absolutely incomparable eternal weight of glory. **18** So we do not focus on what is seen, but on what is unseen. For what is seen is temporary, but what is unseen is eternal.

The persecution – even to the point of death – is temporary, but God's seal is eternal. What's more, this sealing seems to be God's sovereign move to enable and energize his own to persevere through their earthly suffering and temptations to cave. God's people are only able to stand because of God's grace expressed in sealing them. They are inoculated by the truth against the lie

---

[15] Beale, G. K. (1999). *The book of Revelation: a commentary on the Greek text* (p. 409). Grand Rapids, MI; Carlisle, Cumbria: W.B. Eerdmans; Paternoster Press.
[16] Ibid.

(2 Thes 2:11). They are able to stand along with the Lamb that was slain for them (Rv 5:6). They are able to conquer, standing as pillars because of the name of God (3:12).

*How does this sealing by God relate to the PFG of the book **to reveal Jesus Christ so that his servants faithfully endure suffering in order to receive blessing**?*

Some interpretive choices are before us. We must deal once again with the phrase *"after this."* It comes up twice in this chapter. Does the sealing come chronologically after the first six seals? Our answer to that will influence whether we see one group or two in ch.7. A sample of only three commentators illustrates the wide range of options:

> **Beale:** "The introductory Μετὰ τοῦτο ("after this") does not mean that the events of 7:1–8 are chronologically subsequent to those of ch. 6 but only that this vision appeared to John after the vision in ch. 6 (see further on 4:1)."[17]
>
> **A.R. Faussett:** "The two visions in this chapter come in as an episode after the sixth seal, and before the seventh seal. It is clear that, though "Israel" may elsewhere designate the spiritual Israel, "the elect (Church) on earth" [ALFORD], here, where the names of the tribes one by one are specified, these names cannot have any but the literal meaning."[18]
>
> **D.S. Dockery:** "Chapter seven is actually two visions (7:1–8, 9–17), with the second both interpreting and concluding the first. The sealing of the 144,000 (7:1–8) employs starkly Jewish symbols to describe those who know God through Jesus Christ. Clearly John was referring to Christians as the 144,000. For 7:3 refers to the "servants" of God, a term consistently used throughout Revelation to refer either to Christians in general or the Christian prophet, but never to the non-Christian Jew (or Gentile)."[19]

As we can see, some of these interpretations are mutually exclusive. The second interpreter takes the "after this" in 7:1 as not only to refer to a subsequent *vision* but also a subsequent *event*. This approach sees a literal Jewishness to the group in vv.4-8. The other two interpreters take the opposite approach that "after this" only refers to successive *visions* but *not* successive *events*. These interpreters argue that the term "servants of God" is a strong contextual clue that this group is made up of Christians but is being described in Jewish terms.

---

[17] Beale, G. K. (1999). *The book of Revelation: a commentary on the Greek text* (p. 406). Grand Rapids, MI; Carlisle, Cumbria: W.B. Eerdmans; Paternoster Press.
[18] Jamieson, R., Fausset, A. R., & Brown, D. (1997). *Commentary Critical and Explanatory on the Whole Bible* (Vol. 2, p. 569). Oak Harbor, WA: Logos Research Systems, Inc.
[19] Dockery, D. S. (Ed.). (1992). *Holman Bible Handbook* (p. 797). Nashville, TN: Holman Bible Publishers.

The Sealed and the Seventh Seal

Which interpretation is better justified? Reading on will give us more clues:

The Vast Multitude

> **Revelation 7:9-12**
> **9** After this I looked, and there was a vast multitude from every nation, tribe, people, and language, which no one could number, standing before the throne and before the Lamb. They were clothed in white robes with palm branches in their hands. **10** And they cried out in a loud voice:
>
> > Salvation belongs to our God,
> > who is seated on the throne,
> > and to the Lamb!
>
> **11** All the angels stood around the throne, and along with the elders and the four living creatures they fell facedown before the throne and worshiped God, **12** saying,
>
> > Amen! Blessing and glory and wisdom
> > and thanksgiving and honor
> > and power and strength
> > be to our God forever and ever. Amen.

Here is one of those cases – like in the prologue – where John *hears* one thing but then turns to *see* something different. What John *hears* is the numbering of people to be sealed. That number is like an ancient military census of Israel. So, based on what John *hears*, he would expect to see a complete army of God's people, particularly, the fullness of the *Jewish* people. After hearing this description, what *does* he in fact see?

What John *sees* is very different. Not 144,000 but rather a *"vast multitude...which no one could number."* Not thousands from every tribe of *Israel* but those *"from every nation, tribe, people, and language."* This group appears to be the totality of God's redeemed. Their white robes certainly symbolize their righteousness in Christ as they worship the God and the Lamb of their salvation.

Some will argue that both occurrences of "after this" in ch.7 represent a chronological sequence of events. In that case, they would typically see the group of vv.4-8 as separate from that of vv.9ff, the first being a literal number of ethnic Jews and the second being a description of all "true Israel," including Jew and Gentile as one.

If we take the other option, the groups are the same. John *hears* a Jewish accounting, then *sees* a reality that far exceeds his expectation of the magnitude of the people of God. Both "after this" expressions in that case are merely referring to successive visions, and this whole chapter is a sort of parenthesis describing the people of God in two ways as this age concludes with judgment. God seals his (multi-ethnic) people so that they persevere through until their vindication as he brings his wrath on the world.

In this case, why the Jewish census in the first place? The discussion above about Dan and Ephraim's being left out due to idolatry would support the connection to the PFG. The movement from a Jewish collection to a multi-ethnic one would also follow the progress of biblical theology and perhaps connect to the possibility that the 24 elders are twelve tribal representatives of the Old Covenant along with twelve apostolic representatives of the New Covenant. Paul describes the body of Christ as one, now that Christ has demolished the *"wall of hostility"* (Eph 2:14).

There is a good amount of NT support for understanding the two groups of ch.7 as one. James and Peter refer to Christians as *"twelve tribes dispersed abroad"* (Jas 1:1) and *"exiles dispersed"* (1 Pt 1:1), and Peter uses many other OT Jewish terms to refer to the Church in 1 Pt 2:9. Paul clearly argues in Rm 9:6-8 for the use of language to refer to "Israel" as spiritual descendants of Abraham by faith rather than by ethnicity, what he elsewhere calls the *"Israel of God"* (Gal 6:16).

Drawing from the PFG of Revelation, we may find another strong reason to see these groups as one. It does not seem consistent for only Jews to be sealed by God for the purpose of enduring through trial. Coherent arguments to that effect are specific to this text and fairly complex. They tend to depend upon all non-Jewish believers to be absent the earth at this point in time, since all believers are said elsewhere to be sealed (2 Cor 1:22; Eph 1:13; 4:30). A pretribulational "rapture" of all non-Jewish believers (and then the waking up of ethnic Jews Paul described as the "grafting back in" in Rm 11:23) could account in literal terms for John's vision here, but it seems unnecessarily complicated.

Do you think these are 2 distinct groups, or rather 2 visions of one group, and why?

Does one's perspective on that question affect how Revelation accomplishes its purpose? If so, how?

That brings up another interpretive question. Who are *"the ones coming out of the great tribulation"*?

The Sealed and the Seventh Seal

Out of the Great Tribulation

13 Then one of the elders asked me, "Who are these people in white robes, and where did they come from?"

14 I said to him, "Sir, you know."

Then he told me: These are the ones coming out of the great tribulation. They washed their robes and made them white in the blood of the Lamb.

> **15** For this reason they are before the throne of God,
> and they serve him day and night in his temple.
> The one seated on the throne will shelter them:
> **16** They will no longer hunger;
> they will no longer thirst;
> the sun will no longer strike them,
> nor will any scorching heat.
> **17** For the Lamb who is at the center of the throne
> will shepherd them;
> he will guide them to springs of the waters of life,
> and God will wipe away every tear from their eyes.

What is clear is that the question is about the same group of the immediate context, for they are defined as *"these people in white robes."* So, regardless of where we land on the discussion about the Jewish group of vv.4-8, this group now being referenced is multi-ethnic and innumerable (v.9).

We already mentioned the association of white robes with righteousness but now there is a further association. The *"washing"* of the robes in the *"blood of the Lamb"* seems to connotate suffering, likely even bloodshed reminiscent of the *"slaughter"* of those souls in 6:9. The poem of vv.15-17 clearly speaks of suffering: "hunger," "thirst," "scorching heat" and "tears" say a lot. Now those who suffered in these ways will be sheltered, shepherded, guided and comforted. They are said to be coming *"out of"* the great tribulation. What is that, and what is meant by "coming out" of it?

Again, there is a range of views:

> **Beale:** "Dan. 12:1 is acknowledged as the likely origin for the idea of "the great tribulation": "there will be a time of tribulation, such tribulation as has not come about from when a nation was on the earth until that time" (Theod.). That Daniel is in mind is also apparent from the fact that the phrase "great tribulation" occurs in the NT outside Revelation only in Matt. 24:21 (θλῖψις μεγάλη), where it is part of a fuller and more explicit

reference to Dan. 12:1 (cf. likewise Mark 13:19; 1QM 1.11ff. prophesies that God will protect Israelite saints as they pass through the imminent, unprecedented "time of distress" prophesied in Dan. 12:1, after which they will be rewarded with eternal blessing [1QM 1.8–9])."[20]

L. Morris: "The elder explains that the multitudes are those who are coming (present tense) out of the great tribulation. The article in the Greek seems to indicate the great trouble at the end of things (cf. 3:10). But it is likely that it also refers to tribulation in general (cf. John 16:33; Acts 14:22), for not all will undergo the great tribulation."[21]

Dockery: "To have "come out of the great tribulation" (7:14) does not mean that they exited the earth before the hour of tribulation. To the contrary, they did indeed experience the tribulations of this evil age; but now in heaven they enjoy the presence of God (7:15), where they will hunger no more nor thirst any more (7:16)."[22]

According to Dispensationalism, the Church is "raptured" (caught up) off the earth either before a seven-year Great Tribulation or at a midpoint within the seven years that divides the Tribulation from the *Great* Tribulation. This view sees the term "tribulation" as defining a particular short period of time at the end of this age that is primarily characterized by judgment and wrath. It is argued from 1 Thes 5:9 that Christians (at least those who believed before the Rapture) are not appointed to wrath but saved from it, therefore not present during this time.

Other views hold that tribulation also refers to testing and purification and argue that there is no reason to believe that the catching up that Paul writes about takes place in an event (several years) prior to Christ's coming to judge the earth.

What are the interpretive strengths and weaknesses of each view in relation to ch.7, especially given the historical context of temptation to apostatize (as referenced in chs.2-3)?

Regardless of the identification of the group(s) in ch.7, what seems to be the desired impact of these visions of sealing and sheltering on the original audience? On later readers, including us?

---

[20] Beale, G. K. (1999). *The book of Revelation: a commentary on the Greek text* (p. 433). Grand Rapids, MI; Carlisle, Cumbria: W.B. Eerdmans; Paternoster Press.
[21] Morris, L. (1987). *Revelation: an introduction and commentary* (Vol. 20, p. 116). Downers Grove, IL: InterVarsity Press.
[22] Dockery, D. S. (Ed.). (1992). *Holman Bible Handbook* (p. 798). Nashville, TN: Holman Bible Publishers.

The Seventh Seal

Revelation 8:1-5
1 When he opened the seventh seal, there was silence in heaven for about half an hour. **2** Then I saw the seven angels who stand in the presence of God; seven trumpets were given to them. **3** Another angel, with a golden incense burner, came and stood at the altar. He was given a large amount of incense to offer with the prayers of all the saints on the golden altar in front of the throne. **4** The smoke of the incense, with the prayers of the saints, went up in the presence of God from the angel's hand. **5** The angel took the incense burner, filled it with fire from the altar, and hurled it to the earth; there were peals of thunder, rumblings, flashes of lightning, and an earthquake.

What is your immediate reaction to 8:1?

Here are commonly held opinions from several commentators about what is going on with this seal:

Beale: "When the Lamb finally opens the seventh seal the result is "silence in heaven for about half an hour." Many commentators argue that the silence demonstrates that this is the only seal with no content. This interpretation then allows for the idea that the trumpets and bowls, which follow, are then the actual content of the seventh seal.[201] Some have contended that the silence indicates God's rest, while others argue that it represents a temporary suspension of divine revelation. Others see it as humanity's awestruck silence at the end of history in response to God's full revelation of his sovereign, mysterious purposes throughout history.[203] Sometimes the silence is seen as a dramatic pause making more impressive the following series of trumpet judgments. Although this last suggestion may be generally correct, the key to the significance of the "silence" must lie in the connotation that it has in the OT and in Jewish writings, which suggests that the seventh seal had, in fact, significant conceptual content."[23]

Morris: "John now returns to the seals. The final seal is opened. There is an impressive silence, which we cannot but think portends the End. But instead it begins a new series of visions heralded by angels with trumpets. This is typical of John's method. He goes over the ground again and again, each time teaching us something new. There is more to the End than we can readily take in. Every series of visions brings out new facets of it."[24]

---

[23] Beale, G. K. (1999). *The book of Revelation: a commentary on the Greek text* (p. 445). Grand Rapids, MI; Carlisle, Cumbria: W.B. Eerdmans; Paternoster Press.
[24] Morris, L. (1987). *Revelation: an introduction and commentary* (Vol. 20, p. 118). Downers Grove, IL: InterVarsity Press.

Faussett: "The half hour's silence contrasts with the previous jubilant songs of the great multitude, taken up by the angels (Rev 7:9–11). It is the solemn introduction to the employments and enjoyments of the eternal Sabbath-rest of the people of God, commencing with the Lamb's reading the book heretofore sealed up, and which we cannot know till then. In Rev 10:4, similarly at the eve of the sounding of the seventh trumpet, when the seven thunders uttered their voices, John is forbidden to write them. The seventh trumpet (Rev 11:15–19) winds up God's vast plan of providence and grace in redemption, just as the seventh seal brings it to the same consummation. So also the seventh vial, Rev 16:17. Not that the seven seals, the seven trumpets, and the seven vials, though parallel, are repetitions. They each trace the course of divine action up to the grand consummation in which they all meet, under a different aspect."[25]

A. Knowles: "When the seventh seal is opened, there is silence in heaven (8:1–5). Just as God rested on the seventh day of creation and God's people kept the sabbath as a day of rest, so now there is time for absolute stillness and attention to God. Incense is offered to God, together with the prayers of all the saints. Two sequences of visions are now complete: the letters to seven churches and the breaking of seven seals. We, too, fall silent before the great vistas of truth which have been opened before us."[26]

J. Roloff: "The opening of the final seal comes at last. The reader expects an event that in the end surpasses everything to this point. Instead, there is only a half hour's silence in heaven. What does it mean? Many commentators, and not only more ancient ones, wish to understand it as a reflection of the subjective feeling of the seer who portrays here his "ecstatic lockjaw" (W. Bousset): John experienced a disabling silence that felt "immensely oppressive" (E. Lohse) before the visions resumed with the subsequent series of trumpets. But the text says nothing about a subjective feeling of the seer, speaking rather of an objective event in heaven; everything suggests that this event, analogous to the events produced by the other seal openings, must be understood as part of God's end-time plan for history. But what is still absent from this plan for history? The epiphany of the Judge of the world, which follows the end-time catastrophes, was indirectly alluded to in 6:15–17*, and the deliverance of the elect was also described in visionary form in 7:9–17*. What still remains is the coming of a new creation (cf. 21:1–22:5*). In fact, the silence in heaven appears to be a reference to the end-time work of God's new creation."[27]

So, the seventh seal likely either A) pictures final judgment and new creation or B) only sets these things up as events still to come in the trumpets and bowls.

---

[25] Jamieson, R., Fausset, A. R., & Brown, D. (1997). *Commentary Critical and Explanatory on the Whole Bible* (Vol. 2, p. 571). Oak Harbor, WA: Logos Research Systems, Inc.
[26] Knowles, A. (2001). *The Bible guide* (1st Augsburg books ed., pp. 702–703). Minneapolis, MN: Augsburg.
[27] Roloff, J. (1993). *A Continental Commentary: The Revelation of John* (p. 101). Minneapolis, MN: Fortress Press.

The Sealed and the Seventh Seal

Regardless of these options, what seems to be clearly communicated through the trumpets? The incense, altar and prayers? The fire from the heavenly altar along with the thunder, rumblings, lightning and earthquake on the earth?

Reflection

We zoomed in somewhat to view the interpretive options before us in this lesson. Now, let us zoom back a bit so the PFG can guide our thinking.

Sealing

Remember, regardless of your conclusions about who is included in the sealed of 7:4-8, ALL NT believers have the promises quoted earlier that they are sealed by God's Spirit until the day of redemption.

How does the vision of the sealing of God's people speak to your own personal struggle to persevere in your faith through persecution and waiting?

Tribulation

Remember, regardless of whether there is a taking up of the Church prior to the worst days of this age, Jesus told his disciples to expect persecution and suffering (Jn 15:20). James instructed us to count those tests as joyful opportunities for our faith to be refined and proven true (Jas 1:2-4).

If "coming out of the great tribulation" refers to faithful endurance by God's grace, how does this revelation of Jesus Christ draw you toward faithfulness through whatever tribulation YOU must face?

Sheltering

How do all the verbs of the poem of vv.15-17 ("shelter," "shepherd," "guide" and "wipe away every tear") offer comfort for you?

Lesson 8: The First Six Trumpets (Ch.8, V.6 - Ch.9)

Revelation 8:6
6 And the seven angels who had the seven trumpets prepared to blow them.

Now that John has recorded the opening of the seven seals and moves to the seven trumpets, we are faced with two major interpretive camps. Many take the events of the trumpets (and later the bowls) to come chronologically after the seals. On that view, the seventh seal kicks off the next string of events. Many others take John to be doing something he does elsewhere, especially evident in the book of 1 John. There he establishes key themes and then cycles back repeatedly, twisting the prism to refine and expand upon those themes. If this is the case here, then the trumpets may well cover the same ground on the timeline as the seals did, and so might the bowls. This recapitulation theory finds much of its support in the way that each series of sevens seems to climax to a scale that seems end-of-the-age in magnitude.

Succession or Recapitulation?

Imagine each set of sevens (seals, trumpets, bowls) as three consecutive movements of a powerful symphony being played live for an audience through a massive sound system. The volume builds and builds in the first movement (seals), until the orchestra is "cranked to eleven," then BOOM! Speakers blown. Can there be two more movements (trumpets and bowls) to follow with equally dynamic, or even MORE dynamic, climaxes now that the speakers are shot? Possibly. Maybe the speakers have more life in them after all.

The recapitulation idea would see it differently. In this case, the orchestra is playing *one* symphony that is being captured in three different recordings, each with a different focus. There is one dynamic build-up, and the speakers are blown once. (Maybe new heavens and new earth = a new indestructible sound system!) We get to experience this same masterpiece in three renderings, perhaps first experienced from the musicians' seats. Then the performance is rewound and played from, say, the perspective of the audience on the floor. Then finally, we experience the view from the balcony. Three dramatic presentations of one masterpiece. Then imagine the seventh seal's half hour of silence as that grand pause before the audience erupts in a standing ovation (or maybe a kneeling one)!

One commentator presents some of the key issues as he lands on recapitulation, while another reaches the opposite conclusion:

> **J. Roloff:** "At first glance, one might think that successive periods of the end time are being described. Thus, the grouping of the visions of the seven trumpets appears to grow out of the last part of the visions of the seven seals (8:1–5). Arguing against this interpretation, however, is the fact that a corresponding transition from the visions of the seven trumpets to the visions of the seven bowls is absent, that the contents of the three

cycles of sevens are quite similar, and above all, that the visions of the trumpets and those of the bowls are in large part parallel. Thus, the theory of recapitulation, which is represented for the first time by the ancient church interpreter Victorin von Pettan (d. 304), is more probable. It explains these repetitions by maintaining that the same end-time events are described variously from different angles of vision."[28]

T. Constable: "All the trumpet judgments seem to proceed out of the seventh seal judgment. In other words when the Lamb broke the seventh seal John saw not just one judgment but a whole new series of judgments. There is every reason to conclude that these will follow chronologically. We shall see that seven bowl judgments apparently proceed out of the seventh trumpet judgment in the same way."[29]

Remember that Revelation has a clear purpose, **to reveal Jesus Christ so that his servants faithfully endure suffering in order to receive blessing.** We have concluded that we will find this material most helpful in whatever ways it is most clear. This means that regardless of whether the trumpets follow after the seals or they rewind and then offer a different perspective of the same end-time events, John has recorded them to accomplish this clear purpose. So, consider the interpretive options with an open mind regarding issues of timing and chronology. They are not trivial, but neither are they crucial. What is far more important is how Jesus is revealed in these events, and how that revelation is supposed to help us remain faithful. As we said before, if we let the book accomplish its purpose, we will persevere to blessing regardless of which way we see the timeline.

About Trumpets

We discussed how the opening of seals brought to mind matters of authority. Only authorized people could break the seals of a legal document and dispense whatever decrees were contained in the contents. The authoritative seal-breaker could dispense an inheritance and, especially, render official judgments.

What does Jesus – through his Spirit inspiring John – want the reader to associate with trumpet blasts? Thomas Constable gives us a good survey of biblical contexts for trumpet use:

"Trumpets play a major role in God's dealings with His people (cf. Exod. 19:16; 20:18; Isa. 27:13; Jer. 4:5; Joel 2:1; Zeph. 1:16; Matt. 24:31; 1 Cor. 15:51–52; 1 Thess. 4:16). They were part of Israel's ceremonial processions (e.g., Josh. 6:1, 13–16; 1 Kings 1:34, 39; 1 Chron. 15:24), and they assembled the Israelites for war, journeys, and special feasts (e.g., Num. 10:9–10). They also warned of the coming day of the Lord (e.g., Joel 2:1), and they announced the new year in Israel (e.g., Num. 29:1). Here they announce divine judgment in the day of the Lord (cf. Zech. 1:14–16)."[30]

---

[28] Roloff, J. (1993). *A Continental Commentary: The Revelation of John* (p. 15). Minneapolis, MN: Fortress Press.
[29] Constable, T. (2003). *Tom Constable's Expository Notes on the Bible* (Re 8:6). Galaxie Software.
[30] Ibid., (Re 8:2).

The First Six Trumpets

Of all the options, most commentators see the trumpets here in Revelation as signaling warning, especially related to judgment, and in particular, judgment from God in heaven. The judgments unfolding from the release of the seals seemed to focus more on the natural consequences of sin in a fallen world, at least through the first four seals. With the trumpets, the focus seems more on heavenly judgment upon the ungodly. Consequently, these events seem more severe and aimed particularly at punishing those who have refused to repent of sin.

We don't use trumpets much like this these days. Now we have local sirens or EBS broadcasts over radio, television and mobile devices. What immediate reaction would a sudden siren blast or EBS alert bring upon you?

What kind of emergency response do you think the trumpets of Revelation should prompt?

As with the first four seals, the first four trumpets seem to be offered as a collective before John moves on to the last three trumpets. Let's look at these first four trumpets and notice the pattern of threes.

The First Four Trumpets and the Thirds

> **7** The first angel blew his trumpet, and hail and fire, mixed with blood, were hurled to the earth. So a third of the earth was burned up, a third of the trees were burned up, and all the green grass was burned up.
>
> **8** The second angel blew his trumpet, and something like a great mountain ablaze with fire was hurled into the sea. So a third of the sea became blood, **9** a third of the living creatures in the sea died, and a third of the ships were destroyed.
>
> **10** The third angel blew his trumpet, and a great star, blazing like a torch, fell from heaven. It fell on a third of the rivers and springs of water. **11** The name of the star is Wormwood, and a third of the waters became wormwood. So, many of the people died from the waters, because they had been made bitter.

12 The fourth angel blew his trumpet, and a third of the sun was struck, a third of the moon, and a third of the stars, so that a third of them were darkened. A third of the day was without light and also a third of the night.

13 I looked and heard an eagle flying high overhead, crying out in a loud voice, "Woe! Woe! Woe to those who live on the earth, because of the remaining trumpet blasts that the three angels are about to sound!"

First, we see the strong emphasis on threes within these trumpet blasts. These judgments are everywhere expressed in thirds. Trumpet one affects a third of the earth and the trees. Trumpet two impacts a third of the sea, a third of its creatures and a third of its ships. Trumpet three taints a third of the land-locked waters. Trumpet four strikes a third of the celestial objects of sun, moon and stars, with a proportionate impact on day and night. Even the announcement that follows in v.13 groups the last three angels together with their three woes.

Why all the threes and thirds? Commentators widely agree that this is to communicate that these judgments are thus far still *measured*. Mankind's own sin has begun to bring destruction back upon humanity and now God is himself adding his judgment to that distress, but God is still restraining himself somewhat for now. Even the one exception to the fractional decrees – ALL the green grass – seems to be limited, because grass is targeted again in 9:4. Apparently, either the roots or otherwise dormant grasses once again grow up in the period between. Already, though, in 8:7, the terrain would look like a war zone.

Next, note that even though these first trumpets carried a measured judgment in *severity*, as a foursome they carry the symbolism of totality in *scope*. Just as "four corners of the earth" represents the whole earth, this fourfold trumpet series impacts the whole created order. The destruction is not complete, but it is everywhere.

What may be most important to notice in the trumpets is that the focus is different than it was in the seals, as we illustrated with either three symphony movements or recordings. The seals focused more on testing or proving, while the trumpets focus more on judgment.

The first four seals focus on *humanity* in a fallen world system. It depicts the rise of natural consequences of human evil, especially as *a time of testing for believers,* who are then shown to be sealed for faithful endurance. While believers are not specifically addressed in the first four seals, the implication of the fifth seal is that the testing – the proving of faith – is not yet complete for some. They may suffer physical death for their testimony, but they are ensured eternal life and rest. So, in the seals *Christians are being proven by suffering at the hands of evil humans.* (We'll see later on that human evil is being supercharged by demonic power as well.)

The *trumpets*, however, begin with a focus upon the real estate of the earth. Human suffering and death are certainly implied but only explicitly mentioned in the third trumpet. The warning of v.13

The First Six Trumpets

provides a hinge. The first four trumpets have brought devastation to the earth (with collateral human damage), but now the heavenly judgment will target *unbelieving humans*. As we will see in a moment, the tables are turned in the trumpet judgments, for it is those who are *not* sealed by God who are suffering. As we move forward, we will see that in the trumpets the *non-Christians are being judged by suffering at the hands of the God who must vindicate his faithful.*

Before we move forward, it is helpful to look back and note that images associated with divine judgment (burning, darkness and woe) fill this section. There are also many connections back to not only the seals but much further back to the Exodus from Egypt. Here are a few:

- Earth, trees and grass (8:7 & 9:4) echo earth, sea and tree (7:1,3). In both cases the destruction is pronounced first, and then the restraint related to the seal ("do not harm" in 9:4 and 7:3).
- Hail and fire mixed with blood echoes the Exodus plague (Ex 9:13-35).
- A mountain ablaze with fire echoes Sinai in the Exodus (19:18) or may also indicate a wicked kingdom being judged. Similarly, a great star may symbolize an angel being judged (cf. Is 14:12-15).
- Bitter water echoes Exodus (15:23) and the prophets. (Wormwood is mentioned in Jer, Lam and Amos). It may refer to heresy that is symbolically killing many in the "waters" of humanity (in the Greek "destroyed" can mean "corrupted," see Rv 12:4).
- Sun, moon and stars were objects of false worship (Dt 4:19; 17:23; Jer 8:2, cf. Gn 37:9); objects of God's creative work (Ps 148:3; Jer 31:35) and associated with judgment (Ez 32:7; Joel 2:10; 3:15). All these associations may come together here. (Also, since these are associated with God's fixed natural order and used as guarantees of his covenant, they may here symbolize both judgment on covenant *failure* by man and God's covenant *faithfulness*, see Jer 31:35-36; 33:20-26).

How can you relate to the ancient Israelites as being brought by God through your OWN exodus in the following ways: How have you been enslaved? How have you been miraculously saved? What is your promised land? What will God do to your enemies?

Consider the following commentary by Beale on the first four trumpets:

> "All four trumpets have in common that they affect three parts of the created order. The parts that are struck suggest that the basic content of creation is being systematically undone. Though not in the same order as in Genesis 1, the elements affected are light, air, vegetation, sun, moon, stars, sea creatures, and humans. The notion of a "de-creation" is supported by the fact that the Apocalypse climaxes in new creation (21:1ff.) and that the

trumpet series has begun a new overview of history after having spun out of the seventh seal, which partly evoked the silence following the destruction of the old creation."[31]

These events of the first four trumpets *may*, for the most part, be read and understood literally much like when we read the narrative of the Exodus in the OT. In fact, Constable points out that there was a long prophetic tradition of expecting such things to come at the end of the age.

> "The OT prophets understood that the miracles of Egypt were to be repeated in the future (e.g., Isa. 10:22–25; 11:12–16; 30:30; Jer. 16:14–15; 23:7–8; Ezek. 38:22; Mic. 7:15) . . . At several points the prophet Amos uses God's miraculous work of deliverance from Egypt as a reference point for the way He will deal with His people in the future (cf. Amos 2:10; 4:10; 8:8–9; 9:5–7)."[32]

Still, we must remember that John's primary task was to communicate through his *symbols* to accomplish the stated PFG. While these descriptions *may* be literal, they do not *necessarily* have to be. Whether *literal* fire is coming to earth, the *figurative* fire of God's judgment *certainly* is. The genre blend of Revelation does not constrain our interpretation nearly as much as did the historical narrative of Exodus. A strong possibility is that fire is coming *both* literally and figuratively as it did upon Sodom and Gomorrah (Gn 19).

Further, while the trumpets may or may not come chronologically after the seals, John is clearly communicating a different emphasis now. God will judge the world for sin. Just as man's sin has corrupted the whole earth, judgment must come to the earth. Now the wicked inhabitants themselves will begin to suffer for their unrepentant rebellion and violence. An eagle announces the bad news. This may be a literal eagle (perhaps like the massive ones in Tolkien's The Hobbit, though the word may also be translated "vulture") or something like it (some manuscripts have "angel"). Either way, the pronouncement of woes communicates disaster. In the Bible "w-o-e" usually translates quickly to "w-h-o-a!" This will be a dramatic example:

The Fifth Trumpet (The First Woe)

Revelation 9:1–12
1 The fifth angel blew his trumpet, and I saw a star that had fallen from heaven to earth. The key for the shaft to the abyss was given to him. **2** He opened the shaft to the abyss, and smoke came up out of the shaft like smoke from a great furnace so that the sun and the air were darkened by the smoke from the shaft. **3** Then locusts came out of the smoke on to the earth, and power was given to them like the power that scorpions have on the

---

[31] Beale, G. K. (1999). *The book of Revelation: a commentary on the Greek text* (p. 486). Grand Rapids, MI; Carlisle, Cumbria: W.B. Eerdmans; Paternoster Press.
[32] Constable, T. (2003). *Tom Constable's Expository Notes on the Bible* (Re 8:7). Galaxie Software.

The First Six Trumpets

earth. **4** They were told not to harm the grass of the earth, or any green plant, or any tree, but only those people who do not have God's seal on their foreheads. **5** They were not permitted to kill them but were to torment them for five months; their torment is like the torment caused by a scorpion when it stings someone. **6** In those days people will seek death and will not find it; they will long to die, but death will flee from them.

7 The appearance of the locusts was like horses prepared for battle. Something like golden crowns was on their heads; their faces were like human faces; **8** they had hair like women's hair; their teeth were like lions' teeth; **9** they had chests like iron breastplates; the sound of their wings was like the sound of many chariots with horses rushing into battle; **10** and they had tails with stingers like scorpions, so that with their tails they had the power to harm people for five months. **11** They had as their king the angel of the abyss; his name in Hebrew is Abaddon, and in Greek he has the name Apollyon.
12 The first woe has passed. There are still two more woes to come after this.

Okay, we've officially moved into the territory of bizarre. John fills this chapter with more similes than anywhere else in the Bible. He's struggling to record what he sees. It's passages like this that cause many to throw up their hands and flip over to the Gospels or a Bible study on Ephesians or something. We'll stay tethered to the PFG and prayerfully seek to understand the meaning of this trumpet.

Let's look at a few important terms in v.1. The "star" who has "fallen" is given the "key" to the "abyss." That last Greek term is defined as "a supernatural, unfathomable, bottomless gulf or pit regarded as the antithesis to heaven; most often for the detaining and punishment of demons." In this book, "star" has already been used to symbolize angels, and here "key" has already symbolized authority. This star, unlike the apparently inanimate one of 8:10, is personal, and has been given authority.

It may be possible to take "fallen" in a moral sense, that this is a rebellious angel, perhaps Satan himself (cf., 12:12). God allowed Satan limited authority to attack Job (Job chs.1-2), so there is precedent to allow that God might authorize more widespread satanic attacks here. However, the term "fallen" may also simply mean "descended," and this angel doesn't seem active in these attacks but only in releasing them. Further, the attacks are not upon the righteous (who are sealed) but upon the wicked.

Since the nature of the angel is not clear, we can conclude it is not essential. What *is* clear is the nature of the work he performs, and the nature of the authority to perform it. The authority is given, and it is symbolized by the key. The work is to unleash demonic, beastly torture upon the unrepentant.

The "locusts" that are set loose are, like other things John sees, hard to describe and carrying symbolic meaning. Whether the descriptions are literal or not, we get the idea: these creatures are terrifying and powerful. Stingers like scorpions, crowns of power, humanoid faces, teeth like lions', chests like iron and wind-whipping wings. "Hair like women's hair" may not strike us as terrifying, but it almost certainly means long hair and probably conveys a terrible glory or perhaps wildness. What's more, these beasts come "out of the smoke," like scary foes emerge from a swirling dark fog in Harry Potter or Batman movies.

And this is not some helter-skelter mob. This is an organized army mobilized for attack from the bowels of the underworld. It is led by a king, the "angel of the abyss" in v.11. His name means "destruction" (Hebrew: see Jb 26:6; 28:22; 31:12; Ps 88:11; Pr 15:11; 27:20) or "destroyer" (Greek), and he is associated with death, the grave or the netherworld. Locusts are associated with destruction in the OT, but these are on steroids. Ironically, in bringing destruction these beasts are not given permission to kill but only to torture. Death will come, but for those inflicted by this swarm it cannot come soon enough (vv.5-6). Talk about terrifying!

Notice again in v.4 the shift from judgment upon the *earth* (trumpets 1-4) to judgment against the wicked *people* of the earth. Notice, too, both the *presence* and *protection* of God's faithful. This plague can only harm the wicked, those who are not sealed by God. Almost unbelievably, this judgment is, even now, still measured. There are two more woes to come.

How do you suppose John's original audience felt about the statement in v.4, that these terrible scorpion locusts from the abyss cannot harm Christians? How does it make YOU feel?

The Sixth Trumpet (The Second Woe)

> **13** The sixth angel blew his trumpet. From the four horns of the golden altar that is before God, I heard a voice **14** say to the sixth angel who had the trumpet, "Release the four angels bound at the great river Euphrates." **15** So the four angels who were prepared for the hour, day, month, and year were released to kill a third of the human race. **16** The number of mounted troops was two hundred million; I heard their number. **17** This is how I saw the horses and their riders in the vision: They had breastplates that were fiery red, hyacinth blue, and sulfur yellow. The heads of the horses were like the heads of lions, and from their mouths came fire, smoke, and sulfur. **18** A third of the human race was killed by these three plagues—by the fire, the smoke, and the sulfur that came from their mouths. **19** For the power of the horses is in their mouths and in their tails, because their tails, which resemble snakes, have heads that inflict injury.

The First Six Trumpets

Things have gone from extremely bad to much worse for those not sealed by God. The plague of tortuous locusts is now followed by an apparently demonic army that is even worse. This army has been restrained for this exact moment and it has a specific target: "to kill a third of the human race." Just as the key represented a delegated authority for the angel to open the abyss, there is symbolism here in v.16. The golden altar is "before God" and so represents the highest authority. Four horns symbolize the totality of God's power. From this highest power and authority comes the command to release the leaders of this devastating army.

These four angels can almost certainly be seen only as fallen angels, or demons, for faithful angels are not said in Scripture to be bound. Once again, that there are four of them indicates the total scope of their assault. These four angels echo the ones in 7:1 but cannot be them, because there the angels are *doing* the restraining rather than *being* restrained. It is not clear whether these angels themselves do any of the killing, but they are clearly leading a massive army given that task.

Commentators do not agree whether this army numbers a literal two hundred million. Normally, a number expressed with language like the one here communicates an innumerable quantity. It may be that the number was impossibly large for John himself to count, and that might be the significance of his hearing an exact number (if that is the case). Regardless, we get the point. This army is even bigger than the locust swarm, and it is deadly.

It seems the killing is done by the horses rather than the riders, but as with the locusts, these are no mere horses. They are described as having colorful armor and imposing heads that spewed fire, smoke and sulfur, elements associated with judgment and death. In fact, they kill not only with their mouths but also with snake-like tails.

Imagine you have just survived an onslaught of terrifying horse-like locusts coming out of a black smoke. That nightmare went on and on, perhaps for a literal five months. Now a demon army riding fire-breathing horses with snake-tails is killing people all around you!

If you are not a Christian, how do you suppose you are reacting right now?

How about if you are a Christian?

Surely, by now every atheist, every pagan, every person who has trusted in anything but God would now cry out for him to save them, right?

The Revelation of Jesus Christ

20 The rest of the people, who were not killed by these plagues, did not repent of the works of their hands to stop worshiping demons and idols of gold, silver, bronze, stone, and wood, which cannot see, hear, or walk. **21** And they did not repent of their murders, their sorceries, their sexual immorality, or their thefts.

What do you make of this reaction? Does it surprise you? Why or why not?

An angel says in Rv 22:11, "Let the unrighteous go on in unrighteousness; let the filthy still be filthy; let the righteous go on in righteousness; let the holy still be holy." How does the reaction to the first six trumpets relate to this statement by the angel?

Point of No Return?

The reaction of the unbeliever to reject God even in the face of judgment and destruction reminds us of the stubborn pharaoh of the Exodus. It begs the question, "Do unbelievers continue to reject God because they are *unable* to repent, or because they are *unwilling*?" The Bible suggests that "yes" may be the best answer. We are unable to know the heart. We cannot discern the lines of interplay between a creature's hardening of one's own heart and the Creator's hardening of that same heart.

The Bible does repeat the refrain: "Do not harden your hearts" (Ps 95:8; Heb 3:8,15; 4:7). It also indicates that if we ignore the refrain too long, God will harden our hearts in cooperation with our own rebellious desire (Ex 4:21; Is 63:17). When does one cross the line? When are they too far gone? We cannot know, and that is why we are warned to not push it.

The fact that there IS such a point when God's amazing patience is finally and fully exhausted reminds us of our current role as witnesses for Christ. While this Revelation is calling us believers to persevere to our own blessing, it is also reminding us of what is to come for those who refuse to repent. It especially reminds us of the hope that there are still others who WILL repent before it's too late, provided we share the gospel faithfully.

For those yet to repent, we are like singers carrying the message of that classic Larry Norman song from the Jesus Movement, "I wish we'd all been ready." The lyric is ironic because it speaks from the perspective beyond that point of no return. But when we sing it now, anticipating that day but still in advance of it, it is a powerful call to repentance. Right now, there IS still "time to change your mind." So, these pictures from Revelation of coming judgment are for the *Church* but are

The First Six Trumpets

also potentially effective for the *unbelievers* who may be reached by us once we are invigorated in our witness by the reminder of what is to come.

Reflection

What do these first six trumpet judgments reveal about Jesus Christ?

How do these horrific descriptions encourage you as a Christian to endure suffering and be a faithful witness?

How do these trumpet warnings begin to signal the blessings you have, and to which you look forward, in Christ?

Lesson 9: The Mystery of God, the Little Scroll, the Two Witnesses, and the Seventh Trumpet (Chs.10-11)

Opening discussion
Think of your favorite books, shows, movies, etc. where the plot kept you guessing until everything finally was explained in the end (the dénouement). Do you like trying to figure out what will happen? Why or why not?

How do good storytellers use mystery to string us along until the end, and why is it so effective?

Just as there was a break before the seventh seal, John is given an aside here in his visions between the sixth and seventh trumpet. As we have already noted a different focus between the seals and trumpets, so too here. The break before the seventh seal emphasized both the *testing* of and *sealing* of God's faithful. The break here before the seventh trumpet will have a different emphasis. Here the focus is on the prophetic *witness* of the faithful and the unfolding of the mystery of God.

The Mighty Angel and the Mystery of God

Revelation 10:1–7
1 Then I saw another mighty angel coming down from heaven, wrapped in a cloud, with a rainbow over his head. His face was like the sun, his legs were like pillars of fire, **2** and he held a little scroll opened in his hand. He put his right foot on the sea, his left on the land, **3** and he called out with a loud voice like a roaring lion. When he cried out, the seven thunders raised their voices. **4** And when the seven thunders spoke, I was about to write, but I heard a voice from heaven, saying, "Seal up what the seven thunders said, and do not write it down!"

5 Then the angel that I had seen standing on the sea and on the land raised his right hand to heaven. **6** He swore by the one who lives forever and ever, who created heaven and what is in it, the earth and what is in it, and the sea and what is in it, "There will no longer be a delay, **7** but in the days when the seventh angel will blow his trumpet, then the mystery of God will be completed, as he announced to his servants the prophets."

The Revelation of Jesus Christ

The angel described in the beginning of this chapter sounds crazy powerful, so much so that commentators conclude he is either an archangel who represents Christ, that he is a Christological appearance of what the OT calls the Angel of the LORD or that he is Christ himself. This description is similar to OT theophanies (manifestations of God) like happened at Mt. Sinai when Yahweh gave his law to Moses for his people.

The phrase "clothed with a cloud" echoes Dn 7:13 and Rv 4:14. The rainbow here reminds us of 4:3 and echoes Ezek 1:28. It is closely associated with God's glory. "Face like the sun" echoes descriptions of Jesus in Mt 17:2 (at his transfiguration) and Rv 1:16. "Legs" and "pillars" are symbols of strength, especially together and especially when standing on both sea and land. This angel symbolizes power over chaos and the domain of humanity. His voice is powerful and intimidating like a lion's roar, and further, it is associated with seven thunders. Just as the seven spirits seem to represent the sevenfold Spirit of God, these seven thunders may represent the sevenfold voice of God. Here again is the authority to seal or unseal. In this case, John is forbidden to write what the thunders spoke.

What is spoken is apparently intelligible to John, but it is either not for *everyone* and or not for *now*. The other times Scripture records that prophecies were to be sealed all occur in Daniel (8:26; 12:4,9). These revelations were to be kept for later, the last two of them "until the time of the end." Has that time now come, or at least come near, in John's vision? Is the angel saying in vv.6-7 that what John has just now been instructed to *not* write down will be revealed in the seventh trumpet? In that case, what the thunders uttered would be only for the very last days of this age (thus future for John and his original audience). It seems reasonable that what the thunders said, and what John is forbidden to write, may well be the "mystery of God" that will be completed when the seventh angel blows his trumpet.

What is this mystery? It seems pretty important, since this book is a revelation. First, its "[being] completed" in v.7 makes it sound like the days of the 7th trumpet mark the end of the age. This may lend support to the recapitulation theory we discussed earlier. Next, we observe this mystery was "announced" to the prophets. That Greek term is the verb form of the word we translate *evangelism*, and it refers to the proclamation of the gospel.

Next, let's consider the biblical context for "mystery." This is a theme in Daniel (the term occurs seven times). Remember King Nebuchadnezzar's dream? God is declared to be "a revealer of mysteries" (2:28,47; see also Jb 12:22). The Gospels record Jesus telling his disciples, "the divine secret of the kingdom of God has been given to you..." (Mt 13:11; Mk 4:11; Lk 8:10).

Outside of these references and those of Revelation, all the other specific uses of the more specific term "mystery of God" are by Paul. As he closes his letter to the Romans, Paul writes:

The Mystery of God, the Little Scroll, the Two Witnesses, and the Seventh Trumpet

Romans 16:25–27

25 Now to him who is able to strengthen you according to my gospel and the proclamation about Jesus Christ, according to the revelation of the mystery kept silent for long ages **26** but now revealed and made known through the prophetic Scriptures, according to the command of the eternal God to advance the obedience of faith among all the Gentiles— **27** to the only wise God, through Jesus Christ—to him be the glory forever! Amen.

Notice the connection between "the revelation of the mystery" and "the obedience of faith." Ding, ding, ding! That's a direct correlation to the PFG of Revelation! Paul's focus of this letter was for a largely Gentile audience, and so here this mystery is expressed specifically to them.

Elsewhere, Paul writes of the mystery of God as something given via proclamation (1 Cor 2:1) to the Church, one the Church manages (4:1) and administrates, especially as it is proclaimed to the Gentiles (Eph 3:9). Though this component of the unifying of Jew and Gentile is commonly a part of Paul's discussions, this "mystery of God" is ultimately summed up in one word in Col 2:2 – "Christ." Paul says, "In him are hidden all the treasures of wisdom and knowledge" (v.3). Here it is again! The mystery of God has everything to do with the revealing of Jesus Christ.

If the clues of all prior biblical context lead us to think of "the mystery of God" to be bound up in Christ and his Church, then Revelation is totally consistent with that idea, and it refines it further. Christ is being revealed *to* his Church so that he may continue to be revealed *through* his Church until the end of the age. Three of the four mentions of "mystery" in Revelation seem to involve either the true Church (1:20) or the apostate (corrupt) Church (17:5,7). Given the strong connection in the immediate context of Rv.10 to the evangelistic proclamation of the Church (v.9) and the completion of her witness (ch.11), it might be argued that one way to summarize "the mystery of God" is as "the witness of Christ through his Church."

The Little Scroll

8 Then the voice that I heard from heaven spoke to me again and said, "Go, take the scroll that lies open in the hand of the angel who is standing on the sea and on the land."

9 So I went to the angel and asked him to give me the little scroll. He said to me, "Take and eat it; it will be bitter in your stomach, but it will be as sweet as honey in your mouth."

10 Then I took the little scroll from the angel's hand and ate it. It was as sweet as honey in my mouth, but when I ate it, my stomach became bitter. **11** And they said to me, "You must prophesy again about many peoples, nations, languages, and kings."

As with the scroll of ch.5, we understand this "little scroll" to symbolize some part of the unfolding of God's sovereign plan. In fact, some commentators argue this is the same scroll as the one in ch.5, but it seems more likely that this scroll is more limited in its scope, since it is called "little."

Once again, the scroll is associated with the great power and authority that comes from God on his throne, in this case through the mighty angel who stands in power on sea and land. That this scroll is "open" seems to indicate that its contents are already unfolding and would stand in contrast to whatever the seven thunders uttered that was to be "sealed up." The contents of the scroll are closely tied to prophecy. The message of the prophecy would be "sweet" in the mouth of a believer like John but would bring "bitterness" in the stomach as it declared judgment upon the wicked.

The eating of the scroll has a parallel in Ezekiel that is almost surely in the mind of John and his early audience:

Ezekiel 2:8–3:3
8 "And you, son of man, listen to what I tell you: Do not be rebellious like that rebellious house. Open your mouth and eat what I am giving you." **9** So I looked and saw a hand reaching out to me, and there was a written scroll in it. **10** When he unrolled it before me, it was written on the front and back; words of lamentation, mourning, and woe were written on it.

1 He said to me, "Son of man, eat what you find here. Eat this scroll, then go and speak to the house of Israel." **2** So I opened my mouth, and he fed me the scroll. **3** "Son of man," he said to me, "feed your stomach and fill your belly with this scroll I am giving you." So I ate it, and it was as sweet as honey in my mouth.

Notice here in Rv 10 the angel gives the order: "bitter in the stomach" then "sweet in the mouth." John then takes it in, reversing the order: it is sweet in the mouth, then turning his stomach. Since the next statement is about his required prophecy, it seems he has yet to experience the latter "sweet in the mouth" part of the angel's sequence. Why is that?

The editors of the above translation (the CSB) point out that the phrase "prophesy again about" may also be translated "prophesy again against." This is important to note because the context in which this angel says this to John is one of judgment. We'll explore this more in the next section regarding the testimony of the two witnesses, but for now, make note of the fact that prophets executed their office in two primary roles. They spoke God's words both *for* repentance and *against* rebellion. They prophesied *for* the *faithful* in calls to stay faithful or to repent and return to faithfulness, as Jesus did in Rv 2-3. They also prophesied *against* the *unfaithful* in proclamations that judgment would come upon them for their persistent rebellion.

The Mystery of God, the Little Scroll, the Two Witnesses, and the Seventh Trumpet

This seems to indicate that John's prophetic message (which is sweet to him as a believer) is presently gut-wrenching during the struggle under which the Church witnesses, but it will be sweet to finally deliver the message of justice and watch it unfold. This would harmonize with the announcement for those under the altar from ch.6, as well as for a theme of the whole book: *hold on a little longer – sweet vindication is coming.* That he is to prophesy *again* probably relates to prior commissioning for John in 1:10-20 and 4:1-2, and likely also to prior proclamations by OT prophets.

How is the message of the gospel sweet to you?

How is it gut-wrenching to know what it means for those who reject Christ?

Have you ever been knotted up inside, knowing you needed to speak truth to someone? How did it feel when you finally said what you knew you had to say?

The Two Witnesses

As soon as John is told *he* had a message to deliver, the vision turns to a description of two *other* witnesses. John is sent to the temple of God to count those who worship. There seems to be much more going on than the gathering of data for accurate attendance records! Consider these questions before we go on into ch.11:

Why does a witness give a testimony, and what are the possible responses to that testimony?

Why is there such a thing as a "witness protection program" in our day?

The Revelation of Jesus Christ

In the Bible, when the truth is proclaimed (e.g., by prophets), what effect does that truth have on those who believe it? On those who refuse to believe it?

What did Jesus say about his Church and the power of the opposition against her?

Revelation 11:1–14
1 Then I was given a measuring reed like a rod, with these words: "Go and measure the temple of God and the altar, and count those who worship there. **2** But exclude the courtyard outside the temple. Don't measure it, because it is given to the nations, and they will trample the holy city for forty-two months. **3** I will grant my two witnesses authority to prophesy for 1,260 days, dressed in sackcloth." **4** These are the two olive trees and the two lampstands that stand before the Lord of the earth. **5** If anyone wants to harm them, fire comes from their mouths and consumes their enemies; if anyone wants to harm them, he must be killed in this way. **6** They have authority to close up the sky so that it does not rain during the days of their prophecy. They also have power over the waters to turn them into blood and to strike the earth with every plague whenever they want.

7 When they finish their testimony, the beast that comes up out of the abyss will make war on them, conquer them, and kill them. **8** Their dead bodies will lie in the main street of the great city, which figuratively is called Sodom and Egypt, where also their Lord was crucified. **9** And some of the peoples, tribes, languages, and nations will view their bodies for three and a half days and not permit their bodies to be put into a tomb. **10** Those who live on the earth will gloat over them and celebrate and send gifts to one another because these two prophets had tormented those who live on the earth.

11 But after three and a half days, the breath of life from God entered them, and they stood on their feet. Great fear fell on those who saw them. **12** Then they heard a loud voice from heaven saying to them, "Come up here." They went up to heaven in a cloud, while their enemies watched them. **13** At that moment a violent earthquake took place, a tenth of the city fell, and seven thousand people were killed in the earthquake. The survivors were terrified and gave glory to the God of heaven.

14 The second woe has passed. Take note: The third woe is coming soon!

The Mystery of God, the Little Scroll, the Two Witnesses, and the Seventh Trumpet

For context regarding the measuring of the temple and the remarks about the courtyard, compare Ezek chs.40-43. Also, note the following historical information from J. Roloff:

> "The correspondence to the actual events of the year A.D. 70 appears particularly astounding. When the Romans laid siege to Jerusalem, the zealots who were conducting the Jewish revolt took shelter in the inner chambers of the temple in order to make it the center of their defense, "so that the surrounding temple-court from the multitude of dead resembled a common burial-ground and the temple itself a fortress. Into those hallowed and inviolable precincts they rushed in arms ..." (Jos., J.W. 6.3.177 = LCL 3:411)."[33]

It may be that John is borrowing from this historical event to show the Church as the holy remnant that survives the destruction of Jerusalem and the earthly temple. In fact, there are more connections between this opening paragraph of Rv 11 and that historic event of AD 70, says L. Morris:

> "Forty-two months (again in 13:5) is the same period as 1,260 days (11:3; 12:6), or 'a time, times and half a time' (12:14; Dan. 7:25; 12:7; 'a time' = one year, 'times' = two years, 'half a time' = six months). That is to say, the same length of time as in Daniel is allowed for the treading down of the holy city by the Gentiles, the prophesying of the two witnesses, the woman's stay in the wilderness, and the beast's exercise of authority. This is the length of time that Antiochus Epiphanes tyrannized in Jerusalem, a time of unbelievable horror for the pious Jew, but a time which came to its end. So John will mean his readers to discern that the trial of the people of God will be of measurable duration and that they will be delivered out of it."[34]

Morris seems right that John's revelation here is intended to communicate a measured time and context for trial and witness of the people of God.

These witnesses are hard to sort out. So, as before, we will look for what is clear in the symbolism, and we will remember that what we are told here is tied to the PFG, and so it is meant **to reveal Jesus Christ so that his servants faithfully endure suffering in order to receive blessing.**

First, notice the context of worship (v.1). These worshipers are – or symbolize – true worship of the true God. Next, notice their worship and witness are in the context of "trampling" (v.2), "sackcloth" (v.3) and intended "harm" (v.5). Now, notice they have "authority" to testify (v.3), and though they do so for a measured time their testimony is powerful and unthwarted (vv.5-6). Then, observe that once the time of their testimony is concluded, these witnesses are killed by a beastly power and their death is celebrated by all who hated them (vv.7-10).

---

[33] Roloff, J. (1993). *A Continental Commentary: The Revelation of John* (p. 129). Minneapolis, MN: Fortress Press.
[34] Morris, L. (1987). *Revelation: an introduction and commentary* (Vol. 20, p. 143). Downers Grove, IL: InterVarsity Press.

So, who are these two witnesses? Theologians are all over the map on this one, so let's understand the major options and observe some clues. Some see these witnesses as literal humans, say, Elijah and Moses, and there are plenty other candidates offered by those holding to the literal option. Many others think the witnesses symbolize the collective witness of the Church throughout this age, or perhaps a particular portion of it. Whatever the case, most commentators argue that it is hard to see these descriptions of ch.11 as BOTH literal and figurative, and so most conclude one or the other option is best.

What are our clues? For one, the term "lampstands" that is used in v.4 is used elsewhere in Revelation only to refer to churches (1:12,13,20; 2:1,5). Why two? There may be a connection to the fact that under the OT law, two witnesses were required to bring lawbreakers to judgment (Nu 35:30; Dt 17:6; 19:15). Also, it has been suggested that since only two of the seven churches in chs.2-3 were *not* rebuked for shortcomings, it is possible that two represents the *effective* (not failing) or *true* (not apostate) witness of the Church.

The term "olive trees" tells us more. G.K. Beale explains:

> "Olive trees and lampstands together, along with the concluding clause of v 4, come from Zech. 4:14 (cf. 4:2–3, 11–14). In Zechariah's vision the lampstand represented the second temple (the part representing the whole), for which Zerubbabel had laid the foundation (see above on 1:13–15). On either side was an olive tree that provided oil for the lamps. Zechariah interprets the olive trees as "the anointed ones who are standing before the LORD of the whole earth" (4:14), that is, as Joshua the high priest and Zerubbabel."[35]

So, the terminology used here strongly suggests these witnesses are symbolic. There is one more clue that is very telling. The term "dead bodies" in v.8 may be misleading in the English, for the Greek is singular. For this reason, the CSB offers a helpful alternate: "their corpse." These two witnesses have a *singular* corpse. This strongly suggests not two literal persons but a two-fold, unified, symbolic witness.

No matter where one lands on the details of these witnesses, the PFG brings into focus the way that John's material here is supposed to encourage God's people to endure faithfully through suffering. His original audience would recall the fairly recent terror under Antiochus Epiphanes, or similarly, the destruction of the temple in AD 70, in that case, probably even through first-hand experience. But they and all future audiences would understand that a measured suffering will continue for the witnessing Church as long as God has decreed. Finally, God will allow evil to be fully expressed as the witnesses complete their task and succumb to a collective death. That will only signal judgment and vindication. God's witnesses will be resurrected to immortal bodies and the wicked will be judged. Whether interpreting the witnesses literally or symbolically, we must see that John delivers a clear message that is at minimum *applicable* to all believers.

---

[35] Beale, G. K. (1999). *The book of Revelation: a commentary on the Greek text* (p. 577). Grand Rapids, MI; Carlisle, Cumbria: W.B. Eerdmans; Paternoster Press.

The Mystery of God, the Little Scroll, the Two Witnesses, and the Seventh Trumpet

As a witness for Christ, how is it important for you to realize that the opposition cannot stop your testimony (v.5)?

How is it needful and helpful to realize that you are a witness until death (v.7)?

How is it comforting to know that you will be resurrected once the witness of the Church is complete (v.11)?

How do these truths depicted in ch.11 help Revelation accomplish its purpose in you?

The Functions of Testimony

In the last lesson, we considered how it seems possible, if not likely, that no unbelievers repent once God begins to release his judgments on the world. If that's the case, why would witnesses be offering the testimony of the gospel? Why would God employ witnesses to a hopeless task?

Make note that this has happened many times with the OT prophets, most notably Isaiah. God told him explicitly that the people would reject his message. He told him to faithfully proclaim it anyway:

> **Isaiah 6:9–10**
> Go! Say to these people:
> Keep listening, but do not understand;
> keep looking, but do not perceive.
> **10** Make the minds of these people dull;
> deafen their ears and blind their eyes;
> otherwise they might see with their eyes
> and hear with their ears,
> understand with their minds,
> turn back, and be healed.

Isaiah asked how long he must do this. The Lord replies:

> Until cities lie in ruins without inhabitants,
> houses are without people,
> the land is ruined and desolate,
> **12** and the LORD drives the people far away,
> leaving great emptiness in the land.
> **13** Though a tenth will remain in the land,
> it will be burned again.
> Like the terebinth or the oak
> that leaves a stump when felled,
> the holy seed is the stump.

Notice that in Isaiah's day, God promised to leave a remnant to survive the judgment upon those who would not repent. When this cycle repeats in Revelation, it reads like God's remnant is removed from the earth when ultimate and final judgment comes at the hands of the Son. Still, until that moment comes the faithful witness must be offered to vindicate God as righteous in dispensing this judgment.

One hint that some *might* come to faith during the 6th trumpet is in 11:13 when "the survivors... gave glory to the God of heaven." This reaction is clearly different from that of 9:21, though it is not clear whether it is evidence of conversion. There are no explicit indications of repentance after the 5th trumpet.

The Seventh Trumpet

> **15** The seventh angel blew his trumpet, and there were loud voices in heaven saying,
>
>> The kingdom of the world has become the kingdom
>> of our Lord and of his Christ,
>> and he will reign forever and ever.
>
> **16** The twenty-four elders, who were seated before God on their thrones, fell facedown and worshiped God, **17** saying,

The Mystery of God, the Little Scroll, the Two Witnesses, and the Seventh Trumpet

> We give you thanks, Lord God, the Almighty,
> who is and who was,
> because you have taken your great power
> and have begun to reign.
> **18** The nations were angry,
> but your wrath has come.
> The time has come
> for the dead to be judged
> and to give the reward
> to your servants the prophets,
> to the saints, and to those who fear your name,
> both small and great,
> and the time has come to destroy
> those who destroy the earth.

19 Then the temple of God in heaven was opened, and the ark of his covenant appeared in his temple. There were flashes of lightning, rumblings and peals of thunder, an earthquake, and severe hail.

Does the announcement of v.15 – "The kingdom of the world has become the kingdom of our Lord and of his Christ..." – does that announcement seem to carry a positive tone, or a negative tone? Why?

How do the poems of v.15 and vv.17-18 proclaim that Christ is being revealed in the full sense of Heb 2:8, that soon "everything [will be] subjected to him"?

Does the activity of the 7th trumpet seem more like an ending (again), or more like another phase leading to the next events of the bowls? Why?

Reflection

In God's revelation of his redemption plan, how does he act as a master storyteller, revealing key plot themes gradually over time and then bringing everything together at the end?

What then is the effect of the unfolding of the "mystery of God" to 1) the believing saints and 2) the unbelieving idolaters (9:20)?

Lesson 10: The Woman, the Child, and the Dragon (Ch.12)

The seven seals have been opened. The last of the three woes has come with the blast of the seventh trumpet. Whether we see these judgments as consecutive sevens or as two iterations depicting the same climax of the Church Age, there is a sense of exhaustion. The pressure on the faithful is suffocating, and it drags on and on. Still, we have been shown that it is not endless. The testimony is finally coming to completion, and the wickedness of the fallen world has begun to be judged as God pours his wrath on the planet, its creatures and even the whole corrupted cosmos.

A Gospel Flashback

We who are taking in this Revelation need a beat, a chance to take a breath. Once again, God shows his brilliant storytelling as he gives us that chance. John gives us a moment to think back upon God's amazing plan of redemption. God had promised all the way back in the Garden of Eden that he was going to provide a human descendent to bring victory over the serpent and the damage wrought by his deception:

> **Genesis 3:14–15**
> **14** So the Lord God said to the serpent:
> Because you have done this,
> you are cursed more than any livestock
> and more than any wild animal.
> You will move on your belly
> and eat dust all the days of your life.
> **15** I will put hostility between you and the woman,
> and between your offspring and her offspring.
> He will strike your head,
> and you will strike his heel.

Theologians recognize this as the earliest form of the gospel, the good news that God would save mankind through a Son of Man. As human history unfolded following man's rebellion and expulsion from the Garden, God revealed a particular family through whom that descendent would come. The OT chronicles that family and leads to the expectation of that Son. The Gospels record his advent, his life and ministry, his sacrificial death and his resurrection. This book of Revelation is revealing him as the Lord of all.

A Gospel Short Story

Here in ch.12, we get to pause and reflect. John is given a vision that replays God's provision of this promised Son in a short story involving vivid characters called "signs":

The Revelation of Jesus Christ

Revelation 12:1–6
1 A great sign appeared in heaven: a woman clothed with the sun, with the moon under her feet and a crown of twelve stars on her head. **2** She was pregnant and cried out in labor and agony as she was about to give birth. **3** Then another sign appeared in heaven: There was a great fiery red dragon having seven heads and ten horns, and on its heads were seven crowns. **4** Its tail swept away a third of the stars in heaven and hurled them to the earth. And the dragon stood in front of the woman who was about to give birth, so that when she did give birth it might devour her child. **5** She gave birth to a Son, a male who is going to rule all nations with an iron rod. Her child was caught up to God and to his throne. **6** The woman fled into the wilderness, where she had a place prepared by God, to be nourished there for 1,260 days.

At first glance, what would you say this short story is about?

The Interpretation
Let's consider what is most obvious in the signs used in this story and summarize what John seems to be communicating. As we do, remember the gospel in the Garden (Gn 3:15), and remember we are guided by John's purpose **to reveal Jesus Christ so that his servants faithfully endure suffering in order to receive blessing.**

There is no real argument about the broad strokes of this depiction. From Israel comes the Messiah. In spite of all Satan's efforts to devour and destroy, the Son is not prevented from taking his place with God to await his universal rule over all nations. Neither is Satan able to prevent God's provision for his people to endure suffering, at least for an appointed time.

We'll see how the attention turns to the suffering of the woman and the rest of her offspring in a moment. For now, let's dig into these signs and characters a little more.

The Woman and the Son
It is easy to look at the depiction of the woman and immediately think of ethnic Israel. Jesus, the Messiah, was born a Jew, right? The Son comes from the woman Israel. Enough said. That is true, but there is more richness to expose here.

The simple assessment above is justified. The language of v.1 clearly echoes Joseph's dream from Genesis. Remember that dream that made his brothers mad enough to kill? His father Jacob (Israel) was put off too, but he realized there may be something to this dream (he'd had some dreams like that himself):

The Woman, the Child, and the Dragon

Genesis 37:9–11
9 Then he had another dream and told it to his brothers. "Look," he said, "I had another dream, and this time the sun, moon, and eleven stars were bowing down to me."

10 He told his father and brothers, and his father rebuked him. "What kind of dream is this that you have had?" he said. "Am I and your mother and your brothers really going to come and bow down to the ground before you?" **11** His brothers were jealous of him, but his father kept the matter in mind.

Joseph is properly understood as a type of the Christ to come. *Israel* (the man) gave birth to Joseph (through Rachel), and *Israel* (the nation) gave birth to Jesus. Joseph would rule over his family and more, but Jesus would rule over all. "Rule" in Rv 12:5 can also be translated "shepherd." It fuses the two ideas of a shepherd's staff and a king's scepter. "Iron" indicates a rule that is certain and unbreakable (notice he goes to God's throne in v.5). Vv.5-6 have a strong temporal focus. The Son "*is* going to rule" but "*was* caught up to God," and now the woman is in the wilderness where she has fled but is nourished for a period of time. The ascent to the throne is past tense for John's audience (and us), but the universal rule of the Son is future.

In John's vision in Rv 12 there are some tweaks to that flashback with Joseph, but the associations seem to clearly indicate ethnic, or even national, Israel in the sign of the woman. However, this sign seems more subtle and pliable than that. In Gn 3:15, the woman Eve represents *humanity*. So, the woman of Rv 12 may first represent humanity and then represent ethnic Israel. The promised Son was first of humankind and then more particularly of Israel.

In Joseph's dream, "sun" and "moon" were taken by Jacob to symbolize Joseph's parents (himself and Rachel). In John's vision, it may be appropriate to see "sun" and "moon" as representative parents. This would be a two-fold representation of the glory of God expressed in humankind, whom God made in his image as male and female (Gn 1:27). A man-woman interpretation of "sun" and "moon" would be consistent with Paul in 1 Cor 11:7-8, seeing God's glory and beauty expressed in humanity (see also Song 6:10). The "crown of twelve stars" is taken to refer to the twelve tribes of Israel.

The broad symbol of the woman is flexible also in that she seems to initially represent *ethnic* Israel but, more importantly, may also represent "*true* Israel" (see Rm 11). (This would be much like the 144,000 of ch.7 might be taken as a Jewish depiction of all believers.) Of course, Jesus, born as an ethnic Jew in his humanity, would literally be seen as being birthed from ethnic Israel. However, as this chapter unfolds, the attacks of the dragon clearly come to primarily depict his persecution of the Church. History has shown both ethnic and "true" Israel (even *national* Israel) as being in Satan's sights, but we must remember this Revelation is given to and for the Church.

In vv.1-2, the connection between the woman and the Church may seem subtle at first, but it becomes clearer in v.17 with her "offspring" against whom the dragon "makes war." Israel as a nation was certainly in agony in the centuries leading up to the coming of Christ. The faithful among her were surely "crying out" for him. In fact, God explained through Isaiah that his people were unable to save themselves through their own labors:

> **Isaiah 26:17–18**
> **17** As a pregnant woman about to give birth
> writhes and cries out in her pains,
> so we were before you, LORD.
> **18** We became pregnant, we writhed in pain;
> we gave birth to wind.
> We have won no victories on earth,
> and the earth's inhabitants have not fallen.

Israel struggled largely because of her self-reliance. Even in looking for salvation from God, most among Israel looked for it to come on their own terms, a merely political salvation by a warrior king. But the woman also struggles because she has a fierce enemy. If the dragon targets ethnic/national Israel because of the promised seed, he certainly redoubles his efforts against the true Israel of the Church.

The Dragon

Who is this dragon? John will become more explicit in v.9, but we already have a pretty good idea. That he is "fiery" and "red" communicates his adversarial intentions of war. His seven heads and ten horns depict his power, and his crowns represent his glory and authority. That he "swept away a third of the stars in heaven and hurled them to earth" is taken by most to be a reference to an ancient rebellion of angelic beings. So, this formidable enemy has a lot of help. Thankfully, this is not a case of cosmic dualism, a struggle between two equally powerful and equally eternal forces. There is only one ultimate power in ch.12, and it is not the dragon.

It couldn't be clearer that God is the one who brings forth salvation through the Son. His power could not be challenged, nor his salvation thwarted. All of the dragon's power is derived from his creator God, limited by God and used precisely according to God's purposes and timing. The dragon knew the promise of Gn 3:15, and that is why he watched and waited to "devour [the woman's] child" (v.4). But God supervened the miraculous birth, caught the Son up to his throne (as resurrected Lord of all) and made provision for the woman.

Even though God's absolutely sovereign power is on display and the enemy's undoing is expressed in a few brief sentences, that does not mean we should short-circuit John's task here. He is not telling the church that victory will be quick and easy for them, but that it is sure.

At one church where I served on staff, our Executive Pastor bought "Easy" buttons from an office supply store and, as a joke to relieve stress, dispensed them to our administrative staff. On particularly stressful days – perhaps after a difficult conversation or staff meeting – we might

The Woman, the Child, and the Dragon

walk by the receptionist's desk and hit the plastic button and all would be reassured, "That was easy."

John's short story of vv.1-6 might read so far like we just hit the Easy Button. Actually, his purpose as we go further is clearly the opposite. He means to reveal that this will *not* be easy:

The War, the Banishment and the Proclamation

> **7** Then war broke out in heaven: Michael and his angels fought against the dragon. The dragon and his angels also fought, **8** but he could not prevail, and there was no place for them in heaven any longer. **9** So the great dragon was thrown out—the ancient serpent, who is called the devil and Satan, the one who deceives the whole world. He was thrown to earth, and his angels with him. **10** Then I heard a loud voice in heaven say,
>
> > The salvation and the power
> > and the kingdom of our God
> > and the authority of his Christ
> > have now come,
> > because the accuser of our brothers and sisters,
> > who accuses them
> > before our God day and night,
> > has been thrown down.
> > **11** They conquered him
> > by the blood of the Lamb
> > and by the word of their testimony;
> > for they did not love their lives
> > to the point of death.
> > **12** Therefore rejoice, you heavens,
> > and you who dwell in them!
> > Woe to the earth and the sea,
> > because the devil has come down to you
> > with great fury,
> > because he knows his time is short.

Things come into sharper focus now. Some see the "stars" of v.4 as angelic representatives of God's faithful that the dragon has attacked, but many see them as the "angels" of v.7 that have been duped and are now fighting alongside the dragon. Whether or not these evil angels are those stars of v.4, it is clear that they fight against other angels in heaven who are led by Michael and are true to God. It is also now explicit that the dragon is the same person as the ancient serpent of Gn 3:15, also known as the devil and Satan. The connection to Gn 3 is especially strong as he is identified as "the one who deceives the whole world."

The Revelation of Jesus Christ

We see an important event here, the banishment of the dragon and demons from heaven. While this is an apocalyptic vision and we must be careful not to be dogmatic about timing, it is worth noting that this denial of heavenly access seems to follow Christ's ascension to the throne, at least logically if not chronologically. In the ancient account of Satan's attack on the righteous man Job (Job 1-2), the Adversary is presented as having access to the heavenly council but only as an outsider. John's vision here may indicate that Satan no longer has access to accuse Christians before God's throne in heaven (v.10). Even if that is true, he certainly may accuse us to others on earth and perhaps even to ourselves.

Three things are emphasized in vv.10-12: 1) God's power and authority are demonstrated in the casting down of the accuser, 2) God's faithful people also conquer the accuser and 3) in defeat this devil will turn upon the earth in fury. Let's consider each in more detail.

What phrases in vv.7-10 show God as all-powerful in defeating Satan?

In what two ways do the faithful (the "brothers and sisters") conquer their accuser? What phrase describes the level of their commitment to God?

According to v.12, where is there rejoicing at this point and where is there woe, and why?

Notice that the dragon and his angels lose their "place" in heaven. Contrast that with what Jesus told his disciples using the same term:

> **John 14:1–3**
> **1** "Don't let your heart be troubled. Believe in God; believe also in me. **2** In my Father's house are many rooms. If it were not so, would I have told you that I am going to prepare a place for you? **3** If I go away and prepare a place for you, I will come again and take you to myself, so that where I am you may be also.

How does the contrast of losing or gaining a place in heaven help struggling believers persevere?

The Woman, the Child, and the Dragon

The Persecution and Provision

Satan and his demons have been repelled and expelled in their direct heavenly attack. Only one domain remains for them to unleash destruction: the earth. Now, understand that Satan hates humankind in general but he REALLY hates God's chosen. The Easy Button was an illusion, even for the faithful. They have been assured victory by the heavenly voice of vv.10-12, and even given the foolproof strategy to conquer their accuser (v.11), but they have also been prepared for the sacrifice. Like their Savior, they will suffer, possibly even "to the point of death."

> **13** When the dragon saw that he had been thrown down to the earth, he persecuted the woman who had given birth to the male child. **14** The woman was given two wings of a great eagle, so that she could fly from the serpent's presence to her place in the wilderness, where she was nourished for a time, times, and half a time. **15** From his mouth the serpent spewed water like a river flowing after the woman, to sweep her away with a flood. **16** But the earth helped the woman. The earth opened its mouth and swallowed up the river that the dragon had spewed from his mouth. **17** So the dragon was furious with the woman and went off to wage war against the rest of her offspring—those who keep the commands of God and hold firmly to the testimony about Jesus.
>
> **18** The dragon stood on the sand of the sea.

The identity of the woman is more explicit as true Israel at this point because of the phrase that describes "the rest of her offspring." They are "those who keep the commands of God and hold firmly to the testimony of Jesus." Look carefully at that description. It is particularly Christian, so the earlier associations with ethnic Israel fade away at this point. Also, the phrase "rest of her offspring" implies a predecessor. That is no surprise, given the NT doctrine about Christ:

> **Colossians 1:18**
> **18** He is also the head of the body, the church;
> he is the beginning,
> the firstborn from the dead,
> so that he might come to have
> first place in everything.

Christ is the first to be born from the dead ("firstborn"), but more importantly, he is first in his preeminent authority ("first place"). Thus, all who by faith follow his example even to the point of death are "the rest of [the woman's] offspring." These are not mere *professors* of Christianity (of which there have been billions), these are those who *keep* God's commands and *cling* to Jesus. This statement of v.17 is directly tied to the PFG of the prologue.

The focus has definitely shifted to persecution. The dragon is furious in his pursuit of the woman. A "wilderness" is not a fun place even when God blesses with provision, and it brings to mind some really unpleasant parts of the Exodus of Israel. Dockery is very helpful here:

The Revelation of Jesus Christ

"Chapter 12 is crucial for understanding John's view of the sequence of history. The number three and a half was associated by Christians and Jews with times of evil and judgment (see Luke 4:25). John variously referred to the three and a half years as either "42 months" (11:2; 13:5) or "1,260 days" (11:3; 12:6) or "a time, times and half a time" (12:14). For John it was the period of time when the powers of evil will do their oppressive works. But during this time, God will protect His people (12:6, 14) while they both bear witness to their faith (11:3) and simultaneously suffer at the hands of these evil powers (11:2, 7; 12:13–17; 13:5–7)."[36]

Since true believers may suffer even to the point of death, then what is the meaning of the escape of v.14 and the help and provision of vv.14 and 16? We expect dragons to breathe fire, but what is this spewing of a river in v.15?

With a backdrop of passages in the Psalms (18:4,16; 66:12; 69:1-2, 14-15; 124:4-5; 143:7-8, 11) and Isaiah (43:2) as well as non-biblical Jewish commentaries, it seems that this "river" symbolizes the attempts of Satan to destroy God's people. When we recall the context of the PFG, it seems most likely that John is depicting satanic attack on the Church, especially by deception both within and without. The internal deception would be false teaching, while the external deception would be a slanderous propaganda campaign against the Church's reputation. The rescue by the earth's "opening its mouth and swallowing the river" echoes the exodus miracle at the Red Sea. It also reminds us of the swallowing up of those who opposed Moses and Aaron in the wilderness (Nu 16).

The dragon's attempts to wash away the people of God are aggressive, but he is unable to prevail. Still, his power and his deception are prolific. The symbolism of the last statement of ch.12 tells us a lot. "Sand" likely illustrates the shifting foundation of deception and "sea" symbolizes destructive forces or chaos. Given the context of satanic attack through deception, it's hard not to think of Jesus' lesson on foundations:

> **Matthew 7:24–27**
> **24** "Therefore, everyone who hears these words of mine and acts on them will be like a wise man who built his house on the rock. **25** The rain fell, the rivers rose, and the winds blew and pounded that house. Yet it didn't collapse, because its foundation was on the rock. **26** But everyone who hears these words of mine and doesn't act on them will be like a foolish man who built his house on the sand. **27** The rain fell, the rivers rose, the winds blew and pounded that house, and it collapsed. It collapsed with a great crash."

It seems the dragon is poised to sweep away all but the faithful with the shifting sands of his deception and the storm of his wrath. He stands on chaos and lies, vicious in his attack against the church, and he will mobilize the full force of human wickedness too, as we will see his beastly

---

[36] Dockery, D. S. (Ed.). (1992). *Holman Bible Handbook* (p. 800). Nashville, TN: Holman Bible Publishers.

The Woman, the Child, and the Dragon

counterparts engage a proxy war. The question is, will the believers remain faithful in light of this onslaught? Will they stay anchored on the Rock?

Reflection

How has history already shown the people of God to have a bullseye on them?

What do these signs communicate clearly to us about what to expect from the enemy?

What encouragements do these signs offer us now when we sense we are under spiritual attack?

Lesson 11: The Two Beasts (Ch.13)

Opening Discussion

Many personalities have offered advice to those facing adversity. The animated fish, Dory (Ellen DeGeneres), made famous her philosophy, "Just keep swimming." She was echoing Walt Disney's own motto: "We keep moving forward." Martin Luther King, Jr., said, "If you can't fly, then run. If you can't run, then walk. If you can't walk, then crawl. But whatever you do, you have to keep moving forward." Churchill spoke of perseverance in the particular horrific context of world war: "If you're going through hell, keep going."

Churchill's statement references a situation most like what we are seeing in Revelation. The persecuted saints are going through the only hell they'll ever know while the defiant idol-worshipers are beginning to get a taste of the real hell that will soon overtake them for eternity. For the saints, the stress of the test threatens to overwhelm. Can they stand firm? Will they?

What advice does pop culture offer to help people push through struggles? Does it seem to work?

Here's what the NT puts forward:

Philippians 3:12–21

12 Not that I have already reached the goal or am already perfect, but I make every effort to take hold of it because I also have been taken hold of by Christ Jesus. **13** Brothers and sisters, I do not consider myself to have taken hold of it. But one thing I do: Forgetting what is behind and reaching forward to what is ahead, **14** I pursue as my goal the prize promised by God's heavenly call in Christ Jesus. **15** Therefore, let all of us who are mature think this way. And if you think differently about anything, God will reveal this also to you.

16 In any case, we should live up to whatever truth we have attained. **17** Join in imitating me, brothers and sisters, and pay careful attention to those who live according to the example you have in us. **18** For I have often told you, and now say again with tears, that many live as enemies of the cross of Christ. **19** Their end is destruction; their god is their stomach; their glory is in their shame. They are focused on earthly things, **20** but our citizenship is in heaven, and we eagerly wait for a Savior from there, the Lord Jesus Christ. **21** He will transform the body of our humble condition into the likeness of his glorious body, by the power that enables him to subject everything to himself.

The Revelation of Jesus Christ

Hebrews 12:1–2
1 Therefore, since we also have such a large cloud of witnesses surrounding us, let us lay aside every hindrance and the sin that so easily ensnares us. Let us run with endurance the race that lies before us, **2** keeping our eyes on Jesus, the source and perfecter of our faith. For the joy that lay before him, he endured the cross, despising the shame, and sat down at the right hand of the throne of God.

How does the biblical calling to "keep moving forward" compare/contrast to the voices of pop culture?

The Beastly Proxies

As John opens ch.13, we begin to see a new dimension to the dragon's work. Part of his deception is self-concealment. Throughout history he has worked behind the scenes to empower terrible human agents, probably including the likes of Nebuchadnezzar, Antiochus Epiphanes and, more recently, Adolph Hitler. There is no doubt about his empowerment of the earthly rulers in Rev.13. The dragon's war upon heaven has come to earth, and he fights it as a proxy war.

Proxy war has become a well-known strategy in the 20th and 21st centuries. Major (or formerly or wanna-be major) powers covertly throw their support behind minor actors who carry out their agendas. For example, many conflicts in the Middle East have been fought by those native to the region but with the backing of, and at the behest of, major players like Russia and the United States. Proxy wars carry on secret agendas for those powers that want to avoid the political fallout of direct conflict.

Satan likely is not concerned with such fallout. He simply loves using humans to destroy humans. He gives invisible (spiritual) power to his visible (religious and political) proxies. Eventually, he will come out of the shadows, but for now Satan is attacking God's people through these proxies. They are depicted as two beasts.

The pattern for two dangerous beasts reaches all the way back (probably to the era of the patriarchs) to Job 40-41 with Leviathan and Behemoth. In that text, the sea and land beasts represent the height of both earthly power and arrogance (note esp. 41:33-34). Still, without question, God declares his absolute sovereign power over these creatures. It plays out the same in Revelation. The first comes out of the sea:

The Two Beasts

The Beast out of the Sea (Antichrist)

> **Revelation 13**
> **1** And I saw a beast coming up out of the sea. It had ten horns and seven heads. On its horns were ten crowns, and on its heads were blasphemous names. **2** The beast I saw was like a leopard, its feet were like a bear's, and its mouth was like a lion's mouth. The dragon gave the beast his power, his throne, and great authority. **3** One of its heads appeared to be fatally wounded, but its fatal wound was healed.
>
> The whole earth was amazed and followed the beast. **4** They worshiped the dragon because he gave authority to the beast. And they worshiped the beast, saying, "Who is like the beast? Who is able to wage war against it?"
>
> **5** The beast was given a mouth to utter boasts and blasphemies. It was allowed to exercise authority for forty-two months. **6** It began to speak blasphemies against God: to blaspheme his name and his dwelling—those who dwell in heaven. **7** And it was permitted to wage war against the saints and to conquer them. It was also given authority over every tribe, people, language, and nation. **8** All those who live on the earth will worship it, everyone whose name was not written from the foundation of the world in the book of life of the Lamb who was slaughtered.
>
> **9** If anyone has ears to hear, let him listen.
>
>> **10** If anyone is to be taken captive,
>> into captivity he goes.
>> If anyone is to be killed with a sword,
>> with a sword he will be killed.
>> This calls for endurance and faithfulness from the saints.

Symbolism is very important here. Remember, "sea" in ancient literature often represents chaos, an overwhelming force, or a mass of humanity from among the nations. "Ten horns," "seven heads" and "ten crowns" symbolize power and authority. This is the power and authority of the dragon (seven heads, ten horns and seven crowns from 12:3). The numbers seven and ten indicate total dominance.

However, this dominance is offset by a qualified domain ("earth" in v.3) and a limited duration ("forty-two months" in v.5). The clear fact is that this power is derived. In v.5 we see it is "allowed," and in v.7 it is "permitted" and "given." This dominant power of the beast is *over* all on the earth but is especially exercised *against* the saints (v.7).

This beast is characterized by "blasphemy" (vv.1 and 5-6, see also 17:3). This term refers to irreverent speech, that which defames or abuses God or his representatives. Jesus was accused of blasphemy when he claimed to do something only God could do, like forgive sins (Mk 2:7; Lk 5:21). The primary reason for the attack on Jesus by the religious leaders of his day was that he claimed deity (Jn 10:33). Someone's "name" represents his character and power and work. Jesus properly represented God as God, but this beast will defame God and his heavenly creatures (v.6). Jesus properly received worship as God (Lk 19:38-40), but this beast misrepresents himself as worthy of worship (v.8 here).

Who gives authority to this beast in vv.2b & 4?

Who ultimately allows the beast to exercise authority in v.5? Why is this significant?

This beast seems to fuse into one entity a foursome seen by the OT prophet Daniel:

Daniel 7:1–7, 20, 24-27
1 In the first year of King Belshazzar of Babylon, Daniel had a dream with visions in his mind as he was lying in his bed. He wrote down the dream, and here is the summary of his account. **2** Daniel said, "In my vision at night I was watching, and suddenly the four winds of heaven stirred up the great sea. **3** Four huge beasts came up from the sea, each different from the other.

4 "The first was like a lion but had eagle's wings. I continued watching until its wings were torn off. It was lifted up from the ground, set on its feet like a man, and given a human mind.

5 "Suddenly, another beast appeared, a second one, that looked like a bear. It was raised up on one side, with three ribs in its mouth between its teeth. It was told, 'Get up! Gorge yourself on flesh.'

6 "After this, while I was watching, suddenly another beast appeared. It was like a leopard with four wings of a bird on its back. It had four heads, and it was given dominion.

7 "After this, while I was watching in the night visions, suddenly a fourth beast appeared, frightening and dreadful, and incredibly strong, with large iron teeth. It devoured and crushed, and it trampled with its feet whatever was left. It was different from all the beasts before it, and it had ten horns.

The Two Beasts

> **20** I also wanted to know about the ten horns on its head and about the other horn that came up, before which three fell—the horn that had eyes, and a mouth that spoke arrogantly, and that looked bigger than the others.
>
> **24** The ten horns are ten kings who will rise from this kingdom. Another king, different from the previous ones, will rise after them and subdue three kings. **25** He will speak words against the Most High and oppress the holy ones of the Most High. He will intend to change religious festivals and laws, and the holy ones will be handed over to him for a time, times, and half a time. **26** But the court will convene, and his dominion will be taken away, to be completely destroyed forever. **27** The kingdom, dominion, and greatness of the kingdoms under all of heaven will be given to the people, the holy ones of the Most High. His kingdom will be an everlasting kingdom, and all rulers will serve and obey him.'

It makes sense that John's vision is of a singular beast holding the characteristics of Daniel's four. In both prophecies the beasts are representing dominant earthly ruling powers, but by John's day the earlier representatives (probably Babylon, Media-Persia and Greece) have come and gone, swallowed up in the last beast (Rome). John's vision of Rv 13 comes nearer the end of the prophetic timeline, as the beastly kingdoms of this world are beginning to coalesce into a final rebellious system.

The Call for Endurance

With this culmination comes clarity. True and false worship become mutually exclusive on a global scale. This beast from the sea dominates all the people of the earth and demands worship from them. Everyone will go after the counterfeit or the true. All the world will either worship the beast or will be persecuted and conquered for faithfully worshiping only Jesus.

The beast will convince most by his deception. He will appear to be fatally wounded, and then be healed from his supposedly "fatal" wound (v.3). The world will be "amazed" and "follow" the beast, ultimately worshiping him (v.8) and the dragon that empowers him (v.4).

For those who refuse to comply, the beast opposes God and wars against his saints, even conquering them. This conquering will only be temporary, and so the saints are called to endurance (v.10) in light of their eventual victory.

This whole thing seems to be an orchestrated counterfeit to put the beast forth as fulfilling that ancient prediction of Gn 3:15. The world is deceived into worshiping the beast as though he were the promised offspring of the woman. The problem is that this beast only *appears* wounded. He does not possess the true power of an indestructible life as did Jesus (Heb 7:16). The promised seed of Gn 3:15 could not be empowered by the Serpent he came to defeat! That would divide Satan against Satan – how could his kingdom stand? That's exactly the point Jesus made when revealing himself as the true Messiah (Mt 12:26; Mk 3:26; Lk 11:18).

The Revelation of Jesus Christ

This counterfeiting is the ultimate blasphemy. By deception, the beast attempts to *actually* do what the Pharisees *accused* Jesus of doing – to wrongfully set himself up as God. Jesus performed signs and spoke the truth to show himself as the true Son, and this resulted in true worship of God the Son and the Father. The beast will perform false signs and speak blasphemy to appear as though he is the son, and this will result in false worship of the beast and the dragon.

Of course, the counterfeiting would be lost on the pagan or the secularist, but remember this revelation is being given to churches so that Christians will persevere. Without being warned of such deception, those who are already aware of these biblical themes might be in danger of falling away from Jesus and seeing this beast as true. It is worth noting that these chapters of Revelation don't seem to indicate there is much place for secularism. That is probably a striking indication of the dramatic power of the false signs.

To what does "this" refer in the last part of Rv 13:10? What here calls the believer to endure?

Between Christ's resurrection and his second coming, how might Satan APPEAR to have been victorious over Jesus, even though Jesus has risen from the dead?

How then would the claims that Jesus' resurrection was a hoax relate to the success of a faked resurrection by a counterfeit?

Remember the PFG: **<u>to reveal Jesus Christ so that his servants faithfully endure suffering in order to receive blessing</u>**. This chapter's call "for endurance and faithfulness from the saints" comes straight out of that PFG.

How does the exposing of this beast as a counterfeit relate to the PFG?

The Two Beasts

Political and spiritual realms are merged, as this world leader receives – even demands – worship. This is not new. It happened with ancient pharaohs and Caesars, but this case is ultimate. This blending is heightened even more by the second beast from out of the earth:

The Beast out of the Earth (False Prophet)

> **11** Then I saw another beast coming up out of the earth; it had two horns like a lamb, but it spoke like a dragon. **12** It exercises all the authority of the first beast on its behalf and compels the earth and those who live on it to worship the first beast, whose fatal wound was healed. **13** It also performs great signs, even causing fire to come down from heaven to earth in front of people. **14** It deceives those who live on the earth because of the signs that it is permitted to perform in the presence of the beast, telling those who live on the earth to make an image of the beast who was wounded by the sword and yet lived. **15** It was permitted to give breath to the image of the beast, so that the image of the beast could both speak and cause whoever would not worship the image of the beast to be killed. **16** And it makes everyone—small and great, rich and poor, free and slave—to receive a mark on his right hand or on his forehead, **17** so that no one can buy or sell unless he has the mark: the beast's name or the number of its name.

The word "lamb" in v.11 may also be translated "ram," and strongly echoes Dn 8:3. While (political) power and authority are dominant symbols for the first beast, this one seems more characterized by persuasive deceptive speech and false signs. The first beast talks big, and is made to look like deity, but this beast is the one actually performing deceptive signs that seem to show god-like powers. This second beast is the one giving credibility to the first, demanding and enforcing false worship.

Most see this second beast as a false prophet, or perhaps a collective symbol of all false prophets as warned about by Jesus and the NT writers. Others see this beast as representing the apostate church lending credibility to her false God. Many would see this as a fusion of political and religious Rome. Whatever the case, it was clear that such false signs and false worship would characterize the tribulation of the last days.

> **Mark 13:14–23**
> **14** "When you see **the abomination of desolation** standing where it should not be" (let the reader understand), "then those in Judea must flee to the mountains. **15** A man on the housetop must not come down or go in to get anything out of his house, **16** and a man in the field must not go back to get his coat. **17** Woe to pregnant women and nursing mothers in those days!

The Revelation of Jesus Christ

18 "Pray it won't happen in winter. **19** For those will be days of tribulation, the kind that hasn't been from the beginning of creation until now and never will be again. **20** If the Lord had not cut those days short, no one would be saved. But he cut those days short for the sake of the elect, whom he chose.

21 "Then if anyone tells you, 'See, here is the Messiah! See, there!' do not believe it. **22** For false messiahs and false prophets will arise and will perform signs and wonders to lead astray, if possible, the elect. **23** And you must watch! I have told you everything in advance.

2 Thessalonians 2:9–12
9 The coming of the lawless one is based on Satan's working, with every kind of miracle, both signs and wonders serving the lie, **10** and with every wicked deception among those who are perishing. They perish because they did not accept the love of the truth and so be saved. **11** For this reason God sends them a strong delusion so that they will believe the lie, **12** so that all will be condemned—those who did not believe the truth but delighted in unrighteousness.

How does Rv 13 seem to show the fulfillment of these warnings?

How did Jesus and Paul talk about both the potency of the false signs and their limit?

How does the danger of these false signs relate to the PFG of Revelation?

The dragon seems to be parroting the Divine Trinity with his own unholy trinity. He presents himself as like God the Father – the Ancient of Days – who possesses authority and power. He disburses his power and authority to the beast from the sea, just as the Father does with the Son (ch.5; cf. Mt 28:18). The beast from the earth functions much like a counterfeit Holy Spirit in "compel[ling] worship" (Rv 13:12). A close association with the Holy Spirit is seen in the term "give breath" in v.15.

The Two Beasts

The deception of the dragon and his beasts is amazingly strong. Jesus himself used strong language to communicate the danger: these could "lead astray, if possible, even the elect" (Mt 24:24). This is a hypothetical statement to say that this deception could nearly persuade true Christians. Nearly, but not quite. They have been warned, and they have been called to endurance and faithfulness. Jesus is with them through his Spirit, and he will not allow them to be tested beyond their ability (1 Cor 10:13). V.8 of our text affirms that true Christians will not fall for the lie.

Still, it is clear that remaining true in Christian faith will come at the highest cost. The beast marks his followers just as God has marked his faithful. As we learned in Lesson 1, John's audience already knew the socio-political consequences of rejecting the false worship associated with their trade guilds. Under this beast, that insider-outsider division will one day become absolute, according to vv.16-17 of our text. Whatever form this mark takes, this means faithfulness to Christ will be most unusual and most obvious... and most costly.

The call for endurance in v.10 is the focus of Revelation, but there is another call that lends aid to that end:

The Call for Wisdom

> **18** This calls for wisdom: Let the one who has understanding calculate the number of the beast, because it is the number of a person. Its number is 666.

We must be careful that this call for wisdom does not swallow up that call for endurance. The wisdom is supposed to facilitate endurance, but it is not supposed to distract the faithful from their witness by bogging them down in speculations.

Much attention has been given to this number (which, by the way, is 616 in some manuscripts), especially in regard to attempts to identify the beast. Theories have ranged widely over the centuries. Many of these focus on *individuals*, considering various political and or religious leaders of the day. Because of the term "calculate" they use gematria to assign numerical values to names like "Nero" to identify candidates.

Others focus on *entities*, as with one modern proposal that the beast is the worldwide web (taking three Roman numerals "VI" as "www"). One group takes the "mark of the beast" as the resetting of corporate worship rituals from the OT prescribed Sabbath (Saturday) to Sunday. This view identifies the beast as the apostate church (from their perspective, those knowingly rebelling by worshiping on Sunday) or its leader (the Pope, given that he is the figurehead for the traditional church).

Given the incredible diversity of speculations, it seems very appropriate that John said, "This calls for wisdom." It also seems very ironic, since there is so much disagreement about to what this

The Revelation of Jesus Christ

"wisdom" points. Perhaps that is our glaring clue that we may be off-target. Two dominant possibilities emerge.

First, it may be that "the one who has understanding" is restricted to a particular point in history. That means this business about the beast and his mark will be super clear at the right time and to the right people. Many are convinced *now* is the time and *we* are those people. This possibility is weakened somewhat by the fact that there is still lack of agreement and clarity even today. Further, it diminishes the usefulness of this portion of Revelation to accomplish its PFG for the original readers. Even though gematria would reveal Nero as AN antichrist, he was obviously not THE Antichrist.

The second possibility aligns more with the genre blend of Revelation, especially in the immediate context that John is writing about "signs." It is likely that the applied understanding and wisdom involves the *symbolism* of the beast and his number and mark. In fact, we can be quite confident we ARE to draw meaning from the symbolism even if a more literal meaning does become clear at some point. So, we will focus on the symbolism.

The significant thing often overlooked about this number identified with the beast is that it is the number of a PERSON. The word translated "person" in the CSB is the Greek word that means "humankind." Because it appears here in the masculine form, many other translations (ESV, NIV, etc.) opt for "man." The term "its" in the next sentence is gender neutral and does not refer back to "man" but to "number." Taken together, this means that the number does *not* emphasize man as opposed to woman (gender). It also does *not* emphasize one particular human as opposed to another – it does not say "THE" person but "A" person. The emphasis is on the HUMANITY of this person. In fact, it seems more appropriate to understand the emphasis as being on the MERE humanity of this person. Whether one takes the beast as an entity or an individual, this beast is being shown as the epitome of human fallenness, or we might say "short-falling-ness."

Let's review. This book is given to reveal Jesus Christ. We concluded that since Jesus was already revealed as the Lamb of God, the humble Suffering Servant, then this revelation must be about his now exalted state. Jesus is being revealed as the exalted Lord of all. We've already seen it so in heaven, and now he has begun to be revealed upon the earth in depictions of his judgment and vindication.

But Satan, the dragon, is desperately trying to fool the whole world – all of humanity – just as he always has since the Garden. He wants to do a bait-and-switch, substituting a counterfeit god for the true God. He props up a beast, a counterfeit god for humans to worship. Many times, the carved or metal gods man made for himself would suffice as images of invisible, imagined gods, but the deception has always been most powerful when embodied in a human ruler. (That is, after all, the most accurate counterfeit of the real deal.) Throughout history, Satan has no doubt offered *many* of these earthly counterfeit gods: pharaohs, kings, Caesars and modern autocrats too.

The Two Beasts

Since the resurrection of Jesus, Satan's job has been harder. Jesus performed amazing public signs. He did something that only God can do in that he demonstrated his power of an indestructible life, the absolute power of the Creator, the One Who Is. This meant that Satan has been forced to engage a propaganda machine to first defame Christ's real power and resurrection as a hoax and then to create the illusion that Satan's counterfeit god has those same powers.

Satan has been honing his craft. Jesus and his apostles had said the deceiver would present an overwhelmingly convincing case. Now John is being shown – and showing Christians – that Satan has been granted the ability to empower a false prophet, a sort of "wing man" to build the narrative that this beast from the sea is a god who must be worshiped. The wing man is really convincing: fire from heaven, animating inanimate images, death to the rebels. The narrative and the controlling reach are global and overwhelming. Nothing happens without allegiance to this beastly god: no commerce, no freedom of thought or worship, nothing.

Recall vv.3-4: "The whole earth was amazed and followed the beast." "Who is like the beast? Who is able to wage war against it?" Even we who love God tend to get caught up in that deception, to glamorize this beast and search desperately to figure out his identity through the calculations. He must surely be a most impressive leader on the world scene! Who is he?

The people of the world have been fooled, but the Christian must not be. Their supposed god is exposed as a fraud by the truth expressed in one little verse. Don't get caught up in the speculations and miss John's clear meaning! This amazing dominant world leader…

He's just a man. It's what the word means (ἀνθρώπου = human). It's what the number means. God created mankind in his image on day six. Man is not God. If God's perfection is represented in the number seven (for example, seven spirits), then six is man's number, for it is incomplete, short of perfection. Even a false trinity only amounts to three sixes. Six is also associated with the judgments on the beast's followers in the sixth seal, trumpet, and bowl. As impressive as this beast is – even with the power of the dragon and false prophet behind him – he is just a man.

Now JESUS, on the other hand, has already been demonstrated to be both fully man AND fully God. He's the real deal, and the rest of this book will continue to reveal that as John is shown Jesus' victory over all supposed contenders.

John's stated PFG helps us understand what "wisdom" he calls for here in 13:18. It is the kind of wisdom that sees through the deception to see the true God and to discern him from a blasphemous pretender, ANY such pretender.

How are the two "calls" (for endurance in v.10 and for wisdom in v.18) in this chapter related, and how do they relate to the main purpose of Revelation?

The Revelation of Jesus Christ

How do these calls apply to us today, as the deception of the dragon continues to move toward this global climax?

Great Escape or Great Privilege?

I think it is worth taking a moment here to consider once again what I called an unintended consequence of interpretive drift relative to this book. It seems that we may have been accidently telling our children to look for Jesus to come take us away before all these bad things happen. By "we" I mean at least American evangelicals, but probably a good many more who happen to be living in various places as Christians relatively free from harassment in the expression of our faith (so far). I fear many Christians today look for a "great escape" from adversity or persecution.

This is so opposite the perspective of John's original audience (and many readers in various places and times since) that one could imagine John saying, "Are you kidding me? Jesus told me to write this because you should EXPECT persecution, and he wants you to endure it faithfully!"

This understanding was so prevalent in the early church that pastors had to pull Christians back from the error that is opposite that of escapism. Many were not only *expecting* trouble from non-Christians, but they were also *looking* for it. Why would they do that? They had the understanding that it was such a privilege to follow Christ, that greater persecution meant greater honor. Some were literally turning themselves in to the Roman authorities for the chance to proclaim their faith and be executed.

Of course, none of the NT writers – John included – wanted Christians to seek out persecution. But it does come to some degree or another when Christians live faithfully in allegiance to Christ alone. It is inevitable. Jesus said to expect it, and we should. What he is offering through this Revelation of himself is not the prospect of a great escape but one of a great privilege. It is to see Jesus as exalted Lord, and to follow him through whatever suffering we must, with our eyes on him as our prize and goal (Php 3:14; 1 Heb 12:1-2).

Reflection

Treasury agents study real currency for hours upon hours so they can easily spot counterfeit bills. How has this Revelation prepared the Christian to recognize the counterfeit of ch.13?

Do you feel like you study the truth diligently enough to recognize the counterfeit?

The Two Beasts

What kinds of deception and false worship do you see in your culture today?

Can the PFG be accomplished even if the mark and number of the beast don't tell us in advance exactly who (or what) he is? How so?

As many cultures move to a position antagonistic toward Christianity, what particular challenges do you see to living faithfully as a Christian while not actively seeking out trouble? How will it affect you at work, school, in council meetings, in the voting booth, etc.?

Lesson 12: The Lamb, the Redeemed, and the Harvest of Wrath (Ch.14)

The curtain has been peeled back to reveal the posers. The dragon and the two beasts are impressive, so much so that the whole world bows to worship the beast from the sea and the dragon that empowers him. Only the Christians have *understood* the truth (wisdom) and *remained* true to Christ (endurance), the only God worthy of worship. What does John see next in this series of visions between the trumpets and bowls?

The Lamb and the Redeemed

> **Revelation 14:1–5**
> **1** Then I looked, and there was the Lamb, standing on Mount Zion, and with him were 144,000 who had his name and his Father's name written on their foreheads. **2** I heard a sound from heaven like the sound of cascading waters and like the rumbling of loud thunder. The sound I heard was like harpists playing on their harps. **3** They sang a new song before the throne and before the four living creatures and the elders, but no one could learn the song except the 144,000 who had been redeemed from the earth. **4** These are the ones who have not defiled themselves with women, since they remained virgins. These are the ones who follow the Lamb wherever he goes. They were redeemed from humanity as the firstfruits for God and the Lamb. **5** No lie was found in their mouths; they are blameless.

The Lamb

Right away we notice a contrast. In 13:11, when the second beast came out of the earth, it was *"like a lamb, but it spoke like a dragon."* That imposter has been revealed for who he is. Now the *real* Lamb takes the stage.

The Lamb stands on Mount Zion. This is a hill in Jerusalem, a counterpart to Sinai, a place identified with the powerful presence of God. Zion is a symbol that often refers to the whole city of Jerusalem, the "city of David" (2 Sam 5:7; 1 Kgs 8:1; 1 Chr 11:5; 2 Chr 5:2; Jer 26:18). The term was also used to refer to Judah as a tribe (Ps 78:68) but more so as a nation (Ps 48:11; 69:35; 97:8; Is 40:9; Jer 14:19; Lam 5:11). The symbol of Zion depicts God's people as a collective founded and centered on Christ (Is 28:16; Rm 9:33; 11:26) and expressed in the New Jerusalem (Rv 21:2). The Lamb's standing on Zion shows his power and authority being brought to bear in eschatological fulfillment: Christ is bringing his reign to earth.

The Revelation of Jesus Christ

Commentator L. Morris makes a great observation: "We should not overlook the fact that the Lamb is standing on the mountain, whereas the beast stood only on sand (13:1)."[37] What a significant detail, given what Jesus taught in his parable of the builders/foundations in Mt 7:24-27!

The Redeemed

With the Lamb are 144,000 bearing his name and the Father's name. This group corresponds exactly to the group who are sealed in ch.7. Once again it begs the question: Are these ethnic Jews only, or are they representatives including every ethnic group who are all "true" or "spiritual" Israel?

In Rm 11:26 Paul says, "in this way all Israel will be saved." Scripture clearly indicates many ethnic Israelites are NOT saved, so Paul must mean all believing Israel will be saved. The qualifier "who had his name" in Rv 14:1 certainly indicates Christians, and this, coupled with "his Father's name," would complete the tie to Israel. These 144,000 are clearly believers, and there are good reasons to believe they may represent all believers, those who constitute the "true Israel."

The sound (or voice) like "cascading waters" in v.2 ties directly to 1:15 (the voice of the Son of Man) and 19:6 (that of the vast multitude). Coupled with "loud thunder" here, it clearly indicates a massive sound, probably from the 144,000.

The language of vv.2b-3 recounts that of 5:8-10. There, the four living creatures and 24 elders sing the new song, and here the 144,000 learn and sing the new song *before* the creatures and elders. Only redeemed people can learn the song (cf.2:17). This is a fulfillment of Is 35:9-10:

> **Isaiah 35:9–10**
> **9** There will be no lion there,
> and no vicious beast will go up on it;
> they will not be found there.
> But the redeemed will walk on it,
> **10** and the ransomed of the LORD will return
> and come to Zion with singing,
> crowned with unending joy.
> Joy and gladness will overtake them,
> and sorrow and sighing will flee.

Vv.4-5 back in Rv 14 describe these redeemed. Being "undefiled" or "virgins" may refer to physical purity (though it cannot mean that only literal virgins are pure), but it certainly symbolizes spiritual purity. This purity will be contrasted with associating with the harlot Babylon in v.8 (see also 2 Cor 11:2-4). The messages of the OT prophets are replete with references to Israel "playing

---

[37] Morris, L. (1987). *Revelation: an introduction and commentary* (Vol. 20, p. 169). Downers Grove, IL: InterVarsity Press.

The Lamb, the Redeemed, and the Harvest of Wrath

the whore" as symbolizing her spiritual unfaithfulness to Yahweh to serve and worship other gods or her prostituting herself to foreign powers to provide political protection. God even put the prophet Hosea in a marital union with an unfaithful wife expressly to depict Israel's spiritual promiscuity while Hosea's steadfast love depicted God's own. These redeemed in Rv 14 have been faithful to Christ.

The description goes further. They "follow the Lamb." This identifies the redeemed with the language of the Gospels that describes true disciples of Jesus. "Wherever he goes" underscores the ultimate commitment. The Lamb went to death on a cross. His followers go wherever he leads, through persecution even unto death.

These followers are described as "firstfruits." This exact term is used by James (1:18) to refer to any and all believers: "By his own choice, he gave us birth by the word of truth so that we would be a kind of firstfruits of his creatures." This seems to be another clue that these 144,000 may not be limited to ethnic Israel nor to that literal number. John is likely using Jewish terms to describe all believers. The term also reminds us that believers are "living sacrifices" (Rm 12:1-2) like the OT firstfruit offerings.

V.5 is a clear fulfillment of Zeph 3:13: "The remnant of Israel will no longer do wrong or tell lies; a deceitful tongue will not be found in their mouths. They will pasture and lie down, with nothing to make them afraid." Again, the NT (Paul especially) imports the language of Israel's "remnant" to refer at minimum to Jewish Christians and more broadly to all Christians. The truthfulness of Christians is especially descriptive of their witness to the true gospel and Christ, and to their faithfulness – that they remain true to him.

*How do these descriptions of the Lamb and the Redeemed tie into the PFG **to reveal Jesus Christ so that his servants faithfully endure suffering in order to receive blessing**?*

How are those characteristics of vv.4-5 a challenge to us today?

Three Proclamations

After John's vision of the all-powerful Lamb and those he has redeemed, John sees three angels fly overhead and hears them make dramatic proclamations. Notice that these are parallel to the three angelic proclamations of woe in 8:13-11:19. These here are strongly and explicitly tied to the stated PFG of this book. We'll take them one by one. The first angel declares eternal good news:

The Revelation of Jesus Christ

The Eternal Gospel

> **6** Then I saw another angel flying high overhead, with the eternal gospel to announce to the inhabitants of the earth—to every nation, tribe, language, and people. **7** He spoke with a loud voice: "Fear God and give him glory, because the hour of his judgment has come. Worship the one who made heaven and earth, the sea and the springs of water."

Notice this announcement is for the totality of humanity. This is indicated in the repetition of the formula used throughout Revelation: "every nation, tribe, language, and people" (5:9; 7:9; 11:9; 13:7). Further, this announcement is earth-ward, directed to the domain created by God for man to represent his rule and his glory and his image.

For two millennia, the charge of the Church has been to declare the *gospel* (the good news of Jesus), so let's look closely at these verses that contain the only occurrence of that word in this book. What is this good news of Jesus? "The hour of his (God's) judgment has come." We'll consider how and for whom that is good news in a moment. How is this gospel "eternal" if it is characterized here relative to a specific "hour"? It must be that the hour of judgment will yield eternal consequences.

G.K. Beale points out that John's original audience may have in particular picked up on the word "eternal":

> "The "eternal gospel" could be in intentional contrast to the temporary gospel of Caesar. The birthday of Augustus was hailed by the provincial assembly of Asia as having "signaled the beginning of good news for the world" and a new era."[38]

This gospel is not some passing celebration of a pagan ruler. Neither is it one of the many false gospels adopted by those blown around by "winds of doctrine" (Eph 4:14). This gospel is the eternal truth (and consequence) that every human will be judged according to what they have done with Jesus Christ.

That criterion for judgment is given in the form of two parallel commands that are sandwiched around the announcement that "the hour of [God's] judgment has come." The commands are 1) to fear and give glory to God and 2) to worship God.

Fearing God is expressed all throughout Scripture as the proper response to his greatness. It characterized the patriarchs Abraham (Gn 22:12), Isaac and Jacob (31:42,53) and a whole list of God's faithful from Abel to the NT Christians (Heb 11). It is expressed in command form by the Apostle Peter (1 Pt 2:17). In considering "everything under the sun" the Teacher in Ecclesiastes sums up man's whole existence and meaning and duty in this way:

---

[38] Beale, G. K. (1999). *The book of Revelation: a commentary on the Greek text* (p. 750). Grand Rapids, MI; Carlisle, Cumbria: W.B. Eerdmans; Paternoster Press.

The Lamb, the Redeemed, and the Harvest of Wrath

Ecclesiastes 12:13–14
13 When all has been heard, the conclusion of the matter is this: fear God and keep his commands, because this is for all humanity. **14** For God will bring every act to judgment, including every hidden thing, whether good or evil.

Conversely, the reason Paul gives that all humanity is guilty before God – apart from faith and the work of Christ – is because they do *not* fear him:

Romans 3:10–18 (CSB)
10 as it is written:

> There is no one righteous, not even one.
> **11** There is no one who understands;
> there is no one who seeks God.
> **12** All have turned away;
> all alike have become worthless.
> There is no one who does what is good,
> not even one.
> **13** Their throat is an open grave;
> they deceive with their tongues.
> Vipers' venom is under their lips.
> **14** Their mouth is full of cursing and bitterness.
> **15** Their feet are swift to shed blood;
> **16** ruin and wretchedness are in their paths,
> **17** and the path of peace they have not known.
> **18** There is no fear of God before their eyes.

Fearing God is an inward response expressed in outward actions to give him glory. Whether or not someone is characterized by this proper response is the basis of divine judgment, according to v.7 of our text. This is why judgment is given as the reason for the command to fear God. In this context, to give God glory especially carries the idea of confessing and forsaking one's sins. The aspect of confession in this regard was perfectly illustrated in the matter of Achan, who took spoils of war that were forbidden in the battle for Jericho:

Joshua 7:19–20
19 So Joshua said to Achan, "My son, give glory to the Lord, the God of Israel, and make a confession to him. I urge you, tell me what you have done. Don't hide anything from me."
20 Achan replied to Joshua, "It is true. I have sinned against the Lord, the God of Israel.

There was no indication of repentance in Achan's case, only confession. But repentance seems to be the aim of the angel's commands in Rv 14. Confession gives glory to God, but confession coupled with repentance gives him greater glory. Every tongue will confess that Jesus is Lord (Is 45:23; Rm 14:11; Php 2:11), but only those who have repented and been redeemed will have a new song to give glory to God forever (Rv 14:3).

Fearing God and giving him glory are summarized in the parallel command that follows, the command to *worship*. The worship of God commanded in v.7 will contrast with the worship of the beast, which will carry curses in vv.9-11 to follow.

Besides the fear/glory = worship equation, there is another parallel in v.7. This one equates God with being the Creator of all and gives this as a fundamental reason that he is to be worshiped. These statements certainly support worship of the Trinity, but they draw particular attention in this context to the Father and the Son, the Lamb of God. In Revelation Jesus is being revealed as both Creator (3:14; 13:8) and Judge (5:9; 15:3-4), possessing the very authority of the one on the throne in chs.4-5.

To obey the commands of the angel in Rv 14:7 is to do so with and for Jesus. He stated as much himself. Jesus prayed that the Father would glorify him as he did before the world existed (Jn 17:5). Jesus had already asserted that the Father does in fact do this very thing (8:54). That Jesus is in particular the focal point of the judgment in Rv 14:7 was already made clear by Jesus too. He said, "Whoever is ashamed of me and my words, the Son of Man will also be ashamed of him when he comes in his glory and that of the Father and the holy angels" (Lk 9:26; cf. Mk 8:38). That moment is before John now, and the criterion for judgment is declared. Give glory to God in Jesus. Worship the creator God in Jesus.

To those who reject this command, Jesus himself tied all these ideas together to explain their judgment:

> **John 12:48–50**
> **48** The one who rejects me and doesn't receive my sayings has this as his judge: The word I have spoken will judge him on the last day. **49** For I have not spoken on my own, but the Father himself who sent me has given me a command to say everything I have said. **50** I know that his command is eternal life. So the things that I speak, I speak just as the Father has told me."

The gospel is eternal based on this judgment regarding Jesus. This is good news for the faithful, for it is both salvation and vindication. It is finally and forever the removal of all rebellion and evil.

Do you think the call to "worship the one who made the heaven and earth" indicates that repentance is still possible? Why, or why not?

The Lamb, the Redeemed, and the Harvest of Wrath

If the first angel's announcement means there is room yet for repentance and salvation, then there are implications regarding how one sees the timeline. In this case, it would seem that what John is seeing and hearing now falls chronologically before the sixth trumpet (the second "woe") and the sixth seal (which is explicitly identified as the "wrath of...the one seated on the throne and...of the Lamb). As we have seen, those events seem end-of-the-age in scale. What's more, the reaction to the sixth seal by the unbelieving world is not that of seeking mercy or salvation but rather of hiding or escape. And in the sixth trumpet it is explicitly stated, "The rest of the people, who were not killed by these plagues, did not repent..." So, if the angel's announcement of 14:7 allows that repentance and salvation are still possible, it seems it must come chronologically prior to Seal Six and certainly before Trumpet Six.

However, it may be that the commands to give God glory are proclaimed in a moment when the matter is already decided. Pharaoh was told to release the Israelites many times, the last of which was long after his fate was sealed, both by his own hardening of his heart and then by God's hardening of his heart. Jesus explained to his disciples that his teaching by parables was to fulfill the prophecy that the rebellious would listen and not hear (Mt 13:10-15 with Is 6:10). God explained to Isaiah that the truth of the gospel has the effect of condemning the one who does not want it. That may be the function of the proclamation of the angel in Rv 14:7.

The gospel certainly does both things, acquitting the believer and condemning the unbeliever. Does the PFG offer any clues to whether both functions are still in play here? If believers are still on the planet when this announcement is made, this is yet another call to endure in faithfulness to this eternal gospel. In fact, if they are hearing this announcement from John's text at any point in time prior to the event itself, it asserts that call to endure faithfully, and fulfills the purpose for the writing.

For the non-Christian at the moment in question (14:7), we can only hope the door to salvation is still cracked open. If so, this eternal gospel is good news for them too. If not, this announcement of judgment couldn't be worse. And the next announcement will in two grammatical sentences pronounce one eternal sentence:

The Fall of Babylon

> **8** And another, a second angel, followed, saying, "It has fallen, Babylon the Great has fallen. She made all the nations drink the wine of her sexual immorality, which brings wrath."

The pronouncement of wrath here connects strongly to the sixth seal – as we saw above – and to the seventh trumpet (the third woe). The connection between this wrath and both Babylon and sexual immorality will be explained in much more detail in chapters that follow. This pronouncement declares an ultimate fulfillment of Is 21:9 and Jer 51:7-8. The repeating of the phrase "has fallen" probably indicates both initial and ultimate fulfillments but it also serves as

The Revelation of Jesus Christ

an intensification. Not only has a literal entity (city, culture, power) fallen, but so has everything it represents, the height of human and demonic arrogance and rebellion toward God.

As before, "sexual immorality" is very likely to represent actual physical acts (just as with the temple prostitutes of the ancient pagans surrounding Israel), but it is *certain* to symbolize spiritual acts. Her "sexual immorality" is contrasted with the "purity" in v.7 of this chapter. In Babylon is seen the collection of all spiritual prostitution, the offering of oneself to worship false gods. In this case that false worship has culminated in worship of the beast and the dragon.

This ancient – and by then global – system of false worship will collapse. It will not taper off or dissipate into various weaker factions. It will fall. How remarkable that this utter demise is articulated in one little sentence by the mighty angel! Coming chapters will give us much more detail, but even those will emphasize the suddenness of this collapse.

How does this second announcement remind the Christian to endure faithfully through suffering?

Warning and Blessing
With the third proclamation, the PFG is really brought home in no uncertain terms. In fact, "Jesus," "endurance" and "blessing" are all terms from the PFG that are voiced by this angel:

> **9** And another, a third angel, followed them and spoke with a loud voice: "If anyone worships the beast and its image and receives a mark on his forehead or on his hand, **10** he will also drink the wine of God's wrath, which is poured full strength into the cup of his anger. He will be tormented with fire and sulfur in the sight of the holy angels and in the sight of the Lamb, **11** and the smoke of their torment will go up forever and ever. There is no rest day or night for those who worship the beast and its image, or anyone who receives the mark of its name. **12** This calls for endurance from the saints, who keep God's commands and their faith in Jesus."
>
> **13** Then I heard a voice from heaven saying, "Write: Blessed are the dead who die in the Lord from now on."
>
> "Yes," says the Spirit, "so they will rest from their labors, since their works follow them."

As we noted before, there is no room for plurality or syncretism in the end. The options for worship are exactly two, and these are mutually exclusive. Worship the beast or worship the Lamb. The consequence of your choice is clear, and it is eternal. Torment or rest.

The Lamb, the Redeemed, and the Harvest of Wrath

Torment in the Bible never indicates annihilation but only conscious suffering. In the immediate context of two occurrences of the term here, this is clear. What would "fire" and "sulfur" mean to someone who is non-existent? How can these be "in the sight" of both angels and the Lamb (v.10)? How can Babylon's torment be seen by merchants (18:15)? Even taken metaphorically these terms imply ongoing existence. Later, in 18:7, this torment is a punishment parallel to Babylon's self-indulgence and self-glory that she expressed in previous existence. Further, the torment of the devil, beast and false prophet are experienced in temporality expressed as "day and night forever and ever" (20:10). This is not annihilation.

Praise God, the rest allotted for the believer is eternal as well! Eternity for the righteous is not a snapshot of a single blissful moment (contrary to the old song stating "time shall be no more"). It is a ceaseless activity extending throughout all future time (4:8; 7:15). This eternal reality is called "rest."

This rest is directly tied to blessing by Daniel (12:12-13). Rest and blessing are pictured in the seventh day of God's creative work, which he then codified in the command to observe the Sabbath. They are depicted together in the exodus to the promised land by ancient Israel. They are the subject of the writer of Hebrews who reflects on those old stories and symbols (Heb 3-4).

In fact, the call for endurance in Rv 14:11b-13 expresses the same theme as Heb 3:7-4:11. The persecution of Christians will be temporary, though challenging. But the gospel must not be ignored, or rest is lost forever. Those who have heard the gospel must endure in obedient faith. Note the parallel between Rv 14:12 and 12:17b. The blessing on those who die in the Lord emphasizes the presence of enduring faith rather than on the nature of their death (whether martyrdom or natural causes).

This call for endurance in 14:12 is the second such call in two chapters (13:10), and the fourth mention of endurance in the book (1:9; 2:2). The call here is directly tied to the announcement of wrath for false worship. That this calls for *endurance* rather than *repentance* may be cause to further question whether the latter is still a real possibility at this point, but it certainly brings the focus upon the believer more than the unbeliever.

As the PFG directed us to expect, the angel here calls the saints to endure through their suffering (even to the point of death), so that they might enjoy the blessing of eternal rest (v.13). The same eternal gospel issues warning for all but yields two opposite results: torment or rest.

What definition of endurance shows up again in v.12, and how does this tie to the warning?

The Revelation of Jesus Christ

The Harvest

Though the three announcements are aimed at the endurance of the saints, they also are characterized largely by judgment and vindication. This is personified in the Son of Man's being revealed as the authoritative Judge. His judgment begins to come to earth in a symbolic harvest of wrath:

> **14** Then I looked, and there was a white cloud, and one like the Son of Man was seated on the cloud, with a golden crown on his head and a sharp sickle in his hand. **15** Another angel came out of the temple, crying out in a loud voice to the one who was seated on the cloud, "Use your sickle and reap, for the time to reap has come, since the harvest of the earth is ripe." **16** So the one seated on the cloud swung his sickle over the earth, and the earth was harvested.
>
> **17** Then another angel who also had a sharp sickle came out of the temple in heaven. **18** Yet another angel, who had authority over fire, came from the altar, and he called with a loud voice to the one who had the sharp sickle, "Use your sharp sickle and gather the clusters of grapes from the vineyard of the earth, because its grapes have ripened." **19** So the angel swung his sickle at the earth and gathered the grapes from the vineyard of the earth, and he threw them into the great winepress of God's wrath. **20** Then the press was trampled outside the city, and blood flowed out of the press up to the horses' bridles for about 180 miles.

There is a lot of biblical background for harvest as a symbol. It is used to portray judgment as calamity (Is 17:5; 24:13; Hos 6:11; Joel 3:13); judgment as sorting out (Mt 13:30,39); evangelism (Mt 9:37-8; Jn 4:35) and blessing (Is 62:9; Jer 2:3). Our context here in Rv 14 connects linguistically to Joel 3:13 and the negative aspects of judgment, especially as tied to *wrath* (v.19), a *sharp sickle* (vv.14,17-18) and *trampling* (v.20).

The idea of sorting echoes Mt 13:

> **Matthew 13:24–30**
> **24** He presented another parable to them: "The kingdom of heaven may be compared to a man who sowed good seed in his field. **25** But while people were sleeping, his enemy came, sowed weeds among the wheat, and left. **26** When the plants sprouted and produced grain, then the weeds also appeared. **27** The landowner's servants came to him and said, 'Master, didn't you sow good seed in your field? Then where did the weeds come from?'
>
> **28** 'An enemy did this,' he told them.
>
> 'So, do you want us to go and pull them up?' the servants asked him.

The Lamb, the Redeemed, and the Harvest of Wrath

> **29** 'No,' he said. 'When you pull up the weeds, you might also uproot the wheat with them. **30** Let both grow together until the harvest. At harvest time I'll tell the reapers: Gather the weeds first and tie them in bundles to burn them, but collect the wheat in my barn.' "

Applied to our text in Rv 14, the suffering and marking has sorted things out. The function of "authority over fire" (v.18) indicates testing, which sorts out true faith. The wheat (faithful believers) has been marked and so have the weeds (those following the beast). For the latter this harvest is terrible. That this angel comes "from the altar," connects him to the souls who cried out "how long?" (6:10; 8:4). In answer, multiple angels reap with their sickles. Whether taken literally or symbolically, this bloody harvest is horrific. It is no wonder that John's prophecy would turn his stomach (10:10).

The winepress for this harvest is "outside the city" (v.20). This phrase is used repeatedly in Revelation to show the boundary between the redeemed and the rebellious (11:2; 20:9; 21:2; 22:14-15). An outpouring of wrath has happened outside the city before, and that time it was upon Jesus, the Savior. This outpouring will be for all who have refused to identify with Jesus and instead worshiped the beast. This trampling in ch.14 is a complete reversal of the trampling by the nations in 11:2.

This harvest is clearly conducted by the authority of God, but it is not absolutely clear that the "one like the Son of Man" is Jesus himself. The text may read "one like a son of man" but so strong are the connections to Dn 7:13 and Mt 24:30 that the CSB and other translations (NRSV and HCSB) take the phrase to refer specifically to Jesus' favorite title for himself. As in other cases (e.g., Rv 10:1), if it is not Jesus that is meant here, then it is an angel closely associated with God, most likely the Angel of the Lord. If John does mean for us to understand this to be Jesus, then this is another direct tie to the PFG of revealing Jesus as exalted Lord.

Are the statements about the carnage literal? They may well be (compare vv.19-20 to Is 63:1-6 and Joel 3:1-4:16). If so, blood rising up to the horses' bridles is a picture of intense military carnage. 180 miles (Gk. "1600 stadia") is roughly the length of Palestine. Regardless, as before, we can be more certain John intends to communicate through the symbolism of what he writes. L. Morris elaborates:

> "1,600 stadia is a distance of about 184 miles (300 kilometres). But John's interest is rather in the number than in the precise distance it represents. Of the explanations suggested perhaps best is that which sees it as the product of sixteen (the square of four, the number of the earth which is the abode of the wicked) and one hundred (the square of ten, the number of completeness). It is also the square of forty, a number associated with punishment. Blood

stretching for 1,600 stadia thus stands for the complete judgment of the whole earth and the destruction of all the wicked."[39]

After this gruesome account, does it feel like we are back once again to Judgment Day, the Day of the Lord at the end of the world? Many believe we are, and Beale argues that perspective:

> "Vv.1–5 depict the beginning of eternal bliss. Vv.6–7 give a warning to repent. V.8 tells of the judgment at the end of history. Vv.9–11 tell of the eternal consequences of judgment. Vv.12–13 give an exhortation to persevere in the present. And vv.14–20 again tell of judgment at the end of history."[40]

Reflection

Once again, letting the PFG set our zoom level, we can focus on what John clearly communicates in ch.14 and not be too preoccupied with what is less clear. Jesus the Lamb is being revealed as Lord of all upon Mt. Zion, which has long been associated with God's presence and his people. His people are being described and defined as those who are pure in faith, worshiping and giving glory to God alone. They are tested by the full force of this world's spiritual union with false gods, but they are sealed by God and guarded by angelic warnings to all on the earth. The result is that the faithful are sorted out from the faithless. God pours his wrath on those who are judged by the eternal gospel to have rejected Jesus.

In what ways has Jesus been revealed in 1) his appearance on Mt. Zion, 2) the proclamations of the three angels and 3) the harvest of wrath?

How has each of those sections challenged Christians to faithfully endure suffering?

How has each section revealed the promise of blessing?

---

[39] Morris, L. (1987). *Revelation: an introduction and commentary* (Vol. 20, p. 179). Downers Grove, IL: InterVarsity Press.
[40] Beale, G. K. (1999). *The book of Revelation: a commentary on the Greek text* (pp. 783–784). Grand Rapids, MI; Carlisle, Cumbria: W.B. Eerdmans; Paternoster Press.

Lesson 13: The Song, the Temple, and the Bowls (Chs.15-16)

At the conclusion of the seventh trumpet in ch.11 there began a series of seven signs in ch.12 sandwiched between the sevenfold series of trumpets and bowls. All these sevens are communicating completion and fulfillment. Just as with the creation week of Gn 1-2, these sevens are full of activity that will culminate with rest for God's faithful, and they anticipate the promise of new creation.

The first of the seven signs began with the word "appeared" in 12:1. Each one that followed kicked off with the formula "and/then I saw/looked." John has recorded the first six signs: 1) the epic struggle between the dragon and the woman's offspring (ch.12); 2) persecution by the sea beast (13:1-10); 3) persecution by the land beast (13:11-18); 4) the Lamb on Mt. Zion and the 144,000 redeemed (14:1-5); 5) the three angels' proclamations of the eternal gospel and judgment (14:6-13); and 6) the Son of Man's harvest of the earth (14:14-20). Now the series culminates here in ch.15 with the seventh sign introduced by "then I saw" in v.1:

The Song of Moses and of the Lamb

> **Revelation 15:1–4**
> **1** Then I saw another great and awe-inspiring sign in heaven: seven angels with the seven last plagues; for with them God's wrath will be completed. **2** I also saw something like a sea of glass mixed with fire, and those who had won the victory over the beast, its image, and the number of its name, were standing on the sea of glass with harps from God. **3** They sang the song of God's servant Moses and the song of the Lamb:
>
>> Great and awe-inspiring are your works,
>> Lord God, the Almighty;
>> just and true are your ways,
>> King of the nations.
>> **4** Lord, who will not fear
>> and glorify your name?
>> For you alone are holy.
>> All the nations will come
>> and worship before you
>> because your righteous acts
>> have been revealed.

The seven signs began with struggle and end with judgment. The central sign – the fourth – features Jesus, the Lamb standing victorious with his redeemed. With that sign and with this seventh there is celebration and singing of the saints. The fulfilling of God's cosmic plan sorts out into two opposite conditions. The faithful are brought to vindication and joy while the wicked are brought to judgment and despair.

The Awe-inspiring Sign
This seventh sign stands out as the only one called "great and awe-inspiring." The context indicates that this designation is due to the totality and finality of the sign's content. God's wrath will be completed with the seven last plagues.

The *totality* of these seven judgments stands in contrast to the earlier sevens. The restraint prior to the seventh seal – "four angels...restraining the four winds of the earth" in 7:1 – that restraint is gone. The limits assigned to the first six trumpets – all the "thirds" of chs.8-9 – those too are gone. The wrath of the bowls (some translations have "cups" or "vials") is total. The *finality* is emphasized by the sevenfold count of the last plagues and the uninterrupted progression through them, as noted in the Holman Bible Handbook:

> "Between the sixth and seventh seals and the sixth and seventh trumpets we were told of God's protection of, and mission for, the people of God. But with the seven cups there is no break between the sixth and seventh outpourings of judgment. Now only wrath is left; there is no more delay."[41]

For the Christian, God's wrath was satisfied at the cross with the declaration, "It is finished." For everyone else, God's wrath will finally come with these seven last plagues. Before those are dispensed, there is a depiction of the victorious standing on a sea of glass and singing.

The Glassy Sea
This glassy sea seems to roll several ideas together. It seems to be the same sea mentioned in 4:6, but with a new characteristic, the mingling with fire. The danger and chaos of the sea and its monsters echoes those of the Red Sea in the exodus. This is almost surely a depiction of judgment and an ironic one. It is ironic because the saints have been tried by the fire of persecution but now that fire is brought upon those who persecuted them. The saints now stand on the sea of their fiery test. This sea is not in tumult but is calm and peaceful like glass. For those put to death in the early days of the church, their day of martyrdom was often called their "day of victory."[42] So it is now. The faithful stand in victory and sing.

In Boston today there is a memorial to those who suffered and died in the terrors of the concentration camps of the Third Reich. The numbers that were assigned to the victims by their tormentors are inscribed in glass walls in a series of pillars each representing one camp. It is a powerful feeling to walk through these and recall the horrible evil that assaulted these people. This sea in Rv.15 may well serve as a similar memorial, but it does much more than that. The remembering brings justice with it. The fire of the believer's testing is now frozen in the legacy of

---

[41] Dockery, D. S. (Ed.). (1992). *Holman Bible Handbook* (p. 801). Nashville, TN: Holman Bible Publishers.
[42] Morris, L. (1987). *Revelation: an introduction and commentary* (Vol. 20, p. 181). Downers Grove, IL: InterVarsity Press.

The Song, the Temple, and the Bowls

overcoming, but now it will become the fire of judgment upon the demonic world system of those who persecuted them.

Besides the glassy sea, there are other strong connections between ch.15 and the heavenly scene of chs.4-5. The "harps of God" mentioned here in ch.15 point back to the harps of the creatures and elders in 5:8. They held not only harps but golden bowls full of incense, the prayers of the saints. They sang in vv.9-10 of the Lamb's authority to bring judgment for his own slaughter to redeem those saints. Now in ch.15, the saints hold harps and sing to God about the justice he will bring through the bowl judgments to come. Bowls of prayer become bowls of judgment.

Remembering that the PFG is **to reveal Jesus Christ so that his servants faithfully endure suffering in order to receive blessing**, *how would this glassy sea encourage those that are suffering persecution?*

What times of testing in your life can you now look back on in peace, standing on the reality that God has brought you faithfully through?

The Song

So, what is this song being sung by the victors? It might be seen either as two songs or as one. After the subject and verb – "They sang" – the language is parallel. Is this a mash-up or an amalgam? Is the song of the Lamb a reflection upon or a prophetic update to the song of Moses?

There are two songs of Moses recorded in the OT. The first is recorded in Ex 15 immediately following the account of Yahweh's miraculous deliverance of his people from the pharaoh's army at the Red Sea. It is a victory song. The second is found in Dt 32 as Moses gives a history lesson to warn God's people to remain faithful as God works through Joshua to bring them into the Promised Land. This is largely an exhortation song that begins with rebuke and ends with restoration and vindication.

The ideas found in these two songs of Moses are extremely appropriate in Revelation. God's people are being challenged to remain true (as with the song in Dt 32) so that they may be vindicated when God shows his awe-inspiring power in a greater exodus (as celebrated in the Ex 15 song). In the context of Rv 15, that warning to remain faithful is in the background, but the victory song of Ex 15 is in the foreground, for the timeline is approaching final judgment and God's own have now been shown to be faithful.

The Revelation of Jesus Christ

These ideas from Moses and the Exodus are present in the song of Rv 15, but they seem to take on new meaning. So, the song of Moses is not in opposition to the song of the Lamb but rather the old song gets swallowed up into the new and greater reality of this new song as King Jesus brings ultimate victory for his people. This victory is not against an ancient pharaoh but against the dominant world power of the beast. This victory song is about final and ultimate victory. So, it seems appropriate to view vv.3-4 as one song, a "remix" of the song of Moses that is now more properly titled "the song of the Lamb."

How do the themes of Moses' songs (warning, victory and vindication) help Revelation accomplish its PFG for you today?

The song itself draws heavily upon OT language, particularly of the Psalms. It begins with two assertions in v.3 followed by a rhetorical question in 4a. Then it concludes with three proclamations that answer the question.

The first assertion is about power. God is the Almighty who performs great and awe-inspiring works (see Dt 10:17,21; Neh 1:5; 4:14; 9:32; Job 5:9; 9:10; 37:5; Ps 47:2; 66:3; 86:10; 89:7; 92:5; 99:3; 139:14; 145:6; Dn 9:4). "Great" and "awe-inspiring" are descriptions that tie directly back to v.1 of this chapter where they designate the ultimate wonder of the seventh sign. This seventh sign shows the awesome power of God.

The second assertion is about justice. God's ways are "just and true" (see Dt 32:4; Neh 9:13; Ps 18:30; 145:17; Dn 4:37). This designation is tied especially to his just rule as "King of the nations" (see Ps 10:16; 47:8-9; 96:10).

The rhetorical question is cosmic in scope, much like the one of the sixth seal, "Who is able to stand?" (6:17). There it is the wicked crying out but here it is the righteous voicing the question in v.4, "Lord, who will not fear and glorify your name?" This is both a condemnation upon those who have refused to do so and also a pronouncement that all – even they – *will* finally do so. Sadly, in the case of the wicked, to glorify the Lord will not be a salvific confession but a damning one.

The singers proclaim three reasons why the Lord ought to be feared and glorified. Each begins with "for" in the Greek, though the CSB drops the second one, opting to begin a new sentence. In this translation, the "because" of the last couplet is the last "for."

So, the first proclamation is, "For you alone are holy." In the use of the phrase here in v.4, the term "holy" conveys absolute uniqueness and especially perfect purity. It is not the more common Greek term (*hagios*), but a less common one (*hosios*) that is strongly tied to Jesus as Messiah and used in Revelation only here and in 16:5. It resonates from Ps 16:10 where King David states the

The Song, the Temple, and the Bowls

LORD "will not allow his holy one to see decay." Peter makes the connection from that text to Jesus in Acts 2:27 and Paul does the same in Acts 13:35.

So, this song of the Lamb borrows OT language and borrows from Moses' ancient proclamations about Yahweh's amazing exploits and applies them anew to Jesus, King of the nations. Jesus is the Lord whom all will fear and glorify because he is God's Holy One (see 16:5).

The second proclamation is, "For all the nations will come and worship before you." This especially echoes Ps 22:27, a messianic psalm foretelling the salvific suffering of Christ that brings universal worship. It also draws from the language of Ps 86:9 (see also Zep 2:14 and Zec 14:16). This is a statement of fact that fulfills the OT prophets in Jesus, the Lamb.

The third proclamation is, "For your righteous acts have been revealed." The righteous acts of the Lord are particularly seen as acts of judgment. Just as Yahweh's acts at the Red Sea pronounce judgment upon the false gods of Egypt, so the Lamb's acts pronounce judgment upon all false worship. In his righteous acts of judgment, Jesus is revealing true worship and is being revealed as the true object of worship, the Holy One.

Notice that everything lifted up in this song is about the Lord's work. The singers are servants like Moses was a servant (v.3). They do not sing of *their* works in offering testimony, their struggle to be faithful in overcoming the beast. They focus entirely upon their Lord and *his* works.

How then does this song contribute to the first part of the PFG to reveal Jesus Christ?

The Heavenly Temple

> **5** After this I looked, and the heavenly temple—the tabernacle of testimony—was opened. **6** Out of the temple came the seven angels with the seven plagues, dressed in pure, bright linen, with golden sashes wrapped around their chests. **7** One of the four living creatures gave the seven angels seven golden bowls filled with the wrath of God who lives forever and ever. **8** Then the temple was filled with smoke from the glory of God and from his power, and no one could enter the temple until the seven plagues of the seven angels were completed.

What term in v.5 connects to the charge for believers individually and the church collectively to faithfully bear witness to Jesus?

The Revelation of Jesus Christ

What language in v.6 depicts righteous purity? How does it tie back to John's description of the Son of Man in 1:13? What does this communicate about the connection between these angels and Jesus?

In v.5 we begin to see the fulfillment of the model prayer Jesus gave his disciples (Mt 6:9-13). The Father's name is being hallowed in the Son, and his will is about to be done on earth as it is in heaven. The testimony in the heavenly tabernacle is about to flood the earth with final judgment. As Constable points out, "The "tabernacle of testimony" refers to the temple as the building that housed God's law, which the earth-dwellers disregard. God was now going to hold them to it and judge them by it."[43]

In the 1981 movie Raiders of the Lost Ark, a band of power-hungry treasure hunters find and steal the ancient Israelite Ark of the Covenant. In what they believe to be their greatest moment, they open the Ark to lay claim over its mystical powers and dominate the world. It doesn't work out that way. Instead, every last one of them is consumed by God's fire of judgment. It's hard for a sensitive soul to watch! The scene beginning to play out here in Rv 15 will unleash from the heavenly tabernacle a fury to which that old movie pales in comparison.

The seven bowls are patterned after the exodus plagues, and the smoke of God's glory and power in v.8 here echoes that upon Mt. Sinai and especially that of the tabernacle. When Moses completed construction of that tabernacle, recall that he was at first unable to enter because of God's glory:

> **Exodus 40:34–35**
> **34** The cloud covered the tent of meeting, and the glory of the LORD filled the tabernacle. **35** Moses was unable to enter the tent of meeting because the cloud rested on it, and the glory of the LORD filled the tabernacle.

The same thing happened when Solomon consecrated the earthly temple:

> **2 Chronicles 7:1–2**
> **1** When Solomon finished praying, fire descended from heaven and consumed the burnt offering and the sacrifices, and the glory of the LORD filled the temple. **2** The priests were not able to enter the LORD's temple because the glory of the LORD filled the temple of the LORD.

---

[43] Constable, T. (2003). *Tom Constable's Expository Notes on the Bible* (Re 15:5). Galaxie Software.

The Song, the Temple, and the Bowls

If this awesome and terrifying display of power came to the earthly temple, imagine how much more imposing is that display from the heavenly temple! This point is put forward by the writer of Hebrews:

> **Hebrews 12:25–29**
> **25** See to it that you do not reject the one who speaks. For if they did not escape when they rejected him who warned them on earth, even less will we if we turn away from him who warns us from heaven. **26** His voice shook the earth at that time, but now he has promised, **Yet once more I will shake not only the earth but also the heavens. 27** This expression, "Yet once more," indicates the removal of what can be shaken—that is, created things—so that what is not shaken might remain. **28** Therefore, since we are receiving a kingdom that cannot be shaken, let us be thankful. By it, we may serve God acceptably, with reverence and awe, **29** for our God is a consuming fire.

The consuming fire of God's judgment is about to come to earth, and the feeling of impending doom is intense, much like the half hour of the seventh seal (8:1). We seem to be right back where we were with the seventh trumpet, with an open heavenly temple and visions of power and judgment (11:19). Whether this is recapitulation or a progression, with the bowls there is a greater sense of finality. In ch.15 there is an emphasis on *completion* (vv.1 and 8). Further, the idea of *fullness* ("filled" in 15:7 and also in 21:9) amplifies the totality of this judgment. God's remarkable patience has been exhausted. He will now respond to the prayers of his saints ("bowls" and "altar" here tie back to those of 8:3-5). Nothing will stall or interrupt these last plagues that will completely satisfy God's righteous wrath.

It is worth pointing out that even with the bowl judgments interpreters are not universally in agreement that these depictions focus particularly upon an intensification at the very end of this age. The NT writers indicate that the "last days" (Acts 2:17; Heb 1:2) may broadly describe the period bookended by Christ's first and second comings, what we call the Church Age. Still, there seem to be good indications that what is true for this whole age will be more intensely true at the end of it (2 Tm 3:1; Jas 5:3; 2 Pt 3:3). Jesus certainly seems to speak in Mt 24-25 of "that day" when he returns in judgment (see 24:36) as though it intensifies near "the end" just like labor pains come near the end of a pregnancy and signal an imminent birth:

> **Matthew 24:4–8**
> **4** Jesus replied to them, "Watch out that no one deceives you. **5** For many will come in my name, saying, 'I am the Messiah,' and they will deceive many. **6** You are going to hear of wars and rumors of wars. See that you are not alarmed, because these things must take place, but the end is not yet. **7** For nation will rise up against nation, and kingdom against kingdom. There will be famines and earthquakes in various places. **8** All these events are the beginning of labor pains.

The Revelation of Jesus Christ

Jesus seems to indicate that an escalation of persecution will correspond to the global witness of the church, and that these realities bring "the end":

> **Matthew 24:9–14**
> **9** "Then they will hand you over to be persecuted, and they will kill you. You will be hated by all nations because of my name. **10** Then many will fall away, betray one another, and hate one another. **11** Many false prophets will rise up and deceive many. **12** Because lawlessness will multiply, the love of many will grow cold. **13** But the one who endures to the end will be saved. **14** This good news of the kingdom will be proclaimed in all the world as a testimony to all nations, and then the end will come.

These predictions are completely consistent with the thrust of Revelation. (In fact, Revelation may be seen as the extended and final words of Jesus on the matter.) Further, they seem to justify in some measure the futurist view that this age will culminate with an intensification and global scaling of the wickedness of the world and its persecution of the church that has characterized these first two millennia since Christ. As we have said before, Revelation offers its message to every generation of the church. But it does seem that the events of the seal, trumpet and bowl judgments do especially point to ultimate fulfillment just prior to and with Christ's return.

The Seven Bowls

While 15:8 makes it clear that this judgment comes from God alone, he dispatches seven angels to deliver his judgments to the earth. This follows the pattern of a similar OT judgment recorded in Ezek 9:1-10:6 when God sent out seven angels to punish all in Jerusalem who did not bear his mark on their foreheads. However, this occurrence is global.

First, let's read the whole sevenfold account, and then we'll make some observations about these last plagues:

> **Revelation 16:1–21**
> **1** Then I heard a loud voice from the temple saying to the seven angels, "Go and pour out the seven bowls of God's wrath on the earth." **2** The first went and poured out his bowl on the earth, and severely painful sores broke out on the people who had the mark of the beast and who worshiped its image.
>
> **3** The second poured out his bowl into the sea. It turned to blood like that of a dead person, and all life in the sea died.
>
> **4** The third poured out his bowl into the rivers and the springs of water, and they became blood. **5** I heard the angel of the waters say,

The Song, the Temple, and the Bowls

> You are just,
> the Holy One, who is and who was,
> because you have passed judgment on these things.
> **6** Because they poured out
> the blood of the saints and the prophets,
> you have given them blood to drink;
> they deserve it!

7 I heard the altar say,

> Yes, Lord God, the Almighty,
> true and just are your judgments.

8 The fourth poured out his bowl on the sun. It was allowed to scorch people with fire, **9** and people were scorched by the intense heat. So they blasphemed the name of God, who has the power over these plagues, and they did not repent and give him glory.

10 The fifth poured out his bowl on the throne of the beast, and its kingdom was plunged into darkness. People gnawed their tongues because of their pain **11** and blasphemed the God of heaven because of their pains and their sores, but they did not repent of their works.

12 The sixth poured out his bowl on the great river Euphrates, and its water was dried up to prepare the way for the kings from the east. **13** Then I saw three unclean spirits like frogs coming from the dragon's mouth, from the beast's mouth, and from the mouth of the false prophet. **14** For they are demonic spirits performing signs, who travel to the kings of the whole world to assemble them for the battle on the great day of God, the Almighty. **15** "Look, I am coming like a thief. Blessed is the one who is alert and remains clothed so that he may not go around naked and people see his shame." **16** So they assembled the kings at the place called in Hebrew, Armageddon.

17 Then the seventh poured out his bowl into the air, and a loud voice came out of the temple from the throne, saying, "It is done!" **18** There were flashes of lightning, rumblings, and peals of thunder. And a severe earthquake occurred like no other since people have been on the earth, so great was the quake. **19** The great city split into three parts, and the cities of the nations fell. Babylon the Great was remembered in God's presence; he gave her the cup filled with the wine of his fierce anger. **20** Every island fled, and the mountains disappeared. **21** Enormous hailstones, each weighing about a hundred pounds, fell from the sky on people, and they blasphemed God for the plague of hail because that plague was extremely severe.

The Revelation of Jesus Christ

Bowls/Trumpets Parallels

First, make note of the strong parallels between these bowl judgments and those of the trumpets. Beale offers a helpful chart to show these parallels as well as their Exodus background: [44]

Trumpet 1: Hail, fire, and blood fall on the *earth*, one third of which is burned up.	**Bowl 1**: A bowl is poured on the *earth*. Malignant sores come on those who have the mark of the beast and who worship his image.
... corresponding to Exod. 9:22ff. (trumpet), 8ff. (bowl)	
Trumpet 2: A blazing mountain falls into the *sea*. One third of the sea becomes *blood*, a third of *sea creatures die*, and a third of all ships are destroyed.	**Bowl 2**: A bowl is poured on the *seas*, which become *blood*, and *every living thing in them dies*.
... corresponding to Exod. 7:17ff.	
Trumpet 3: A blazing star (Wormwood) falls on a third of *rivers and fountains;* their waters are poisoned and many die.	**Bowl 3**: A bowl is poured on *rivers and fountains*, and they become blood.
... corresponding to Exod. 7:17ff.	
Trumpet 4: A third of *sun, moon, and stars* are struck. Darkness results for a third of a night and day.	**Bowl 4**: A bowl is poured on the *sun*, which scorches people with fire.
... corresponding to Exod. 10:21ff. (trumpet); 9:22ff. (bowl)	
Trumpet 5: The shaft of the pit is opened. Sun and air are *darkened* with smoke from which locusts emerge to *torment* people without the seal of God.	**Bowl 5**: A bowl is poured on the throne of the beast. His kingdom is *darkened* and people are in *anguish*.
... corresponding to Exod. 10:4ff. (trumpet), 21ff. (trumpet and bowl)	
Trumpet 6: Four angels bound at *the Euphrates* are released, with their cavalry of two hundred million, which kills a third of humanity.	**Bowl 6**: A bowl is poured on *the Euphrates*, which dries up for kings from the east. Demonic frogs deceive the kings of the world to assemble for battle at Armageddon.
... corresponding to Exod. 8:2ff. (bowl)	
Trumpet 7: *Loud voices in heaven* announce the coming of the kingdom of God and of Christ. *Lightning, thunder, earthquake*, and *hail* occur.	**Bowl 7**: A bowl is poured into the air, and *a loud voice from God's throne* announces "It is done." *Lightning, thunder*, and an unprecedented *earthquake* occur, and terrible *hail* falls.
... corresponding to Exod. 9:22ff. and the Sinai theophany (19:16–19)	

---

[44] Beale, G. K. (1999). *The book of Revelation: a commentary on the Greek text* (pp. 809–810). Grand Rapids, MI; Carlisle, Cumbria: W.B. Eerdmans; Paternoster Press.

The Song, the Temple, and the Bowls

Notice how the progression for the impact of the bowls echoes that of the trumpets: 1) earth, 2) sea, 3) rivers, 4) sun, 5) darkness/torment, 6) Euphrates/warriors and 7) global cataclysmic judgment. The first four bowl plagues are focused on natural elements, but they directly target those who worship the beast. The last three plagues target political dominions and ultimately draw in all the world's rulers. The fifth plague engulfs the whole kingdom of the beast in darkness and torment. The sixth plague brings deception to unite all earthly rulers against God. Then the seventh plague rocks the globe with cataclysmic doom.

The Angel and the Altar

With the third bowl, there is a pronouncement of the angel of the waters and a response from the altar that are strongly tied once again to that cry of "How long?" from 6:10. The angel declares that those who suffer now are getting what they deserve. The punishment fits the crime. The victims are now being vindicated.

The title "holy one" used by the angel in v.5 is used dozens of times in the OT, especially by Isaiah recording Yahweh's pronouncements about his sovereign work. As we saw earlier, the term is now being applied to Jesus as well. The connection of the phrase "holy one" to Jesus is strengthened further by his own use of the phrase to identify his authority in speaking to the church at Philadelphia. In bringing these judgments, the Holy One is doubly declared just by both the angel (v.5) and by the altar (v.7). God is demonstrated to be righteous particularly *because* he judges the wicked.

How does it make you feel to think about God's punishment of evil? Does it seem right to rejoice about it? Why, or why not?

What would be the theological consequences of a God that did NOT judge evil?

The Holman Bible Handbook offers this perspective:

> "God longs to see His rebellious children lay down their arms and come home to Him. God has mercifully acted by all possible means—even to the extent of taking to Himself, through His Only Begotten Son, the very penalty that He has prescribed for sin—to bring His wayward children home. Wrath brings grief even to the heart of God, but God will not coerce our love of Him.

The Revelation of Jesus Christ

But we must neither deny nor even lament the wisdom of God for His past or future assertions of wrath. Our God evidently loves righteousness, justice, and mercy to such an extent that He will not brook our cowardly tolerance of evil. We may not lightly dismiss the fact that heaven is neither silent nor embarrassed when evil is punished. Heaven rejoices at the justice and judgment of God (19:1–6)."[45]

Blaspheming God

The fourth and fifth plagues result in the same reactions. People blaspheme God and they refuse to repent and give him glory. The dual blasphemy of God and his heavenly dwelling echoes that of the beast in 13:6. Those who worship the beast follow him in doing what he does. They will share his tortuous fate too. These plagues are not redemptive, they are punitive.

How is the suffering of the unrepentant different from that of the redeemed? How is the result different?

Since Satan likes to create counterfeits, then his PFG would be something like the following: to deceive the world about the beast so that everyone he can fool will persist in their blasphemy and rebellion in order to be cursed under wrath. His deception is working, for the servants of the beast are holding onto their rebellion all the way to the point of a cursed death under God's wrath.

Darkness

The fifth bowl is poured out "on the throne of the beast." This phrase directly echoes the "throne of Satan" from 2:13 and is a reminder that even these latter portions of Revelation were relevant to the original audience.

The darkness of this plague sounds like the Egyptian plague of darkness that completely isolated individuals (Ex 10:21-23). That darkness was palpable and crippling. They were paralyzed for three days. This latter darkness is worse. It is surely just as isolating, but it is also tortuous. It is undoubtedly symbolic (though, once again, it may well also be literal). This darkness barely begins to depict the torment and loneliness of the eternal separation from God for which the rebels are destined upon final judgment.

Euphrates and Armageddon

In the sixth bowl, God does something he has done before to execute judgment. His prophets had said God would dry up waters for this purpose. He did it with the Red Sea (Ex 14:21), with the Jordan (Josh 3:16-17) and would do it again (Is 11:15; 44:27-28; Zec 10:11). History records that

---

[45] Dockery, D. S. (Ed.). (1992). *Holman Bible Handbook* (p. 802). Nashville, TN: Holman Bible Publishers.

The Song, the Temple, and the Bowls

Cyrus fulfilled Isaiah's prophecy by diverting the Euphrates in a surprise attack to defeat ancient Babylon.

Some take John's writing here literally, that the Euphrates will be dried up to allow distant kings to assemble for a great battle, the Battle of Armageddon. One difficulty is that there is no such place known by the name Armageddon. The Hebrew term apparently refers to the "mountain of Megiddo" or "city of Megiddo" (see Jgs 5:19; 2 Kgs 23:29; 2 Chr 35:22). Others escape this difficulty by taking John to be writing only symbolically of a sort of coalescing political disunity among the rebellious powers of the world.

As elsewhere, the symbolism is what is clear, so we will focus on that. In the fifth bowl individual rebels are isolated by darkness. In this sixth bowl it seems that whole kingdoms are polarized by deception. This deception comes from unclean spirits whose work is patterned after that of the false prophets that enticed wicked King Ahab to march into the battle that would take his life (1 Kgs 22:20-23). The frog simile ties back to the exodus plagues and probably emphasizes that these spirits are unclean and loathsome.

The result of the deception is global disunity. The only thing unified at this point is that all oppose God, but these kings are not assembling as a single force. This is not a case of "the enemy of my enemy is my friend." This seems to be World War "n," whatever number we've reached by then. The infighting of these evil forces will be explicitly affirmed in the latter part of ch.17. So, deception leads only to disunity. That'll preach.

Ironically, the assembly of the world's kings for battle is assigned a special designation, but it is not "World War" Anything. It is rather, "the great day of God, the Almighty." Deception and pride will draw the assembly, but they will be utterly helpless regarding this day's outcome. It is God's day.

"Like A Thief"

Suddenly interjected in the description of this sixth bowl judgment is a warning and challenge by Christ himself (v.15). This repeats the language he used to the seven churches:

> **Revelation 3:3–5, 18**
> **3** Remember, then, what you have received and heard; keep it, and repent. If you are not alert, I will come like a thief, and you have no idea at what hour I will come upon you. **4** But you have a few people in Sardis who have not defiled their clothes, and they will walk with me in white, because they are worthy.
> **5** "In the same way, the one who conquers will be dressed in white clothes, and I will never erase his name from the book of life but will acknowledge his name before my Father and before his angels.

18 I advise you to buy from me gold refined in the fire so that you may be rich, white clothes so that you may be dressed and your shameful nakedness not be exposed, and ointment to spread on your eyes so that you may see.

That Christ will come like a thief is also asserted by Paul:

1 Thessalonians 5:1–4
1 About the times and the seasons: Brothers and sisters, you do not need anything to be written to you. **2** For you yourselves know very well that the day of the Lord will come just like a thief in the night. **3** When they say, "Peace and security," then sudden destruction will come upon them, like labor pains on a pregnant woman, and they will not escape. **4** But you, brothers and sisters, are not in the dark, for this day to surprise you like a thief.

The Doctrine of Imminence rings out loudly and clearly from Jesus in Rv 16:15. Right in the thick of God's last plagues, he gives warning and assures blessing. Notice this wakeup call comes right after the description of spiritual deception. Blessing once again is tied to wisdom. Be alert, stay gospel-focused.

Many modern interpreters take Jesus' coming like a thief to refer to a separate event from his second coming. They see this event as his taking up, or "rapture," of the church, and most of them see it as happening years before Christ's coming as a victorious warrior. For most of church history, Christians did not see these as two events but one unified one. Whichever is the case, we must be careful to not misunderstand Jesus in Rv 16:15. He is not telling Christians, "I'm coming to sneak you out!" He is telling them, "Don't get caught with your pants down!"

How is this statement, stuck in the middle of this description of the Day of the Lord, intended to help along the PFG of the book?

How does a Christian follow the mandate to remain alert and clothed? How might many today be failing to keep this mandate?

"It Is Done"
The seventh angel pours out his bowl, and like the third angel he makes a proclamation: "It is done!" The seven last plagues were said to complete the wrath of God (15:1), and now we come to the last of the seven.

The Song, the Temple, and the Bowls

How is the seventh bowl (vv.17-21) similar to the seventh trumpet (11:13-19) and the seventh seal (8:1-5)? How is it different?

How does the pronouncement, "It is done!" in v.17 relate to the one by John in Rv 15:1, to the one by Jesus in his model prayer in Mt 6:10, to the one by him on the cross in Jn 19:30 and finally, to the statement by the one on the throne in Rv 21:6? How does it relate to the cry of the souls under the altar in Rv 6:10? To the purpose of the book?

In Eph 2:2 Paul reminded believers that they used to live "according to the ways of this world, according to the ruler of the power of the air, the spirit now working in the disobedient." In Rv 16:17 wrath is being poured out on this power. God's judgment is deconstructing the world. John uses the most extreme language. Seven times in this bowl he uses the term *megas*: "loud"; "severe" (2x); "great" (3x) and "enormous." This is "mega" judgment! John uses a term only here in the book to say the plague of hail was "extremely" severe. In summary, as Jesus predicted, this day of God's wrath is like no day the earth has ever known!

The height of all earthly and demonic rebellion has been exposed and God's wrath has been completed. What more is there to see? It seems we will back up (once again) as an angel will show John more detail of this judgment of the evil powers that oppose God. A glimpse of that final blessed state promised to the faithful is just around the corner. But first, we will see the undoing of all evil and the judgment of everyone. Until then, we must keep clinging to Jesus Christ so that we faithfully endure suffering in order to receive that blessing.

Lesson 14: The Prostitute and the Beast (Ch.17)

In the last lesson we saw that with the pouring out of the seven bowls God's judgment comes to the earth suddenly and completely. A loud voice from the heavenly temple declares, "It is done!" (16:17). The wicked have persisted in their wickedness, and even as God's wrath pours down on them, they blaspheme, refusing to acknowledge him as true God.

As before, it seems now that this Revelation will rewind a bit as John is given an expanded, more detailed vision. Just like the enhanced slow-motion replay of today's sporting broadcasts, John seems to be given a chance to see a frame-by-frame perspective of this sudden judgment of all evil powers. The vision turns about to watch the collapse of each major player. Beale points out that chs.16-18 begin to show a reversal of the dramatic rise of all these evil powers:

> "The preceding chapters envisioned the rise of the dragon (ch.12), followed by the beast (13:1–10), the false prophet (or second beast, 13:11–18), and finally Babylon (14:6–11). Ch.16 begins a segment that reverses the order of the careers of these evil protagonists. Babylon is mentioned first in the explanation of their demise (16:17–21; chs.17–18), followed by the beast and the false prophet (19:17–20) and finally the dragon himself (20:10)."[46]

This is not to say that these powers necessarily fall one after the other in a stretched out chronological sequence, for they are judged suddenly, and so it is probably more accurate to see these next few chapters as expanded details of a more unified, condensed collapse of earthly and demonic evil. Either way, these chapters depict the utter destruction of every power that opposes God and of every person who follows after them in misplaced trust and false worship.

As we said before, Revelation peels back layers to expose these powers behind false worship even as it reveals Jesus as the one worthy of true worship. The antagonists are now being exposed in a rise-and-fall narrative. Their fall comes with the final judgment and wrath of God in which Jesus destroys all enemies and establishes his eternal cosmic reign.

The Prostitute

The first power John sees depicted in its fall is Babylon. She is depicted as a prostitute that is closely associated with the power and rule of the beast, or Antichrist:

---

[46] Beale, G. K. (1999). *The book of Revelation: a commentary on the Greek text* (p. 812). Grand Rapids, MI; Carlisle, Cumbria: W.B. Eerdmans; Paternoster Press.

The Revelation of Jesus Christ

> **Revelation 17:1–3**
> **1** Then one of the seven angels who had the seven bowls came and spoke with me: "Come, I will show you the judgment of the notorious prostitute who is seated on many waters. **2** The kings of the earth committed sexual immorality with her, and those who live on the earth became drunk on the wine of her sexual immorality." **3** Then he carried me away in the Spirit to a wilderness.

Seven angels had been charged with carrying out God's judgments on the earth. It is appropriate that one of these is authorized to walk John through this vision (v.1). The vision is about judgment, and that term here carries a negative sense. The object of that judgment is a prostitute. The Greek term that describes the prostitute (that term *mega* again) means "remarkable" or "great" but carries a negative sense – great in a *bad* way – and so the CSB translates it "notorious."

This whore is seated upon (or beside) "many waters." That phrase will be explained in v.15 to mean "peoples, multitudes, nations, and languages." In other words, she holds sway among the sea of humanity that is all of the earth's peoples. She seduces not only the common masses but also the "kings of the earth" (v.2). She has charmed the whole earth with her wiles, luring both the great and the many into immorality, especially *spiritual* immorality.

What does this woman symbolize? The angel will have to show her relationship to another symbol – the beast – to give the full picture. Further, to help John see more clearly, the angel then carries him into a wilderness. We'll see why in a moment. It is directly related to the PFG.

> I saw a woman sitting on a scarlet beast that was covered with blasphemous names and had seven heads and ten horns. **4** The woman was dressed in purple and scarlet, adorned with gold, jewels, and pearls. She had a golden cup in her hand filled with everything detestable and with the impurities of her prostitution. **5** On her forehead was written a name, a mystery: Babylon the Great, the Mother of Prostitutes and of the Detestable Things of the Earth. **6** Then I saw that the woman was drunk with the blood of the saints and with the blood of the witnesses to Jesus. When I saw her, I was greatly astonished.

The "Other" Woman

This woman is set in direct contrast to the woman of ch.12 and the bride of chs.21-22. Whereas those are depictions of true Israel and the Church clothed in the purity of Christ and true worship, this woman is Babylon, the filthy, impure opposite. Christ has a Bride – those who are true to him – but this temptress makes her play as the "other woman," seducing people away from Christ with her "detestable impurities." That is not to say that the prostitute isn't attractive.

In fact, she beautifies herself in the shrewdest ways. Her purple clothes and jewelry speak of wealth and glory, even of royalty. (She says of herself that she "sits as a queen" in 18:7.) She sells herself to those in power to amplify her allure. Her "scarlet" clothing associates her with the scarlet of the beast and the red of the dragon. She dresses up to steal hearts from what is truly glorious.

The Prostitute and the Beast

The harlot is the city Babylon trying to steal hearts and passion from Christ to take the place of the pure Bride that is New Jerusalem (21:2, 9-23). These dress-up clothes of hers are reminiscent of the high priests' garments and parts of the OT sanctuary (Ex 25:3-7; 28:5-9; 15-20; 35:6; 36:9-12; 15-21). These emphasize her association with worship. Further, the high priest wore a cap that declared him "holy to the LORD" (Ex 39:30-31), which is directly contrasted to the forehead here of "Babylon the Great, the Mother of Prostitutes and of the Detestable Things of the Earth."

The Symbolic Background

In his depictions, John draws from OT pictures of unfaithful Israel as she was seduced by pagan idolatry and economic and political security. Over and over again ancient Israel turned away from the LORD to trust in political and military alliances, and her heart was always quickly drawn into worship of false gods. God spoke repeatedly through his prophets to describe Israel as adulterous, so much so that she was more like a prostitute than a bride (e.g., Jer 3:9; Ez 16:32; Hos 2:5; compare Jer 4-6 with what happens to Babylon in Rv). The prophets also used the language of prostitution to describe pagan worship. Non-Jewish powers like Tyre (Is 23:16-17) and Nineveh (Nah 3:4) were depicted as seductive harlots that pulled the world – even the Jews – into the worst kinds of idolatry.

The OT prophets especially connected God's judgment upon the false worship of his people to the pursuit and abuse of economic power through political means. For example, hear the words of Micah:

Micah 1:2–7
2 Listen, all you peoples;
pay attention, earth and everyone in it!
The Lord GOD will be a witness against you,
the Lord, from his holy temple.
3 Look, the LORD is leaving his place
and coming down to trample
the heights of the earth.
4 The mountains will melt beneath him,
and the valleys will split apart,
like wax near a fire,
like water cascading down a mountainside.
5 All this will happen because of Jacob's rebellion
and the sins of the house of Israel.
What is the rebellion of Jacob?
Isn't it Samaria?
And what is the high place of Judah?
Isn't it Jerusalem?

> **6** Therefore, I will make Samaria
> a heap of ruins in the countryside,
> a planting area for a vineyard.
> I will roll her stones into the valley
> and expose her foundations.
> **7** All her carved images will be smashed to pieces;
> all her wages will be burned in the fire,
> and I will destroy all her idols.
> Since she collected the wages of a prostitute,
> they will be used again for a prostitute.

This pronouncement is to the whole earth about the witness of God from his heavenly temple (v.2). Judgment is coming (vv.3-4) because of rebellion (v.5a). This rebellion is idolatry (vv.5b-7). Notice this idolatry is described as a prostitute's wages.

The prophet goes on to describe the oppression by the leaders for economic gain:

> **Micah 2:1–3**
> **1** Woe to those who dream up wickedness
> and prepare evil plans on their beds!
> At morning light they accomplish it
> because the power is in their hands.
> **2** They covet fields and seize them;
> they also take houses.
> They deprive a man of his home,
> a person of his inheritance.
> **3** Therefore, the LORD says:
> I am now planning a disaster
> against this nation;
> you cannot free your necks from it.
> Then you will not walk so proudly
> because it will be an evil time.

God will not put up with this forever:

> **Micah 2:9–10; 3:9-12**
> **9** You force the women of my people
> out of their comfortable homes,
> and you take my blessing
> from their children forever.

The Prostitute and the Beast

10 Get up and leave,
for this is not your place of rest
because defilement brings destruction—
a grievous destruction!

9 Listen to this, leaders of the house of Jacob,
you rulers of the house of Israel,
who abhor justice
and pervert everything that is right,
10 who build Zion with bloodshed
and Jerusalem with injustice.
11 Her leaders issue rulings for a bribe,
her priests teach for payment,
and her prophets practice divination for silver.
Yet they lean on the LORD, saying,
"Isn't the LORD among us?
No disaster will overtake us."
12 Therefore, because of you,
Zion will be plowed like a field,
Jerusalem will become ruins,
and the temple's mountain
will be a high thicket.

John's Apocalypse picks up where Micah leaves off. Those who pervert worship and justice, who oppress the innocent and who lead people into idolatry will come to destruction. This turn of events will be the salvation of those who are true to God who will establish his righteous rule:

Micah 4:1–2
1 In the last days
the mountain of the LORD's house
will be established
at the top of the mountains
and will be raised above the hills.
Peoples will stream to it,
2 and many nations will come and say,
"Come, let's go up to the mountain of the LORD,
to the house of the God of Jacob.
He will teach us about his ways
so we may walk in his paths."
For instruction will go out of Zion
and the word of the LORD from Jerusalem.

The Revelation of Jesus Christ

The language of spiritual prostitution also finds expression in the NT with the false teachers that have plagued the church since its early days. Jude, in his short letter, traced a line of deviant worship and spiritual seduction all the way back to Balaam up until his own day. That's why he exposes these deviants and exhorts Christians to be faithful:

> **Jude 20–25**
> **20** But you, dear friends, as you build yourselves up in your most holy faith, praying in the Holy Spirit, **21** keep yourselves in the love of God, waiting expectantly for the mercy of our Lord Jesus Christ for eternal life. **22** Have mercy on those who waver; **23** save others by snatching them from the fire; have mercy on others but with fear, hating even the garment defiled by the flesh.
>
> **24** Now to him who is able to protect you from stumbling and to make you stand in the presence of his glory, without blemish and with great joy, **25** to the only God our Savior, through Jesus Christ our Lord, be glory, majesty, power, and authority before all time, now and forever. Amen.

Jude is confident that God will protect his own from stumbling, but that protection comes through his warning, their own spiritual discipline and prayer. It is the same in Revelation. The rebukes from Jesus to the churches in Rv 2-3 make it clear that these issues were widely present in the first century. The very nature of the PFG confirms that these seductions are the struggle of the entire Church Age. The allure of false worship threatens the faithfulness of Christ's servants and so threatens their blessing.

We could summarize this way: The notorious prostitute, Babylon, symbolizes the fusion between false worship and economic power. This false worship would include secular humanism, apostate forms of Christianity, all forms of spiritism and mysticism, false monotheisms and the occult ("everything detestable" in v.4). In short, the whore Babylon is the ultimate form of syncretism, where everything but true Christianity coalesces into false worship. False religion blends with greed and unites with political power to get what she wants.

In John's day the economic power of Rome worked through the trade guilds to express this false worship in largely pagan ways. Things shifted in the fourth century as Constantine made Christianity accepted as a religion of Rome. So, by the time of the Protestant Reformation false worship found much wider expression in the excesses of (impure) Christianity. One of the primary practices that set Luther off on his mission to reform the Church was the selling of indulgences. Supposedly, if you had enough money, your spiritual security could be bought.

In our own day, it is hard not to think of the machinery of prosperity theologians. *Send your money, and you will find healing and comfort, the best life can offer you now.* The proponents accumulate huge mansions, global networks and air-conditioned dog houses. The message of

The Prostitute and the Beast

comfort at any cost is exactly opposite the message of Revelation, which calls for the true believer to bear up faithfully under suffering and persecution for the testimony of Jesus.

What personalities or entities or movements today should set off our "Babylon alarms"?

The Mysterious Name

The glue that holds this false worship together is pride. Pride is what drives humanity to worship anyone or anything but God. This pride is evident in the name given the woman. "Babylon the Great" (v.5 of our text) has already been mentioned in Rv 14:8, and it draws from an ancient source. King Nebuchadnezzar lifted the title up as a monument to his pride in Dn 4:30:

> **30** the king exclaimed, "Is this not Babylon the Great that I have built to be a royal residence by my vast power and for my majestic glory?"

Notice God's immediate response to this pride:

> **31** While the words were still in the king's mouth, a voice came from heaven: "King Nebuchadnezzar, to you it is declared that the kingdom has departed from you. **32** You will be driven away from people to live with the wild animals, and you will feed on grass like cattle for seven periods of time, until you acknowledge that the Most High is ruler over human kingdoms, and he gives them to anyone he wants."

> **33** At that moment the message against Nebuchadnezzar was fulfilled. He was driven away from people. He ate grass like cattle, and his body was drenched with dew from the sky, until his hair grew like eagles' feathers and his nails like birds' claws.

This same pride is behind every form of defiant and deviant worship throughout the ages. It finds ultimate expression in this symbolic Babylon that is the Mother of All Prostitutes. She lures into false worship everyone who proudly resists the true God. That her name is a "mystery" ties back to the Daniel passage above. It also points to the ironic way that Babylon falls victim to the self-destructive forces of evil even before Christ brings ultimate defeat. The political forces turn against the religious-economic forces and destroy them.

This is ironic because the false worship of the woman is completely intertwined with the pursuit of wealth and security and pleasure. Just like ancient Israel "went a-whoring" after the wealth and security of political alliances by adopting the gods of the nations around her, so will the whole world be seduced by the promises of Babylon's detestable beast-worship.

The Revelation of Jesus Christ

The golden cup in Babylon's hand represents her intoxicating power to seduce, but she is herself a cup in the hand of God to accomplish his purposes just like ancient Babylon was:

> **Jeremiah 51:7–8**
> **7** Babylon was a gold cup in the LORD's hand,
> making the whole earth drunk.
> The nations drank her wine;
> therefore, the nations go mad.
> **8** Suddenly Babylon fell and was shattered.

History is about to repeat itself. This time Babylon's influence is global. This time her destruction will be final.

In what ways do we see this prostitute, Babylon, at work to corrupt true worship today?

In what ways are false religions uniting against true Christianity?

Astonishment

John had been taken into a wilderness to see this vision. It seems likely that the primary reason for this move is that he must see the temptress out of her element (the city) to see her for what she really is. Even then, it seems to take a rebuke by the angel for him to pick up his jaw from the ground. The Greek for "I was greatly astonished" (v.6) literally means, "I marveled a great marvel."

While it is not explicit that John's astonishment approaches nearly to worship, the language is loaded with that possibility. Another possibility is that this could be a strong reaction to the prostitute's effect, the horrifying statement that the whore is the "Mother of...the Detestable Things of the Earth" who is "drunk with the blood of the saints" (v.6). The rebuke of the angel at minimum means that John has been more impressed than he ought to be, whether it is because he is nearly seduced or because he is overly horrified.

The reason John is rebuked by the angel becomes clear as we read on:

The Prostitute and the Beast

> **7** Then the angel said to me, "Why are you astonished? I will explain to you the mystery of the woman and of the beast, with the seven heads and the ten horns, that carries her. **8** The beast that you saw was, and is not, and is about to come up from the abyss and go to destruction. Those who live on the earth whose names have not been written in the book of life from the foundation of the world will be astonished when they see the beast that was, and is not, and is to come. **9** This calls for a mind that has wisdom.

John's astonishment is inappropriate because it is exactly that same reaction by the unbelieving world that will draw them into the harlot's seductive trap (v.8). The implicit rebuke of the angel in v.7, "Why are you astonished?" is bookended with a warning: "This calls for a mind that has wisdom." What a humbling truth to realize that even John himself needed to draw wisdom from this revelation he was being given so that he too would resist the seduction of the prostitute!

If John was temporarily or nearly fooled by this woman, it was because she manages to appear so much like the real deal. As Paul warned, Satan and his agents can be very convincing:

> **2 Corinthians 11:13–15**
> **13** For such people are false apostles, deceitful workers, disguising themselves as apostles of Christ. **14** And no wonder! For Satan disguises himself as an angel of light. **15** So it is no great surprise if his servants also disguise themselves as servants of righteousness. Their end will be according to their works.

Makeup can make someone appear beautiful from a distance, but the truth is exposed up close. Sometime around the late 1980's (when records were still commonly on vinyl) I remember seeing in a store a record jacket of a glam rock band. From a few feet away, the cover looked like a group of attractive women. Upon closer inspection, every one of them was a man wearing a lot of makeup exactly to fool people into this misperception. Just like that cover, this prostitute Babylon is not what she seems. This is lipstick on a pig. The angel is helping John see her for what she is.

Daniel had prophesied that an evil ruler would employ his forces to establish abominable worship (Dn 11:31). He said he would deceive his followers but that the people of God would have insight and would suffer for a time by standing in strength against the deception (vv.34). They would be refined but would not be fooled (v.35). The same kind of insight leads to faithful endurance and then rest and reward at the end of days (12:10-13).

The warning of Rv 17:9, to have wisdom and not be fooled, echoes the parallel one back in Jr 51:6:

> Leave Babylon;
> save your lives, each of you!
> Don't perish because of her guilt.
> For this is the time of the LORD's vengeance—
> he will pay her what she deserves.

That warning will be repeated in Rv 18:4, and it is how the PFG functions to provide insight for God's people:

> Come out of her, my people,
> so that you will not share in her sins
> or receive any of her plagues.

How is the harlot at work today, disguising herself as true religion?

Where do we get the wisdom we need to not be fooled by her disguise?

How do we look closely and carefully enough to see what is true about any such potential "prostitutes" while still keeping a safe distance from her allure?

The Beast

The angel has said he will "explain the mystery of the woman and the beast" because the two are so closely associated. The seductive power of the harlot is catalyzed by the false sign of the beast, who appears to rise from the dead. Remember, the second beast, the false prophet, lends credibility to the beast with false signs that are (or at least seem to be) miraculous. This collaboration seems to give the prostitute overwhelming influence. Her influence is particularly religious but is expressed in the economic arena. As we learned, this was already a challenge to the first century Christians. Beale reminds us:

> "The connection between economic factors and idolatry is well attested elsewhere in the Apocalypse and in first-century Asia Minor (see, e.g., on 2:14, 20–22). Customarily each trade guild had patron gods to which members had to pay homage as well as to the Roman emperor. If Christians did not participate in such homage, they were economically ostracized and prevented from practicing their trade. The whore of ch.17 represents these religious-economic aspects of society, which often work in conjunction with the political state."[47]

---

[47] Beale, G. K. (1999). *The book of Revelation: a commentary on the Greek text* (p. 856). Grand Rapids, MI; Carlisle, Cumbria: W.B. Eerdmans; Paternoster Press.

The Prostitute and the Beast

Mountains, Kings and Horns

The interaction of evil powers will find global expression in the woman's collaboration with the *political* powers of the beast. John goes on in Rv 17:

> "The seven heads are seven mountains on which the woman is seated. They are also seven kings: **10** Five have fallen, one is, the other has not yet come, and when he comes, he must remain for only a little while. **11** The beast that was and is not, is itself an eighth king, but it belongs to the seven and is going to destruction. **12** The ten horns you saw are ten kings who have not yet received a kingdom, but they will receive authority as kings with the beast for one hour. **13** These have one purpose, and they give their power and authority to the beast. **14** These will make war against the Lamb, but the Lamb will conquer them because he is Lord of lords and King of kings. Those with him are called, chosen, and faithful."

"Seven mountains" (v.9) was a common reference to Rome in John's day. He combines that reference with "seven heads" to symbolize authority and power. "Seven kings" is lumped in to complete the symbol. Some take these kings to be a succession of Roman rulers, while others see it as a summary of historic earthly superpower kingdoms like Daniel saw in his visions. Whatever the case, the beast is symbolically present throughout all history in every evil ruler but will especially be so at the end. John is clearly depicting the totality of evil earthly political power that in his day was still looking forward to its final expression.

This symbol goes into further detail with the connection to the beast and ten kings who are given authority with him for "one hour." The beast (already introduced in ch.13) seems to dominate the earthly scene at the end of the age. This term "one hour" seems to indicate a particular, relatively short-term period of rule. This rule has already been shown to be empowered by the dragon. The kings and the beast are a united front against the Lamb. We have seen that this means they attack the Lamb first by attacking his people, the "called, chosen, and faithful" of v.14. We saw that this attack will temporarily overwhelm the saints (13:7), but here the end is made clear: "the Lamb will conquer them (the kings and the beast) because he is Lord of lords and King of kings."

How have we seen political powers throughout history and today cooperate with religious powers? Has that usually worked out to be a good thing, or a bad thing?

How does the progression through the three terms "called, chosen, and faithful" tie to the PFG, <u>**to reveal Jesus Christ so that his servants faithfully endure suffering in order to receive blessing**</u>*?*

The Revelation of Jesus Christ

The Mocking Formula
Just like the woman's beauty is deceptive, the beast's power is deceptive. In fact, the angel in ch.17 uses a formula to mock the beast. God has several times in this revelation been referred to with different forms of a formula: "the one who was, who is, and who is to come" (1:4,8; 4:8; 11:17; 16:5). Now, the formula is applied to the beast two times in 17:8 and again in v.11. But there is a clear difference.

The beast formula finishes with "going to destruction" (vv.8,11), whereas with Christ the formula finishes with "is to come." His coming results in an everlasting kingdom. The beast (representing all evil) *appears* to rise when Christ is crucified, but we could hear on Jesus' lips the words of a recent song that says, "A cross meant to kill is my victory." That victory is sure for Christ, the "one who is to come," and that coming is depicted in these last chapters of Revelation. Jesus will come to deal once and for all with the beast and with Satan himself.

So, just as the faithful need wisdom to discern the harlot from the true Bride (v.9), they also need wisdom to discern the beast from the true Lamb. Jesus was truly dead and came to life, while the beast will only appear to resurrect but will ultimately go to eternal destruction.

How does this formula (rightfully applied to Jesus and mockingly to the beast) help along the PFG?

One Purpose
The seduction of Babylon's corrupt idolatry has taken in the world. All the powers of the world are united against the Lamb and his faithful. This all sounds overwhelming, if it weren't for the statement in v.14 about the Lamb's sure victory. This victory is sure because everything is going exactly according to God's plan:

> **15** He also said to me, "The waters you saw, where the prostitute was seated, are peoples, multitudes, nations, and languages. **16** The ten horns you saw, and the beast, will hate the prostitute. They will make her desolate and naked, devour her flesh, and burn her up with fire. **17** For God has put it into their hearts to carry out his plan by having one purpose and to give their kingdom to the beast until the words of God are fulfilled. **18** And the woman you saw is the great city that has royal power over the kings of the earth."

The Great City
As we noted earlier, the prostitute has surrounded herself with the "waters" of the earth's peoples. She has corrupted all but the faithful. She has peddled her deceptions to even the highest powers of the earth in order to gain her luxury and comfort (more on that in the next chapter). But these powers will turn on her. The "great city" has held sway over kings, using her deception to control

The Prostitute and the Beast

and manipulate their political and military power for her own ends (v.18). But now they will turn on her and devour her (v.16).

Betrayal and Destruction
Why would these political powers turn against the religious system that has helped them control the world? Why would the leaders of the false religion build her wealth and status upon political alliances that could not be trusted? Because all of this has been exactly according to God's plan. All that human and demonic wickedness can ever do – even at their very pinnacle! – all they can do is fulfill God's word and his purpose.

God has repeatedly used human powers as agents to bring judgment, even upon his own people, in their case to test them and reveal who was true. Israel was God's agent to judge the Canaanite peoples. Assyria was his agent against Israel. Then Babylon. Then the Medes and Persians against Babylon. Then the Greeks. Then the Romans. This pattern always accomplishes God's purposes, and it only stops when God himself brings final judgment.

God's plan was already at work long before John wrote, as we saw with Micah's prophecies earlier. Notice the parallels in the latter part of his message:

> **Micah 4:10–13**
> **10** Writhe and cry out, Daughter Zion,
> like a woman in labor,
> for now you will leave the city
> and camp in the open fields.
> You will go to Babylon;
> there you will be rescued;
> there the LORD will redeem you
> from the grasp of your enemies!
> **11** Many nations have now assembled against you;
> they say, "Let her be defiled,
> and let us feast our eyes on Zion."
> **12** But they do not know the LORD's intentions
> or understand his plan,
> that he has gathered them
> like sheaves to the threshing floor.
> **13** Rise and thresh, Daughter Zion,
> for I will make your horns iron
> and your hooves bronze
> so you can crush many peoples.
> Then you will set apart their plunder
> for the LORD,
> their wealth for the Lord of the whole earth.

The Revelation of Jesus Christ

Now John is shown that the last Babylon has rallied the nations against God's people. She has made herself drunk with the blood of the martyrs. Now God is bringing his harvest of wrath upon her. The kings of the earth have made her wealthy, but now they turn and destroy her. Now, as the angel said in 17:1, comes "the judgment of the notorious prostitute."

Reflection

Let's think back through this chapter to consider how it contributes to the PFG.

What key statements in ch.17 reveal Jesus?

How does this chapter help the saints faithfully endure persecution?

How does it point to the believer's blessing?

Lesson 15: The Judgment of Babylon, Earthly Laments, and Heavenly Praise (Ch.18 – Ch.19, V.10)

We saw in the last lesson that the harlot Babylon and the beast have worked together to perform their evil. So, just as they have shared in their detestable and rebellious activities they will share in judgment and destruction. It has been revealed to John that God's plan all along was to use the political and military powers of the beast as his agents to destroy Babylon. He will turn the earth's rulers against the great city that is the epitome of human pride and rebellion. She is guilty of the most detestable blasphemies and demonic worship, and she has exploited the world to lift herself up in riches and to spill the blood of the saints. Now God will use those beastly powers with which she has prostituted herself to destroy her. Then Christ himself will destroy these powers.

We have repeatedly made note of the nature of apocalyptic-prophetic literature, that it often seems to make jumps in time and that we should be careful not to assume it is laying events out in chronological sequence. This is especially apparent in chs.18-19, as the verbs will change tense several times. In 18:2 Babylon *has* fallen. In v.8 her plagues *will* come in "just one" day and she *will* be burned up. Then again, in v.10 her judgment *has* come, but in v.21 she *will be* thrown down.

Remember we have seen that these evil forces find expression throughout the whole church age – indeed through all recorded history – but that their final judgment is said to come quickly, or suddenly. The power of the beastly kingdoms lasts for "one hour" (17:12) and Babylon's judgment comes in "a single hour" (18:10,17,19). Remember too that John is recording successive visions that may or may not be successive as events. It seems that judgment and destruction come upon Babylon and the beast essentially together, even if it unfolds in rapid succession.

John's next vision comes with another "after this" and with another angel from heaven:

The Initial Decree from Heaven

Revelation 18:1–3
1 After this I saw another angel with great authority coming down from heaven, and the earth was illuminated by his splendor. **2** He called out in a mighty voice:

> It has fallen,
> Babylon the Great has fallen!
> She has become a home for demons,
> a haunt for every unclean spirit,
> a haunt for every unclean bird,
> and a haunt for every unclean and despicable beast.

> **3** For all the nations have drunk
> the wine of her sexual immorality,
> which brings wrath.
> The kings of the earth
> have committed sexual immorality with her,
> and the merchants of the earth
> have grown wealthy from her sensuality and excess.

How is this angel described, and what does this description tell us about his proclamation?

How does the past tense "has fallen" speak to the certainty of this judgment?

How is Babylon described spiritually? Politically? Economically?

The proclamation that Babylon has fallen was initially given in 14:8:

> **8** And another, a second angel, followed, saying, "It has fallen, Babylon the Great has fallen. She made all the nations drink the wine of her sexual immorality, which brings wrath."

That proclamation cited Babylon's spiritual immorality with the national powers as the reason for God's wrath. Then in 17:2 her judgment was again announced for the same reason. Now ch.18 develops this proclamation of Babylon's fall. A heavenly voice gives warning and then declares that she is getting what she deserves. Then from the earth comes a series of lament poems patterned after those of the OT prophets against Tyre (Ezek 26-28) and ancient Babylon (Is 13; 14; 21; Jer 50; 51). Babylon has not fulfilled God's purpose for her but instead has given herself over to self-promotion and worship of the beast. Earth laments because they have lost her (and consequently their own) prosperity, glamour and pleasures.

The double statement that Babylon is fallen probably denotes surety and suddenness. It may also indicate both initial (historical) and final (ultimate) fulfillment. In this case, it would recall ancient

The Judgment of Babylon, Earthly Laments, and Heavenly Praise

Babylon's fall while depicting final Babylon's fall. The OT prophet Isaiah made the same double pronouncement (Is 21:9) but from his perspective looking forward to the final fulfillment.

The phrases that describe Babylon in her already fallen state seem primarily aimed at showing her utter desolation. They echo Isaiah's descriptions of Babylon and Edom as being inhabited by beasts and birds (Is 13:21-22; 34:11,14), which Jewish interpreters took to be demonic figures (see also Zech 2:14-15 regarding Nineveh; Jer 9:11 against Jerusalem and 27:39 and 50:39 against Babylon). These phrases also reflect the demonic power behind Babylon's idolatry. That power that facilitated her rise is now the ghostly residue of her demise.

The reason for this demise is spelled out once again as in 14:8. She has drawn the nations into her corruptions. She has climbed to despicable greatness through sensuality and excess (v.3), and this calls for God's wrath. Notice again that Babylon is primarily seen as a blend of religious perversion and economic extravagance. More on that in a bit. This contrasts with the faithful saints who have been oppressed and slaughtered by her for their true worship of Christ alone.

Following the decree comes a turn. We move from a backward look upon Babylon in her already fallen state to a previous position where her fall is imminent but has not yet come. The reason for coming back prior to her fall is to issue a warning. This warning comes from another voice in heaven, and is addressed to God's people:

The Calling out of God's People

> **4** Then I heard another voice from heaven:
>
>> Come out of her, my people,
>> so that you will not share in her sins
>> or receive any of her plagues.
>>
>> **5** For her sins are piled up to heaven,
>> and God has remembered her crimes.
>> **6** Pay her back the way she also paid,
>> and double it according to her works.
>> In the cup in which she mixed,
>> mix a double portion for her.
>> **7** As much as she glorified herself and indulged her sensual and excessive ways,
>> give her that much torment and grief.
>> For she says in her heart,
>> "I sit as a queen;
>> I am not a widow,
>> and I will never see grief."

The Revelation of Jesus Christ

> **8** For this reason her plagues will come in just one day—
> death and grief and famine.
> She will be burned up with fire,
> because the Lord God who judges her is mighty.

The heavenly exhortation of v.4 ties directly to the PFG, **to reveal Jesus Christ so that his servants faithfully endure suffering in order to receive blessing**. It is a wakeup call once again for the saints to stay pure and faithful. *Don't compromise.* They must be wise and not be fooled by the façade. *Stay pure and true to Christ.* The message draws strongly from Isaiah's and Jeremiah's nearly identical messages for God's people to separate themselves from ancient Babylon's idolatry in light of her impending judgment:

> **Isaiah 52:11**
> **11** Leave, leave, go out from there!
> Do not touch anything unclean;
> go out from her, purify yourselves,
> you who carry the vessels of the Lord.

> **Jeremiah 51:6**
> **6** Leave Babylon;
> save your lives, each of you!
> Don't perish because of her guilt.
> For this is the time of the Lord's vengeance—
> he will pay her what she deserves.

Paul, in writing to the Corinthians, cited the above passage from Isaiah to issue his own warning for Christians to refuse to compromise and blend into the corrupt world system:

> **2 Corinthians 6:16–18**
> **16** And what agreement does the temple of God have with idols? For we are the temple of the living God, as God said:
>
> > **I will dwell
> > and walk among them,
> > and I will be their God,
> > and they will be my people.**
>
> **17** Therefore, **come out from among them
> and be separate, says the Lord;
> do not touch any unclean thing,
> and I will welcome you.**

The Judgment of Babylon, Earthly Laments, and Heavenly Praise

> **18** And **I will be a Father** to you,
> **and** you will be **sons** and daughters **to me,**
> **says the Lord Almighty.**

Also behind this warning of Rv 18:4 is the one given to Lot before the destruction of Sodom and Gomorrah:

> **Genesis 19:14–15**
> **14** So Lot went out and spoke to his sons-in-law, who were going to marry his daughters. "Get up," he said. "Get out of this place, for the Lord is about to destroy the city!" But his sons-in-law thought he was joking.
> **15** At daybreak the angels urged Lot on: "Get up! Take your wife and your two daughters who are here, or you will be swept away in the punishment of the city."

The emphasis of that ancient incident was upon physical separation from the wicked city's literal destruction. The emphasis of the warning recorded by John is elevated to a symbolic one – for saints to be uncompromising in an anti-Christian world system – though the judgment to come will bring literal destruction once again.

As we have seen before, the options are mutually exclusive. The people of earth either associate with Babylon and the Beast OR with New Jerusalem and Jesus Christ. To share in Babylon's corrupt worship and wealth is to share in her sins and plagues. To come out of her is to be an outcast for the name of Jesus, to suffer at her hand but to find rest and safety when her crimes come around in full payback.

What ways are Christians tempted to compromise or blend in with today's Babylon?

What does "coming out of her" look like for you in your own daily life?

What Babylon mixed in her cup was corruption and oppression, a mixture of impurities. But her judgment is pure and just, and it will be exactly what she deserves (v.6). Like ancient Babel, she has built herself a tower, and she thinks it is a monument to her greatness. It is only her sins piled sky high, and – as with that ancient tower – God will not allow it to continue.

Notice that following the warning of v.4 this heavenly voice offers a sort of sandwich of God's sovereign power and righteousness to bring justice upon Babylon. "God has remembered her crimes" (v.5) and "she will be burned up with fire because the Lord God who judges her is mighty" (v.8). At the heart of this sandwich is the heart of her problem, or better, the problem of her heart. Babylon's pride is the single core reason for her destruction by God (v.7). Remember that Babylon is the symbol for all forms of rebellion and corrupt worship, which means that she ultimately boils down to individual rebels who will each stand in judgment before God.

The heart of pride is an internal thing only God sees and knows, but it is expressed in outward deeds that are apparent to all. Babylon "glorified herself and indulged her sensual and excessive ways" (v.7). This is important because these outward characteristics are how the saints can recognize her inward corruption, even through all that makeup and glamour. The true Bride is called to worship in spirit and truth (Jn 4:23-24), and so she looks for what glorifies Christ and speaks the truth about Christ. She worships in sacrifice and suffering. The harlot Babylon has glorified herself and has lied about Christ (often in very subtle ways). She worships in luxurious excess and comfort (which is scarily similar to the description of Laodicea in 3:17).

How is self-glorification being expressed and promoted in our society today?

How have luxury and comfort corrupted true worship today, even in the name of Christianity?

The Earthly Laments
From heaven, judgment has been proclaimed and God's people have been warned. Now from the earth come the laments:

...of the Kings

> **Revelation 18:9-10**
> **9** The kings of the earth who have committed sexual immorality and shared her sensual and excessive ways will weep and mourn over her when they see the smoke from her burning. **10** They will stand far off in fear of her torment, saying,
>
> > Woe, woe, the great city,
> > Babylon, the mighty city!
> > For in a single hour
> > your judgment has come.

The Judgment of Babylon, Earthly Laments, and Heavenly Praise

Morris makes the shrewd observation that not one of the earthly groups lamenting Babylon's fall is depicted as loving the city for herself, but only for what they could get out of her. She might seduce and enrich people but there was nothing truly lovely in her.[48]

The kings of the earth have lent their political and military support so they might participate in Babylon's sensuality and luxury. We learned in the previous lesson that some of these kingly powers are the agents of her destruction, but here kings mourn the loss of the pleasures she provided. These apparently are different kings from those of 17:16 and seem to broadly represent earthly rulers. They have separated themselves far off from her torment in fear of her judgment.

This lament follows the pattern of Ezek 26:16-18 and 27:29-36, where the same three groups (kings, merchants, and mariners) mourn Tyre's fall. These kings are not mourning Babylon's destruction for *her* sake but for their *own*. They are "in fear of her torment," meaning they are watching the fires from a distance and wondering, *Oh shoot! Are we next?* At the very least, it is clear that their political base and lavish lifestyles are going up in smoke along with the great city.

The suddenness of Babylon's fall has been intensified. The "one day" of v.8 is now "one hour" (vv.10,17,19). These kings seem to see it for what it is: judgment. They aren't the only ones watching and weeping:

...of the Merchants

> **11** The merchants of the earth will weep and mourn over her, because no one buys their cargo any longer—**12** cargo of gold, silver, jewels, and pearls; fine linen, purple, silk, and scarlet; all kinds of fragrant wood products; objects of ivory; objects of expensive wood, brass, iron, and marble; **13** cinnamon, spice, incense, myrrh, and frankincense; wine, olive oil, fine flour, and grain; cattle and sheep; horses and carriages; and slaves—human lives.
>
> > **14** The fruit you craved has left you.
> > All your splendid and glamorous things are gone;
> > they will never find them again.
>
> **15** The merchants of these things, who became rich from her, will stand far off in fear of her torment, weeping and mourning, **16** saying,
>
> > Woe, woe, the great city,
> > dressed in fine linen, purple, and scarlet,
> > adorned with gold, jewels, and pearls;
> > **17** for in a single hour
> > such fabulous wealth was destroyed!

---

[48] Morris, L. (1987). *Revelation: an introduction and commentary* (Vol. 20, p. 209). Downers Grove, IL: InterVarsity Press.

As with the kings, the merchants do not lament for Babylon's loss but for their own. Babylon has made them rich (v.15), but now they have no buyer for their cargo (v.11). Also like the kings, these merchants stand "far off from her torment" (v.15). It is important to realize that only one item on their cargo list is inherently deplorable: human lives (v.13). Babylon traded in human lives, and this points to the fact that she (and her merchants) had no scruples about building their wealth on the backs of others whom they exploited and oppressed.

The other items traded with Babylon were not themselves bad things. Many of these were used at God's command to beautify his temple in Jerusalem. The problem with these trades is rooted in v.7, that they were traded for the purpose of self-glorification, sensuality, and excess. It is worth noting the similarity to lists of goods that Solomon traded to accumulate (1 Kgs 10), as his fame and glory grew until his heart was pulled away to false gods (ch.11). This was exactly the underlying character and effect of Babylon's trade.

The kings had lost their political base. The merchants had lost their economic base. And these weren't the only ones to mourn the riches that were burning with the great city:

...and of the Mariners

> And every shipmaster, seafarer, the sailors, and all who do business by sea, stood far off **18** as they watched the smoke from her burning and kept crying out, "Who was like the great city?" **19** They threw dust on their heads and kept crying out, weeping, and mourning,
>
>> Woe, woe, the great city,
>> where all those who have ships on the sea
>> became rich from her wealth;
>> for in a single hour she was destroyed.

As with the others, this final group of mourners stands "far off" to watch their great business venture go up in smoke. Once again, this catastrophe is said to come in "a single hour" (v.19). And once again, the lament is focused on how this destruction will ruin their own prosperity. Babylon's partners care only for themselves.

All three groups have repeated the twofold "Woe, woe, the great city" (vv.10,16,19). As with the repeated "has fallen" of v.2, the double pronouncement intensifies the severity. This is finally and ultimately the end of everything Babylon symbolizes, as we shall see in the last poem of this chapter.

How do 1) the coming desolation of Babylon and 2) the self-centered responses of her cohorts serve the PFG to dissuade Christians from compromise and infidelity?

The Judgment of Babylon, Earthly Laments, and Heavenly Praise

At this point, there is a complete reversal from the lament to a call for rejoicing:

> **20** Rejoice over her, heaven,
> and you saints, apostles, and prophets,
> because God has pronounced on her the judgment she passed on you!

This call for rejoicing may come from the voice of the angel of v.1, the other voice of v.4 or perhaps from John himself. Whatever the case, it is surely not the voice of the mariners who were mourning in v.19. Angels are not explicitly listed, but the call for rejoicing seems to extend to all who love righteousness and justice in heaven and on earth.

For the saints, apostles and prophets this rejoicing is particularly for their vindication. God has turned the tables on the religious and economic power that had pronounced judgment on his faithful. It is important to note that the call is not vindictive. It is not for revenge but for justice. The difference is in the ironic way that Revelation calls Christians to *conquer*. It is not through power or violence but through faithful endurance through suffering. This kind of conquering was prescribed by Paul to the Romans, who were living in the heart of the Babylon of John's day:

> **Romans 12:19–21**
> **19** Friends, do not avenge yourselves; instead, leave room for God's wrath, because it is written, **Vengeance belongs to me; I will repay,** says the Lord. **20** But
> > **If your enemy is hungry, feed him.**
> > **If he is thirsty, give him something to drink.**
> > **For in so doing**
> > **you will be heaping fiery coals on his head.**
>
> **21** Do not be conquered by evil, but conquer evil with good.

The call to rejoice in Rv 18:20 is for those conquerors who have "left room for God's wrath." Now that wrath is coming, and the enemies are being judged. Therefore, and appropriately so, the righteous are to rejoice in God's carrying out justice.

Have you ever found it unsatisfying to personally "get back" at someone? How so?

How is it different to root for judges to punish the wicked for their crimes?

How is the rejoicing for God's judging Babylon connected to the blessing of Revelation's PFG?

The Revelation of Jesus Christ

The Final Decree

After recording the laments of Babylon's earthly cohorts, John observes a mighty angel giving a most dramatic object lesson to declare the utter finality of the great city's fate:

> **21** Then a mighty angel picked up a stone like a large millstone and threw it into the sea, saying,
>
> > In this way, Babylon the great city
> > will be thrown down violently
> > and never be found again.
> > **22** The sound of harpists, musicians,
> > flutists, and trumpeters
> > will never be heard in you again;
> > no craftsman of any trade
> > will ever be found in you again;
> > the sound of a mill
> > will never be heard in you again;
> > **23** the light of a lamp
> > will never shine in you again;
> > and the voice of a groom and bride
> > will never be heard in you again.
> > All this will happen
> > because your merchants
> > were the nobility of the earth,
> > because all the nations were deceived
> > by your sorcery.
> > **24** In her was found the blood of prophets and saints,
> > and of all those slaughtered on the earth.

V.21 draws from Jer 51:61-64, where the prophet pronounces judgment upon ancient Babylon:

> **Jeremiah 51:61–64**
> **61** Jeremiah told Seraiah, "When you get to Babylon, see that you read all these words aloud. **62** Say, 'LORD, you have threatened to cut off this place so that no one will live in it—people or animals. Indeed, it will remain desolate forever.' **63** When you have finished reading this scroll, tie a stone to it and throw it into the middle of the Euphrates River. **64** Then say, 'In the same way, Babylon will sink and never rise again because of the disaster I am bringing on her. They will grow weary.' "

Now a powerful angel repeats this symbolic action and applies it to the final Babylon (see also Ezek 26:12,21 regarding Tyre).

The Judgment of Babylon, Earthly Laments, and Heavenly Praise

The use of the millstone for this object lesson is appropriate for several reasons. First, the millstone in ancient times symbolized daily sustenance of life. These stones were used in pairs to grind grain for food and were so important to a family that the law of Moses said, "Do not take a pair of grindstones or even the upper millstone as security for a debt, because that is like taking a life as security" (Dt 24:6). Second, these stones were heavy, so to throw them down was a violent act – the point of the metaphor in v.21. Third, one had been used in a famous act of judgment. In the time of Israel's judges, a woman (who was apparently pretty strong or resourceful) threw one down on a vengeful man named Abimelech and crushed his skull. This was said to be the way "God brought back Abimelech's evil" – on his head, you might say!

Most relevant to this angel's depiction is the warning of Jesus: "Whoever causes these little ones who believe in me to fall away – it would be better for him if a heavy millstone were hung around his neck and he were drowned in the depths of the sea" (Mt 18:6; see also Mk 9:42; Lk 17:2). That a "mighty" angel performs this object lesson with a "large" millstone exaggerates the meaning of this symbol. That meaning is clear. Babylon has led the unbelieving world to fall away from Jesus. She has stripped the mortal life away from the prophets and saints whom she has slaughtered (v.24) and the eternal life away from all the nations whom she has deceived (v.23), and so she will be thrown down in judgment. Stones don't float, and this one is sunk forever.

The finality of the destruction and loss is expressed six times in vv.21-23 in the formula "never again" ("ever again" in v.22b). The great city falls short of true perfection and so fails at lasting glory. Beale explains how the punishment fits the crimes against the saints:

> "Just as Babylon thus removed Christian workers from the marketplace and persecuted them, so God will remove Babylon's own loyal workers: "by no means will any artisan of any craft be found in you again."[49] Just as the means of making a living was earlier removed from the believing community, so now it will be taken from Babylon: "the sound of a mill will by no means be heard in you again, and the light of a lamp will by no means shine in you again" (vv.22–23). Just as the daily pleasures of economic prosperity were taken from God's people through economic (2:9; 13:16–17) or political persecution (2:9–10; 6:10; 16:6; 17:6), so "the sound of harpists and musicians and flutists and trumpeters will by no means be heard in you again" (18:22), and "the voice of the bridegroom and of the bride by no means will be heard in you again" (v.23)."[50]

Collectively these things represent vitality, beauty, joy and enlightenment. All are lost forever in Babylon because they were illusory. In her they were corrupt. Vv.23c-24 give three reasons for this judgment: self-glorification (with the nobility); deception (of all the nations) and violence (in slaughtering the saints).

---

[49] Beale, G. K. (1999). *The book of Revelation: a commentary on the Greek text* (p. 919). Grand Rapids, MI; Carlisle, Cumbria: W.B. Eerdmans; Paternoster Press.
[50] Ibid., p. 920.

The Revelation of Jesus Christ

How is our own culture today filled with the appearance of vitality, beauty, joy and enlightenment? How does this impression often prove illusory?

Even when propped up by demonic powers, the height of human pride always and ultimately leads to the depths of destruction. Babylon's glory is a mirage. It turns out to be an earthy stone, cast down and lost forever in the watery depths. While the earth mourns, heaven and all the faithful have been called to rejoice, and so they do:

The Hallelujah Chorus

> **Revelation 19:1–10**
> **1** After this I heard something like the loud voice of a vast multitude in heaven, saying,
>
>> Hallelujah!
>> Salvation, glory, and power belong to our God,
>> **2** because his judgments are true and righteous,
>> because he has judged the notorious prostitute
>> who corrupted the earth with her sexual immorality;
>> and he has avenged the blood of his servants
>> that was on her hands.
>
> **3** A second time they said,
>
>> Hallelujah!
>> Her smoke ascends forever and ever!
>
> **4** Then the twenty-four elders and the four living creatures fell down and worshiped God, who is seated on the throne, saying,
>
>> Amen! Hallelujah!
>
> **5** A voice came from the throne, saying,
>
>> Praise our God,
>> all his servants, and the ones who fear him,
>> both small and great!

The Judgment of Babylon, Earthly Laments, and Heavenly Praise

> **6** Then I heard something like the voice of a vast multitude, like the sound of cascading waters, and like the rumbling of loud thunder, saying,
>
>> Hallelujah, because our Lord God, the Almighty, reigns!
>> **7** Let us be glad, rejoice, and give him glory, because the marriage of the Lamb has come, and his bride has prepared herself.
>> **8** She was given fine linen to wear, bright and pure.
>
> For the fine linen represents the righteous acts of the saints.

Remarkably, the four occurrences of the term *hallelujah* here are the only ones in the NT. This is a common expression of praise in Hebrew that means "praise God" (literally, "praise Jah"), and it is found peppered throughout Books IV and V of the Psalms. Psalm 104:35 in particular associates the term with God's removal of wickedness from the earth:

> **35** May sinners vanish from the earth
> and wicked people be no more.
> My soul, bless the LORD!
> Hallelujah!

Beale notes that there is good reason to think an extrabiblical Jewish writing may provide a backdrop for these hallelujahs:

> "In Tob. 13:15–17 the streets of end-time Jerusalem shout "hallelujah" because the city has been rebuilt and ornamented with "sapphire, emerald, and precious stones: your walls ... with pure gold ... and the streets ... paved ... with ruby and stones of Ophir." This is striking since the "hallelujah" of Rev. 19:1, 3, 6 is sung by the bride of Christ (v.7), who will be equated with the new Jerusalem (21:2, 9–10), the walls and street of which are made of most of the precious metals mentioned in Tobit (21:18–21)."[51]

The first two hallelujahs come from a "loud voice" that John describes as being like that of "a vast multitude." John may be saying it sounds like this is coming from the vast multitude from every nation, tribe, people, and language that he described in 7:9. Or it may be that this loud voice is that of angelic beings. It may well be a collection that includes both of these and all other heavenly voices.

---

[51] Beale, G. K. (1999). *The book of Revelation: a commentary on the Greek text* (p. 927). Grand Rapids, MI; Carlisle, Cumbria: W.B. Eerdmans; Paternoster Press.

The Revelation of Jesus Christ

What reasons are given in vv.1-2 for why God is worthy of praise?

What seems to be the emphasis behind this praise? How does the second hallelujah in v.3 support that emphasis?

The third hallelujah comes from a specific group mentioned earlier in Revelation. Remember, the twenty-four elders represent all of God's faithful among humanity, and the four living creatures represent all living creatures. These give double affirmation of God's worthiness to receive praise. First, their "Amen!" is a formal way of voicing agreement, like saying, "Yes, absolutely!" Second, they issue their own hallelujah.

In between the third and fourth hallelujahs comes a call to praise that both affirms the first three and gives occasion for the last, most resounding one. It also brings a shift from negative to positive. The first hallelujahs were offered because God "has judged the notorious prostitute" (v.2), but the fourth is because God "reigns" (v.6) and "the bride has prepared herself" (v.7). More on that in a moment.

This call to praise that brings the turn in v.5 is issued "from the throne" which directly follows the worship of the elders and four living creatures before the throne in v.4. While it is clear that the voice in v.5 comes with God's authority, it is not clear whose voice it is. John has in his Gospel written that Jesus referred to God the Father as "my God and your God" (Jn 20:17). For more direct context, in this very Revelation John has penned that Jesus used "my God" four times in his address to Philadelphia (3:12). Still, these references are not exact equivalents. Perhaps "from the throne" communicates *from the throne area*. As elsewhere, we are wise to focus on what is clear, and what is clear here is that the voice issues this command to praise God with the highest authority, that of the one on the throne.

The call to praise is voiced to "all God's servants." This emphasizes the universality of God's praise and also the lowliness of the servant status. The following phrases – "the ones who fear him" and "both small and great" – further define the servants as equally humble and reverent before the Lord. These phrases appeared together already in the heavenly worship that followed the blast of the seventh trumpet (11:18). All God's servants are on equally humble footing before him, but this results in their blessing. This call for praise is anchored in their cause for great joy.

That cause for joy is voiced in the fourth hallelujah (v.6). The call to praise is answered by an even bigger response. The "voice of a vast multitude" is amplified with other similes, "cascading waters"

The Judgment of Babylon, Earthly Laments, and Heavenly Praise

and "rumbling of loud thunder." The reason for this climactic hallelujah is because God reigns, or more specifically, that his reign is now coming to earth. It is being expressed in his union with his people, and that is why the cause for joy is also expressed in the picture of a marriage celebration (v.7). The reign of Christ the Lamb is now coming in his universal rule with his bride, the Church, by his side. There is rich theology in vv.7-8. The bride was *given* fine linen to wear. This bright and pure linen symbolizes righteousness, and John's comment in v.8b confirms this. The term he uses typically is a legal reference, a court sentence declaring *justification*.

So, why does the CSB translate this gift as righteous *acts* (as with NASB, NIV, HCSB, and "deeds" in ESV and NET)? The translation is rightfully colored by the phrase in v.7, that the bride "has prepared herself," and by the context of the PFG. The saints (who make up the bride) have been given a righteous standing, but they have performed the righteous acts of perseverance *from* that standing *to* prepare themselves for Christ's return and blessing.

The relationship of salvation as a gift that yields godly works was very carefully explained by Paul:

> **Ephesians 2:8–10**
> **8** For you are saved by grace through faith, and this is not from yourselves; it is God's gift—**9** not from works, so that no one can boast. **10** For we are his workmanship, created in Christ Jesus for good works, which God prepared ahead of time for us to do.

How does the PFG assume the gift of justification by faith? How does it draw the believer into the good works that come from and express that faith?

The Marriage Feast

The hallelujahs have contrasted the condemned prostitute with the blessed bride. This latter picture draws from well-known marriage rituals in the ancient Near-East to depict the beauty and blessing of Christ's union with his Church. Constable gives helpful background:

> "There were three main events involved in a marriage. First, the parents chose a bride for the groom. Second, when the time for marriage had come, the groom would leave His home with His friends, go to the home of the bride, and escort her from her home to his. The bride did not know when this would occur. Third, the groom provided a feast for his bride and his friends at his home that lasted several days. The present verse (v. 7) describes the wedding proper, stage two (cf. vv. 8, 14), which had taken place in John's vision. It also announces that the bride is ready for the feast, stage three."[52]

---

[52] Constable, T. (2003). *Tom Constable's Expository Notes on the Bible* (Re 19:7). Galaxie Software.

The Revelation of Jesus Christ

The first stage would represent the drawing of the Holy Spirit to call out God's elect. The second stage correlates to Christ's coming for his Church. The third stage is now anticipated in John's vision, the celebration feast. Revelation's PFG is being realized in the consummated union of the "called, chosen, and faithful" (17:14) with the Lamb. The collective metaphor of the bride now gets more personal, as John is given a statement to write to individual Christians. John himself has personally sat at a feast with Jesus before. Now, *all* the faithful will experience this in an ultimate way. And so, quite naturally, there is a pronouncement of blessing:

> **Rev 19:9-10**
> **9** Then he said to me, "Write: Blessed are those invited to the marriage feast of the Lamb!" He also said to me, "These words of God are true." **10** Then I fell at his feet to worship him, but he said to me, "Don't do that! I am a fellow servant with you and your brothers and sisters who hold firmly to the testimony of Jesus. Worship God, because the testimony of Jesus is the spirit of prophecy."

The first statement in v.9 is doubly stressed. First, John has already been commanded in general to write down this whole Revelation. The repeat of the command means that the statement dictated is very important. Second, that dictation is followed by the assertion, "These words of God are true." This statement itself has a double emphasis, for the words are words of God and are therefore true, for God cannot lie (Ti 1:2). What is so important for John to write? A message of blessing. This is the *goal* of the PFG.

The curious thing about this passage is the ambiguity about who is speaking. Who is the "he" of v.9? As with the voice from the throne in v.5, the lack of clarity leads us to consider what else is the focus. This voice is likely that of an angel, and is certainly from a visible present figure, but the important thing is his sure message of blessing. What we *can* know about the speaker is that he is not Christ, for when John falls down to worship him, he forbids it. Further, he describes himself as a "fellow servant" and speaks of Jesus and God in the third person perspective.

How could an apostle, a close friend of Jesus, nearly stumble into false worship? It seems that these visions are characterized by such authority and close association with Christ that such an authoritative message would seem to come from Jesus himself. Whatever the reason for John's confusion, the reminder is clear: worship is for God alone. Note the contrast with the last near misstep on this matter. If John was overly impressed with the prostitute Babylon in 17:6, she would have gladly welcomed his blasphemous worship. Here, however, the faithful fellow servant forbids it.

The speaker says in v.10 that "the testimony of Jesus is the spirit of prophecy." This is the reason given why John should not worship this fellow servant, because he too clings to this testimony. As with the "revelation of Jesus" in ch.1, there are multiple options. Is this the testimony *about* Jesus? Is it *belonging* to Jesus? Is it *from* Jesus? As before, we are probably meant to understand it as all these. Jesus is the spirit (or Spirit) behind, or the engine driving, all true prophecy. He is also

The Judgment of Babylon, Earthly Laments, and Heavenly Praise

the focus of prophecy, the destination where all true prophetic roads lead. Letting the PFG guide us again, the main point is that clinging to the testimony of Jesus is the key to the blessing this speaker is pronouncing.

Reflection
How has this lesson revealed Jesus Christ?

How has this lesson called Christians to remain faithful?

How has it pointed to blessing?

Lesson 16: Victory, the Millennium, and the White Throne Judgment (Ch.19, V.11 – Ch.20)

Victory over the Beast

In the last lesson we saw Babylon fall once and for all. This was God's judgment upon the first power of the unholy trinity. Now John is shown how judgment comes to the beast and the dragon to finally judge all wickedness, deception, and rebellion. Jesus himself will bring this judgment:

The Rider on a White Horse

> **Rev 19:11-16**
> **11** Then I saw heaven opened, and there was a white horse. Its rider is called Faithful and True, and with justice he judges and makes war. **12** His eyes were like a fiery flame, and many crowns were on his head. He had a name written that no one knows except himself. **13** He wore a robe dipped in blood, and his name is called the Word of God. **14** The armies that were in heaven followed him on white horses, wearing pure white linen. **15** A sharp sword came from his mouth, so that he might strike the nations with it. He will rule them with an iron rod. He will also trample the winepress of the fierce anger of God, the Almighty. **16** And he has a name written on his robe and on his thigh: KING OF KINGS AND LORD OF LORDS.

This Rider proceeds from heaven, the seat of all power and authority. That he is on a white horse denotes purity and power. These are tied also to the army of horsemen in "pure white linen" who are also on white horses. These horsemen may be angels, but 17:14 suggests they may be – or at least may include – the faithful saints. The horse as a symbol of power is a stark contrast to the donkey upon which Jesus rode into Jerusalem to make his humble sacrifice for sin.

Nowhere in these verses is this Rider explicitly called Jesus, but John's descriptions and titles leave no doubt. In the context of this Revelation alone the identity is clear. The greater witness of other Scriptures only adds to the clarity.

Jesus already identified himself as the "faithful and true" witness in 3:14 when he spoke to the church of Laodicea (notably the *least* faithful among the seven churches). Before that, John had called Jesus the "faithful" witness in 1:5. To Philadelphia, Jesus identifies himself as the "true" one in 3:7. The song of Jesus the Lamb in 15:3 declares that his ways are "just and true," which pulls in the next key term in v.11 above, that of "justice." In fact, we've seen all through the book that the statements about God's justice are rightfully applied to Jesus and are carried out through him. Beale catches the most direct tie of this title to the PFG: "Christ has promised to judge the wicked in order to vindicate his name and his followers, and he will be "faithful and true" in fulfilling this promise."[53]

The description of the Rider's "fiery eyes" ties directly to Jesus in 1:14 and 2:18. As in those cases, it seems here to especially emphasize Christ's ability to see into and judge hearts. His piercing "I know" voiced toward the churches is now turned upon the godless nations.

Jesus is not with absolute certainty described as wearing any crown until now. Still, we did see that the crowned one in the harvest of 14:14 is likely either Jesus himself or an angel closely identified with him ("one like the Son of Man" or "one like a son of man"). We have also seen that the 24 elders cast their crowns before the throne just before the Lamb approached it to open the seals. The ambiguity regarding Jesus and crowns up to this point may be meant to reinforce that it is in Christ's coming in judgment and war that his kingly rule is fully realized. Notice the numberless crowns upon Jesus' head versus the limited numbers on those of the dragon and beast (12:3 and 13:1). Christ's dominion is over all and for all eternity.

John got us looking for the Bridegroom, but first he presents a warrior (see Is 11:4). This warrior does not come in fallen human bloodlust, but rather comes in righteous justice to bring the war of liberation for the downtrodden, his faithful.

The "name no one knows except himself" is closely associated with Jesus who promised the same kind of name to the conquerors at Pergamum (2:17). In that case, the meaning of the name points to blessing in a very personal way. Here, it probably is intended to communicate that Christ – even as God in human flesh – possesses depths that are beyond our knowing. Another possibility is that for the ancients (and many since) it was believed that to know someone's name was to have power over them. In this case, it would symbolize that Jesus is the highest power. This reference seems to draw from Isaiah where the LORD is revealing himself in judgment:

> **Isaiah 63:1–3**
> **1** Who is this coming from Edom
> in crimson-stained garments from Bozrah—
> this one who is splendid in his apparel,
> striding in his formidable might?
> It is I, proclaiming vindication,
> powerful to save.
> **2** Why are your clothes red,
> and your garments like one who treads a winepress?

---

[53] Beale, G. K. (1999). *The book of Revelation: a commentary on the Greek text* (p. 950). Grand Rapids, MI; Carlisle, Cumbria: W.B. Eerdmans; Paternoster Press.

Victory, the Millennium, and the White Throne Judgment

> **3** I trampled the winepress alone,
> and no one from the nations was with me.
> I trampled them in my anger
> and ground them underfoot in my fury;
> their blood spattered my garments,
> and all my clothes were stained.

"Robes" and "blood" have already been associated with Jesus in the persecution of his followers in 7:14. Their robes are said to be "washed" and "made white" in the "blood of the Lamb." That Jesus' robe is dipped in blood, then, is primarily to be understood as his own blood, that of his suffering as the "firstborn from among the dead" (Col 1:18). That association of the blood is then secondarily understood to be the blood of those he judges, as that from the harvest of Rv 14. Blood will be spilled here in ch.19, but his robes are already said to be bloody before that. In fact, the trampling of "the winepress" in v.15c seems to look back at the bloody harvest of ch.14 as though it is still future, which emphasizes that the blood on his robe is Christ's own and is meant to symbolize his own martyrdom.

The "word of God" is a common phrase in Revelation but used only here as a proper name. Still, the close association of this phrase with "the testimony of Jesus Christ" in 1:2 sets the two ideas as parallel. Of course, John explicitly connects the phrase to Jesus in his Gospel, which opens with the declaration that Jesus is the Word who was "in the beginning," who "was God" and who "was with God." This one is a no-brainer.

The "great sign" in ch.12 depicted Jesus as the Son "who is going to rule all nations with an iron rod" (v.5). Ps 2 prophesies in the same way about Jesus, the Son who will break the nations "with an iron scepter and establish his rule, his inheritance from the LORD. In fact, this whole Psalm seems to provide a prophetic backdrop for Rv.19.

The "sharp sword" from his mouth is the weapon with which Jesus strikes the nations. This phrase echoes 1:16 and 2:12,16. The power of Jesus is the power of the Word. This sword is not only the truth about Jesus' identity, but it is the power of the Son who created all by his word. Jesus is and possesses the power of God to create and to judge, to give life and to take it and to dispense wrath (19:15).

The last identifier in this description is the ultimate title. Jesus is "KING OF KINGS AND LORD OF LORDS" (v.16). Forms of this title were used of Yahweh by the great Israelite leader Moses (Dt 10:17) and, remarkably, by the terrible Babylonian king Nebuchadnezzar (Dn 2:47). Paul uses it in 1 Tm 6:15 regarding Christ's "appearing." In this case, Paul may already be using the title of Jesus himself or of God the Father. But Jesus is explicitly given this title in Rv 17:14, and it is the reason given that he will conquer all the powers of evil, "because he is Lord of lords and King of kings." Beale summaries the symbolic meaning:

The Revelation of Jesus Christ

"The thigh was the typical location of the warrior's sword (e.g., Exod. 32:27; Judg. 3:16, 21; Ps. 45:3) and the symbolic place under which the hand was placed to swear oaths (e.g., Gen. 24:2, 9; 47:29). Christ's victory over the wicked will be a fulfillment of God's promise to judge."[54]

How is the revelation of Jesus in vv.11-16 different from the way he is revealed in the Gospels?

How does "with justice" contrast with the way everyone else has "judged and made war"?

Imprisonment and the Terrible Feast

Heaven is opened, and Jesus comes forth in all power and authority with the armies of heaven on white horses. He is the Lord of Hosts (Ps 24:10; 46:7,11; 48:8; 59:5; etc.). He comes to "strike the nations," destroying the powers of evil with the word of his mouth (2 Thes 2:8) and dispensing God's wrath. The tension builds as the beast and the kings of the earth rally to make war, but almost as quickly as the outcome is predicted, this glorious Rider brings victory:

> **17** Then I saw an angel standing in the sun, and he called out in a loud voice, saying to all the birds flying high overhead, "Come, gather together for the great supper of God, **18** so that you may eat the flesh of kings, the flesh of military commanders, the flesh of the mighty, the flesh of horses and of their riders, and the flesh of everyone, both free and slave, small and great."
>
> **19** Then I saw the beast, the kings of the earth, and their armies gathered together to wage war against the rider on the horse and against his army. **20** But the beast was taken prisoner, and along with it the false prophet, who had performed the signs in its presence. He deceived those who accepted the mark of the beast and those who worshiped its image with these signs. Both of them were thrown alive into the lake of fire that burns with sulfur. **21** The rest were killed with the sword that came from the mouth of the rider on the horse, and all the birds ate their fill of their flesh.

In v.9 of this chapter an angel pronounced blessing upon those invited to the marriage feast of the Lamb. Now in v.17 an angel announces an invitation to a very different feast. This invitation is for birds of prey, and this feast is a horrific one. The phrase "standing in the sun" seems to

---

[54] Beale, G. K. (1999). *The book of Revelation: a commentary on the Greek text* (p. 963). Grand Rapids, MI; Carlisle, Cumbria: W.B. Eerdmans; Paternoster Press.

Victory, the Millennium, and the White Throne Judgment

mainly indicate the position of this angel high in the sky to issue his call, but it may also color the announcement with heavenly glory and authority. This supper of doom could not provide a clearer contrast to the celebration feast of the Lamb, and with these the fates of the faithful and the rebellious are in sharp contrast as well.

This battle is like none before it. It is unique in its *totality*. All the categories of the victims in v.18 are summarized in the central idea, "the flesh of everyone," to emphasize the universality of this macabre feast. No one – from greatest to least – no one who opposes the Lamb will survive this warrior's onslaught. This battle is also unique in its *brevity*. In fact, we may take John to mean there essentially is no battle at all. The beast, the kings and their armies are rallied together in v.19, but there is no record of combat.

There is none of the usual drama of warfare here. None of the ebb and flow of one force temporarily gaining the upper hand only to succumb to the surge of the overwhelming odds, or perhaps to the surge of the underdog against those odds. There are no odds because there is only one real power here.

The supposedly massive powers of mankind are assembled against the Rider and his army (recall Ps 2:2: "The kings of the earth take their stand, and the rulers conspire together against the LORD and his Anointed One"). The wording of v.19 indicates this gathering may very well be the same one occurring already in 16:14 and also still ahead in 20:8. This possibility is strengthened in that "war" in each instance has in the Greek the article "the" and so reads: "THE war."

Despite this build-up, the next thing John records is the simple capture of two prisoners: the beast and the false prophet (the beast from the sea, or Antichrist, from 13:1 and the beast from the earth in 13:11). No nail-biting narrative of an epic struggle or near escape. These two are simply "thrown alive into the lake of fire that burns with sulfur" (v.20). The significance of "alive" here probably is to emphasize the swiftness and severity of the event, as with the sons of Korah in Nu 16:33.

And what of all those kings and warriors in the rebellious armies of the earth? Killed with just the Rider's word, the "sword from his mouth" (vv.15,21, see also Is 11:4; 49:2). No hint of the slightest skirmish. Simply instantaneous decimation with the Word's voicing of a decree of death. The gruesome feast ensues. A similar passage in Ezek 39:17-20 (written against Gog and Magog) may cause us to think of the fallen here as a holy sacrifice:

The Revelation of Jesus Christ

> **Ezekiel 39:17–20**
> **17** "Son of man, this is what the Lord God says: Tell every kind of bird and all the wild animals, 'Assemble and come! Gather from all around to my sacrificial feast that I am slaughtering for you, a great feast on the mountains of Israel; you will eat flesh and drink blood. **18** You will eat the flesh of mighty men and drink the blood of the earth's princes: rams, lambs, male goats, and all the fattened bulls of Bashan. **19** You will eat fat until you are satisfied and drink blood until you are drunk, at my sacrificial feast that I have prepared for you. **20** At my table you will eat your fill of horses and riders, of mighty men and all the warriors. This is the declaration of the Lord God.'

The faithful have offered themselves willingly to God as a living sacrifice (Rm 12:1). Many have been slaughtered by the beast and his followers. Now, their persecutors are offered as unwilling sacrifices to God as he vindicates his faithful.

Even if one takes a completely idealistic interpretation of this passage, the images are powerful and communicate with great clarity. The harlot Babylon has been judged, and now, just as surely and swiftly, the beast and his wingman are cast into judgment fire.

Recall that the PFG is **to reveal Jesus Christ so that his servants faithfully endure suffering in order to receive blessing**.

Why then do you suppose that John makes a point of reminding us in v.20 that the false prophet performed signs to deceive people into worshiping the beast? Why would he put this reminder of that powerful deception right in the middle of his brief description of their destruction?

The Millennium

With ch.20 come some of the deepest interpretive waters of this book. The major camps vary widely about what is communicated in the first few verses of this chapter, especially regarding the binding of Satan and the Millennial Reign. These two subjects are united in duration, and the parallels seem to present them as simultaneous and interdependent epochs. While we need to understand and consider the major interpretive options, we also need to listen carefully to the PFG as a lighthouse to keep us from drifting off too far in these waters. We won't always have to find land, but we must stay afloat and keep navigating toward our blessing.

The Binding of Satan

The first two powers of the evil trio have been dealt with. What about the ancient evil behind the whole rebellious world system?

Victory, the Millennium, and the White Throne Judgment

Revelation 20:1–3
1 Then I saw an angel coming down from heaven holding the key to the abyss and a great chain in his hand. **2** He seized the dragon, that ancient serpent who is the devil and Satan, and bound him for a thousand years. **3** He threw him into the abyss, closed it, and put a seal on it so that he would no longer deceive the nations until the thousand years were completed. After that, he must be released for a short time.

Satan is bound, to be sure. But what are the nature and degree of this binding? When does it happen, and how long does it last? Why does he have to be released? There are several coherent and biblically sound systems of interpretation to answer these questions. Each has some strengths and some challenges to overcome. Each has been and is held by brilliant and committed biblical scholars, so we are wise to consider them carefully and hold any conclusions loosely. As we said in the beginning of this study, the points of disagreement here involve important, but non-essential doctrines. A faithful Christian may hold any of these sound positions.

It may seem like this binding of Satan happens after both the fall of Babylon (which is God's judgment through human agency) and the imprisonment of the beast and false prophet in the lake of fire. However, as we have seen repeatedly before, the "Then" in v.1 ("And" in the Greek) that begins this portion of narrative indicates a successive scene in John's vision but not necessarily a chronological sequence of events. We will have to consider other clues as to whether the binding follows the other judgments.

This act of binding is performed by an angel from heaven who is not otherwise described except that he has "keys" and "a great chain." Keys have already symbolized authority elsewhere in this book (1:18; 3:7; 9:1) and elsewhere in Scripture (Is 22:22; Mt 16:19). In particular, Rv 3:7 reflects upon Is 22:22 to speak of opening and shutting, which, along with the great chain here, complete the idea of binding. This passage in Matthew is especially relevant:

Matthew 16:16–19
16 Simon Peter answered, "You are the Messiah, the Son of the living God."
17 Jesus responded, "Blessed are you, Simon son of Jonah, because flesh and blood did not reveal this to you, but my Father in heaven. **18** And I also say to you that you are Peter, and on this rock I will build my church, and the gates of Hades will not overpower it. **19** I will give you the keys of the kingdom of heaven, and whatever you bind on earth will have been bound in heaven, and whatever you loose on earth will have been loosed in heaven."

Now, in this text, it is a *what* that is being bound, not a *who*, but the ideas are related. Jesus says that the revelation of himself as the Son of God (v.16) will be the basis for his building of and securing of his church. Even the gates of Hades will not overpower her, as Rv 1:18 bears out, for there Jesus tells John, "I hold the keys of death and Hades." The idea of gates "overpowering" often confuses people, because we think of gates as defensive measures repelling an attack from *outside.*

But gates are also designed to prevent jailbreak. Christ holds authority over Hades. Its gates cannot prevent those who cling to him from escaping death and being raised up and seated in the heavens with Christ (Eph 2:6). Those who hold to the testimony about Christ – those who "keep his words" – are given power of his resurrection life to conquer the grave.

Gates are also security against theft. Jesus used this analogy to show the Pharisees that he drove out demons by God's authority rather than Satan's:

> **Matthew 12:28–30**
> **28** If I drive out demons by the Spirit of God, then the kingdom of God has come upon you. **29** How can someone enter a strong man's house and steal his possessions unless he first ties up the strong man? Then he can plunder his house. **30** Anyone who is not with me is against me, and anyone who does not gather with me scatters.

Of course, Jesus was not saying he was a thief. All things belong to him because he is creator of all. The point of his analogy is that Jesus is able to "gather" (v.30) those whom Satan held under his dominion because he has the power of God. In revealing himself, Jesus exercises his power to bind Satan so that his captives may be liberated by the true gospel.

How do these ideas relate directly to the PFG?

The "whatever" that is bound or loosed in Mt 16:19 does seem to connect to the binding of Satan in Rv. 20. Commentator Leon Morris asserts this "whatever" is about "what things are forbidden and what things are permitted."[55] This understanding seems correct, and it seems to bear out in the church's council at Jerusalem in Acts 15. The Jewish Christians repelled an attempt by some Pharisees (often called Judaizers) to add circumcision to faith in Christ for salvation (v.4, see also Paul's letter to the Galatians). These wanted to demand Gentiles practice the law of Moses even though their receiving of the Holy Spirit already demonstrated they had been saved by faith in Christ (vv.8-11). James and the other church leaders rejected this corruption of the gospel of salvation by grace alone, but they did suggest the Gentile converts refrain from some activities that would be particularly offensive to many Jews:

---

[55] Morris, L. (1992). *The Gospel according to Matthew* (p. 426). Grand Rapids, MI; Leicester, England: W.B. Eerdmans; Inter-Varsity Press.

Victory, the Millennium, and the White Throne Judgment

> **Acts 15:19–20**
> **19** Therefore, in my judgment, we should not cause difficulties for those among the Gentiles who turn to God, **20** but instead we should write to them to abstain from things polluted by idols, from sexual immorality, from eating anything that has been strangled, and from blood.

Every item in the list above was associated with pagan worship. So, the church leadership was exercising its authority *to safeguard the gospel and prevent corruption of the church, whether by Jewish legalism or by paganism.*

The faithful witness of the gospel of Jesus binds the deception of Satan so that those who believe it may be loosed from his dominion. It is for the safeguarding and proclaiming of this gospel that Christ gives the keys of his authority to his church.

John is performing the same task in Revelation. He is revealing the true Christ so that Christians will hold to the faithful witness of the gospel and not be deceived by the lies of false religion. And the connection between deception and binding brings us back to Rv 20. The binding of Satan is specifically "so that he would no longer deceive the nations" (v.3). Nothing in this statement indicates clearly that Satan is completely incapacitated. Some propose that he may still have influence much like a mafia boss or gang leader can exert great influence even from prison.

The language of this verse is directly parallel to that of 12:9, where John was writing of the "great sign in heaven" about the woman, the child and the dragon:

> **9** So the great dragon was thrown out—the ancient serpent, who is called the devil and Satan, the one who deceives the whole world. He was thrown to earth, and his angels with him.

In both places: "dragon, serpent, devil, Satan." In both places, the emphasis is on deception: "the whole world" in ch.12 is parallel to "the nations" in ch.20. "Thrown to earth" is parallel to "threw him into the abyss." The abyss in earlier passages likely symbolized the underworld, the realm of the dead, and so here too. The "time is short" of 12:12 corresponds to the "short time" of 20:3. We also argued in earlier lessons that "sealing" likely has much to do with deception or protection from deception.

The leftover parts of ch.20's account bring us back to questions of timing and duration. When are these "thousand years" of Satan's binding, and when is the "short time" of his release? Are chs.12 and 20 referring to separate periods of satanic deception or the same period? What, if anything, does the binding of Satan have to do with the present age and the church?

Many interpreters take this "binding" of Satan as different from the "casting out" of ch.12, and as sequentially following the judgments of Babylon and the beast and false prophet. While they acknowledge the "chain" of v.1 should be taken figuratively (a spiritual being cannot be held by a literal chain), they interpret the thousand years as literal and as coming chronologically after the seal, trumpet, and bowl judgments. They see the binding as total incapacitation of Satan. (Nothing is said here about the binding of other demonic agents, but Satan's binding is usually taken to mean broadly that all demonic influence is prevented.) This period of binding is usually taken to correspond exactly with the thousand-year reign of Christ on earth described in the next section. Christ's second coming, then, comes *before* this millennial period *(premillennialism)*.

One key passage related to this discussion is found in Paul's letter to the Thessalonians:

> **2 Thessalonians 2:5–12**
> **5** Don't you remember that when I was still with you I used to tell you about this? **6** And you know what currently restrains him, so that he will be revealed in his time. **7** For the mystery of lawlessness is already at work, but the one now restraining will do so until he is out of the way, **8** and then the lawless one will be revealed. The Lord Jesus will destroy him with the breath of his mouth and will bring him to nothing at the appearance of his coming. **9** The coming of the lawless one is based on Satan's working, with every kind of miracle, both signs and wonders serving the lie, **10** and with every wicked deception among those who are perishing. They perish because they did not accept the love of the truth and so be saved. **11** For this reason God sends them a strong delusion so that they will believe the lie, **12** so that all will be condemned—those who did not believe the truth but delighted in unrighteousness.

Premillennialists today commonly take Paul in this passage to be talking about God's restraining of Satan's deceptive influence through the Antichrist, and they understand Paul to be speaking of this present Church Age, but they do not see this restraint as the binding of Rv 20:1-3. On this view, the restraining is occurring now and will be removed during the Tribulation – usually taken to be seven literal years of extremely powerful deception – that ends with Christ's victorious return. And *then* comes the binding of Satan for a literal thousand years. So, the cycle of *restraining* and satanic *freedom* precedes and is distinct from that of *binding* and *releasing*.

Many others understand this period of satanic binding and Christ's reign as the same situation Paul described to the Thessalonians, and one corresponding to this present age between Christ's two advents. These would take the binding as the limitation on Satan to deceive, especially that he cannot deceive the elect of God. The seal of Satan's prison corresponds to the sealing of the saints against his deception. The "short time" that he is loosed is the end of this age when the restraining power is taken away and his deception is overwhelming for any but true Christians. On this view, the Millennium is *now*, and it was inaugurated with Christ's resurrection and ascension *(amillennialism or inaugurated millennialism)*.

Still others take Rv 20:1-3 to communicate to Christians that Satan is powerless to stop the march of the Church and her gospel. The gospel will eventually spread and radicalize cultures and nations

Victory, the Millennium, and the White Throne Judgment

until a largely Christian world will bring in the millennial reign of Christ through his Church, and then *after* this he will return *(postmillennialism)*. Postmillennialists tend to de-emphasize the role of Satan's deceptions.

Regardless of one's view, how do the restraining and binding of Satan relate to the function of the PFG to ensure that Christians persevere faithfully?

How do we decide among the options? First, we need to consider more clues from the next verses.

Reigning with Christ and the First Resurrection

The binding of Satan is only part of the picture of this millennium. It corresponds to another key piece, the reign of Jesus and his faithful:

> **4** Then I saw thrones, and people seated on them who were given authority to judge. I also saw the souls of those who had been beheaded because of their testimony about Jesus and because of the word of God, who had not worshiped the beast or his image, and who had not accepted the mark on their foreheads or their hands. They came to life and reigned with Christ for a thousand years. **5** The rest of the dead did not come to life until the thousand years were completed.
>
> This is the first resurrection. **6** Blessed and holy is the one who shares in the first resurrection! The second death has no power over them, but they will be priests of God and of Christ, and they will reign with him for a thousand years.

John has written of thrones nearly four dozen times in this book. Only three of those occurrences (2:13; 13:2; 16:10) seem to clearly indicate thrones on earth. Many interpreters take this thousand-year reign as an earthly reign, but this is difficult to support conclusively in this passage. An eternal earthly reign is clearly indicated in ch.22 as Christ rules the entire cosmos.

Some important terminology in these verses brings up another major point of disagreement. "Resurrection" in vv.5 and 6 translates the Greek term *anastasis*, the very common term for bodily resurrection. This is different from the "came to life" of vv.4 and 5. Many take this as a clue that the "coming to life" and the "reigning" of this passage are spiritual realities.

"Coming to life" may make either of two distinctions. It could refer to a subset of saints – "martyrs" who come to life spiritually to share in the "first resurrection." In this case, all other believers would be resurrected at the end of the thousand years with the non-believers. More likely, "coming to life" describes all believers, for they are all "blessed and holy" and unharmed by the "second death" (2:11; 20:14; 21:8). In this case, the "rest of the dead" refers to unbelievers.

The Revelation of Jesus Christ

Against the view that the first resurrection is a spiritual one, many argue that the context demands only a physical resurrection be in view throughout this chapter, as Constable argues, and then cites Alford in support:

> "Amillennialists usually take the first resurrection as a reference to spiritual regeneration. They believe the second resurrection describes a general resurrection of all the dead at the end of time. This view is inconsistent in that it takes "resurrection" figuratively in one case but literally in the other.
>
> If, in a passage where **two** resurrections are mentioned . . . the first resurrection may be understood to mean **spiritual** rising with Christ, while the second means **literal** rising from the grave;—then there is an end of all significance in language, and Scripture is wiped out as a definite testimony to any thing."[56]

In considering the above statements, it must be noted that "spiritual" and "literal" are not opposites. A spiritual resurrection is still literal but is simply not physical. Every time we assure a believer that they have eternal life we are affirming a *literal* life. Further, Alford overstates his case, because we have already seen that two different pairs of terms are used in Rv 20 for "coming to life" and being "resurrected." And these pairs are used in other NT contexts to refer to alternately spiritual and physical realities within the same contexts, as Beale observes:

> "Rom. 6:4–13 reads: "just as Christ was **raised** from the dead ... so also we should walk in newness of **life**. For if we have become united with the likeness of his death, certainly also we will be in the likeness of his **resurrection**.... For if we have died with Christ, we believe that also **we will live** with him ... but the life **he** [Christ] **lives, he lives** to God. So also you reckon yourselves to be dead to sin but **living** to God in Christ Jesus ... present yourselves to God as **those alive** from the dead" (cf. similarly Rom. 8:10–11). Likewise, John 5:24–29 has the following: "the one believing him who sent me has eternal **life** and does not come into judgment, but has passed from death into **life** ... an hour comes and now is when the dead will hear the voice of the Son of God and those hearing **will live**. For just as the Father has **life** in himself, so also he has given the Son to have **life** in himself ... an hour comes in which all those in the tombs will hear his voice, and they will come forth, those having done good deeds to a **resurrection of life**, those having practiced evil deeds to a **resurrection** of judgment."[57]

This does not mean the literal approach must be wrong but only that the possibility that Rv 20:4-6 is speaking of a spiritual resurrection cannot be ruled out by grammar or literary context. The "coming to life" may express the spiritual reality for the believer and then the physical one for the unbeliever. And then the "first resurrection" would be the physical one of the believer while the

---

[56] Constable, T. (2003). <u>Tom Constable's Expository Notes on the Bible</u> (Re 20:5). Galaxie Software.
[57] Beale, G. K. (1999). <u>The book of Revelation: a commentary on the Greek text</u> (pp. 1004–1005). Grand Rapids, MI; Carlisle, Cumbria: W.B. Eerdmans; Paternoster Press.

unbeliever would experience eternal death. The believer would experience two kinds of resurrection, while the unbeliever two kinds of death. It does not violate ch.20 grammatically to understand it to say that Christians experience a spiritual resurrection and then a physical one while the unbelievers experience a physical resurrection and then spiritual death (the "second death" of 2:11; 20:6,14; 21:8).

How does the blessing of the first resurrection relate directly to the PFG of Revelation?

Victory over Satan

This millennial period – when Satan is bound and the saints rule with Christ – it does not last forever. Upon his release, Satan does what he has always done, and this time on the grandest scale:

> **7** When the thousand years are completed, Satan will be released from his prison **8** and will go out to deceive the nations at the four corners of the earth, Gog and Magog, to gather them for battle. Their number is like the sand of the sea. **9** They came up across the breadth of the earth and surrounded the encampment of the saints, the beloved city. Then fire came down from heaven and consumed them. **10** The devil who deceived them was thrown into the lake of fire and sulfur where the beast and the false prophet are, and they will be tormented day and night forever and ever.

There is direct correlation: Satan was restricted "so that he would no longer deceive the nations until the thousand years were completed" (v.3) and now that the thousand years are completed, he "will go out to deceive the nations" (v.8). The "When" of v.7 is actually "Whenever" and may support the possibility that these thousand years describe an unspecified period. This would emphasize that the period lasts exactly as long as it is supposed to. This deception is presented as a part of God's sovereign plan that *must* occur (v.3) and will accomplish exactly what God decrees. Those among all the nations who reject the gospel *will* be deceived.

We have already learned that "four corners" is a way of saying "the whole earth." "Gog and Magog" are references from the OT that originally refer to people groups (Gn 10:2; 1 Chr 1:5; 5:4) and their land (Ezek 38-39) that together came to symbolize the collective forces of evil.[58] The overwhelming magnitude of this force is clear from their number being "like the sand of the sea" and is probably also with "the breadth of the earth." The armies that surround the saints spread as far as the eye can see. This "encampment of the saints" is set parallel to, and so identified as, the "beloved city" (v.9). This is in direct contrast to the "great city" of Babylon. So, while it may or

---

[58] Morris, L. (1987). *Revelation: an introduction and commentary* (Vol. 20, p. 227). Downers Grove, IL: InterVarsity Press.

may not be a literal city – say, Jerusalem – John seems more focused on identifying those who are collectively the faithful "encampment" rather than on naming this city.

How do the overwhelming odds depicted in v.9 resonate with church history? With today?

We saw in the fifth bowl judgment (16:12-16) that the kings and armies were drawn together, at first probably to fight one another, but then to coalesce into a unified force of rebellion against God. Here in ch.20 it is clear that their target is the saints. Some take these to be two distinct events, while others will argue they are the same. Regardless, the accounts are broadly the same with different emphases, and so are the results: complete destruction of God's (and the saints') enemies. In this case, the destruction comes through fire from heaven. The devil is thrown into the lake of fire, a fate already assigned to the beast and false prophet in 19:20.

Notice again the emphasis on Satan's deception. It was the reason for his binding (v.3), and once he is freed, it is the activity that leads all the wicked to destruction (vv.8,10), including his own. As we have seen, the language of "day and night forever and ever" makes it clear that the unholy trinity suffer a real and unending torment. They are not annihilated. Sadly, those whom they deceived will share the same fate, as we will see in the last section of this chapter.

The Problem of Why

So, why is there a Millennium at all? The Postmillennialist has to explain in what sense Satan is ever loosed to deceive and lead a multi-national rebellion if the Church prevails to the extent that the world is already Christian before Christ returns. The Premillennialist has to explain why Satan is allowed to deceive a second world population (20:7-8) after the first one is destroyed (19:21). How can God's wrath be said in 15:7 to be "completed" with the bowl judgments, but then come down in fire on a later rebellion in 20:9?

One particular answer to the "problem of why" creates its own questions. It says that the Millennium serves to satisfy all the OT promises made to ethnic Israel. The Jews were promised an earthly reign by a descendant of David (2 Sam 7:10-13), and so this must be carried out in the earthly rule of Christ. But these promises are for an eternal rule, so how does a thousand-year rule advance the issue? If Christ reigns visibly on earth forever, what is the significance of this temporary reign? Some propose that it is to allow a special reward for those who are martyred for the name of Christ. They get the unique privilege of reigning with him during this period. While this is possible, it must be noted that Paul affirmed as trustworthy the truth that ALL who endure in faith will reign with Christ (2 Tm 2:11-13).

Some, like Wiersbe, would say the Millennium's rebellion offers "final proof that the heart of man is desperately wicked and can be changed only by God's grace." He says, "In one sense, the

Victory, the Millennium, and the White Throne Judgment

millennial kingdom will 'sum up' all that God has said about the heart of man during the various periods of history [dispensations]. It will be a reign of law, and yet law will not change man's sinful heart. Man will still revolt against God."[59] Didn't we already learn about our rebellious hearts through the Fall in the Garden? Isn't the insufficiency of the law to save the exact point of Christ's ushering in the New Covenant? What new offering does the Millennium bring to these truths? Many people end up concluding with Thomas, "The final answer as to why God sees this as a necessity with its fruition in another rebellion is hidden in the counsels of God."[60]

This "question of why" is simpler to overcome for the Amillennialist. Under this view, the Millennium describes the spiritual reign of Christ in this present age when Satan is limited in his power to deceive until the full number of the elect are brought into belief. His reign is already inaugurated, and merely awaits full realization as the eternal, visible, and earthly rule that the prophets foretold. In this case, the Millennium's function is to fulfill God's plan to redeem the elect through the gospel witness of the church and to condemn the rebellious by their rejection of that witness.

Dayton Hartman reminds us that various interpretations of the Millennium are nearly as old as the church: "Shortly after the deaths of the apostles, basic interpretations of the millennium appeared in early Christian histories and letters."[61] He also gives us some nearly two millennia of history to consider:

> "Justin Martyr points out that the early church—before Eusebius apparently—tolerated both premillennialism and amillennialism. But this early church diversity converged into an amillennial consensus.
>
> "The Reformers, like Martin Luther and John Calvin, were also amillennial, following in Augustine's footsteps. They found the premillennialism of some of the Radical Reformers repulsive, as if these folks sought to understand God's categories through human categories. Sort of like Eusebius' estimation of Papias.
>
> Amillennialism remained the only show in town until the Puritans introduced some variety. (Around the same time, premillennialism was revived by Pietists.) Some Puritans envisioned the New World as a guiding light to the nations. And so theologians like John Owen popularized the hopeful eschatology of postmillennialism. Jonathan Edwards—who didn't speak publicly about his millennial speculation—reimagined America as a bastion of gospel hope: a people that would lead the nations into the millennial age and beyond."[62]

---

[59] Constable, T. (2003). *Tom Constable's Expository Notes on the Bible* (Re 20:8). Galaxie Software.
[60] Ibid., Re 20:3
[61] Hartman, D. (2019). *Jesus Wins: The Good News of the End Times* (p. 38). Bellingham, WA: Lexham Press.
[62] Ibid., p. 40.

"But postmillennialism's advance came to a grinding halt around the time of the American Civil War. The conflict was a serious blow to the hope that this nation was the impetus for Christ's millennial reign. As the nineteenth century turned into the twentieth century, the future of the world was uncertain. Optimism faded as fear and pessimism reigned. Americans grappled with the devastation left by the Civil War, the terrors of World War I, the Great Depression, and the difficulties of modernization. People wanted an explanation for what was happening, and American postmillennialism wasn't doing the trick. Enter the new kid on the block: dispensationalism. With its eye always on the current news cycle, dispensationalism supplied a mechanism for explaining the world."[63]

As Hartman notes, in thinking through these options we must be careful not to be won over solely by which view is oldest, which is held by the majority, which is the most novel or recent. If we seek to land, we must see which interpretive system seems to most coherently bring to bear all that Scripture says. More importantly, we need to realize that in the finer points we do not really need to land at all. Since John has given us a clear purpose, function, and goal for this Revelation, we should seek to understand it – and especially these difficult parts – according to that PFG.

Interpreting according to the PFG

The Islands of Eschatology
There are many islands in the Sea of Last Things. The Premillennial Islands alone include several: the Classics and the Dispensationals, which themselves include Pre-Trib Island, Mid-Trib Island and Post-Trib Island. And there are also the Postmillennial and Amillennial Islands. And there are many others, too – Preterist Island, Futurist Island, the Eclectics, and more – large and small, some mostly deserted, others with large settlements, even well-advertised tourist traps.

The PFG reminds us that we are heading to a mainland. The Goal of Revelation is none of these Islands. It is the Mainland of Blessing. It is helpful – even needful to some extent – to explore the islands on our way, but whichever of them seems best to us, the more important thing is that we continue to chart our course forward to Blessing.

Charting A Clear Course
So, how does the PFG steer us? What is John clearly communicating to all Christians in these visions? This is where we find the common ground central to all the islands.

Regarding the binding of Satan: *God is sovereign over the timing, scope and effectiveness of Satan's deception. Believers will not be deceived by Satan.*

---

[63] Hartman, D. (2019). *Jesus Wins: The Good News of the End Times* (pp. 41-42). Bellingham, WA: Lexham Press.

Victory, the Millennium, and the White Throne Judgment

Regarding the reign of saints: *Saints who have died in Christ are blessed in sharing the first resurrection and the second death has no power over them. Believers will not fall victim to the second death. Ultimately all saints are assured they will reign with Christ.*

How are these clear truths governed by the PFG, and how do they help it along?

The White Throne Judgment and the Second Death

The promise of judgment against evil and vindication of Christ and his faithful has nearly played out. The beast and false prophet and even Satan himself have been thrown into the lake of fire. All of those of the earth who have rejected God and set themselves against his people have been killed. One last event stands between mankind and his eternal destiny – judgment:

> **11** Then I saw a great white throne and one seated on it. Earth and heaven fled from his presence, and no place was found for them. **12** I also saw the dead, the great and the small, standing before the throne, and books were opened. Another book was opened, which is the book of life, and the dead were judged according to their works by what was written in the books. **13** Then the sea gave up the dead that were in it, and death and Hades gave up the dead that were in them; each one was judged according to their works. **14** Death and Hades were thrown into the lake of fire. This is the second death, the lake of fire. **15** And anyone whose name was not found written in the book of life was thrown into the lake of fire.

The throne here represents the height of majesty and authority as well as pure justice. The one seated on it is clearly God, and, given the pattern of this book (4:2,3,9,10; 5:1,7,13; 6:16; 7:10; etc.) and that of the OT (Is 6:1; Ezek 1:26; Dn 7:9), we would best understand this to be the Father. Still, the NT affirms that Christ has been given all judgment by the Father (Mt 25:31-34; Jn 5:22; 2 Cor 5:10; Rm 14:10). So, as Morris says, "We should understand that the Father is the Judge, but that he judges through the Son (he 'has entrusted all judgment to the Son')."[64]

The language of v.11b echoes the cataclysmic effect of judgment upon heaven and earth in 6:14 and 16:20 and anticipates the new heaven and new earth of ch.21. The White Throne Judgment is the ultimate matter of life and death, though the emphasis in these verses is more on the latter. Whatever is going on with the resurrections of the earlier verses, it is clear that the grave has surrendered everyone for judgment.

Now we have another clear statement to record as we chart our way to final blessing: *Every person from everywhere is brought before God's throne for judgment.*

---

[64] Morris, L. (1987). *Revelation: an introduction and commentary* (Vol. 20, p. 228). Downers Grove, IL: InterVarsity Press.

The Revelation of Jesus Christ

The basis for judgment is two-fold: books and works. Daniel saw this coming before John did:

> **Daniel 7:9–10**
> **9** "As I kept watching,
>
>> thrones were set in place,
>> and the Ancient of Days took his seat.
>> His clothing was white like snow,
>> and the hair of his head like whitest wool.
>> His throne was flaming fire;
>> its wheels were blazing fire.
>> **10** A river of fire was flowing,
>> coming out from his presence.
>> Thousands upon thousands served him;
>> ten thousand times ten thousand stood before him.
>> The court was convened,
>> and the books were opened.

Daniel records an angel talking again of judgment in ch.12, where he says, "all your people who are found written in the book will escape" (v.1). That singular book is apparently John's "book of life" in Rv 20:12. It makes all the difference, for only names written there indicate rescue from the lake of fire. All are said to be judged by works, and judgment is meted out accordingly and perfectly.

Rv 3:5 has already given us a template for understanding this judgment:

> "In the same way, the one who conquers will be dressed in white clothes, and I will never erase his name from the book of life but will acknowledge his name before my Father and before his angels."

From this we understand that condemnation is based on rejection. One's name must be blotted out (Ps 69:28), though God may speak of it as already missing from the "foundation of the world" (Rv 17:8). Having one's name erased is a result of a conscious decision to reject the gospel and reject Christ (Jn 12:48; Acts 13:46; Heb 12:25). This is why the book of life is the book of the Lamb (Rv 13:8). Either your sins are blotted out through faith in Jesus, or your name is blotted out from his book of life through your rejection of Jesus. No one partakes of eternal blessing without having their name in this book (Rv 21:27).

For those who do confess Jesus as the Son of God, and by faith declare him Lord, he will acknowledge their names before the Father (3:5 above). This does not mean that believers are not judged. The indication of the depiction of the Great White Throne is that we too are judged according to our works. We are guaranteed eternal life and blessing, but Paul helps us understand

Victory, the Millennium, and the White Throne Judgment

more clearly that we will gain or lose particular rewards according to how we live out our lives of faith:

> **1 Corinthians 3:11–15**
> **11** For no one can lay any foundation other than what has been laid down. That foundation is Jesus Christ. **12** If anyone builds on the foundation with gold, silver, costly stones, wood, hay, or straw, **13** each one's work will become obvious. For the day will disclose it, because it will be revealed by fire; the fire will test the quality of each one's work. **14** If anyone's work that he has built survives, he will receive a reward. **15** If anyone's work is burned up, he will experience loss, but he himself will be saved—but only as through fire.

Just as every unbeliever's judgment will exactly fit his or her works but will all be experienced in the lake of fire, so every believer's judgment will exactly fit his or her works but will be experienced in eternal blessing.

John will begin to try to describe that blessing in ch.21, but for now, the focus has largely been on the judgment of the wicked. More than that, we have been shown the removal of all kinds of evil. All demonic and human agents of destruction have been thrown into the lake of fire forever. So too have Death and Hades. Every enemy of the glorious life promised by God for the faithful has been cast away.

Reflection

How has Christ been revealed in this lesson?

How can these passages help you persevere through persecution by Christ's enemies?

How do the truths of this lesson give us a taste of the blessing to come in Christ?

Lesson 17: The New Heaven, the New Earth, and the New Jerusalem (Ch.21 – Ch.22, V.5)

This Revelation of Jesus Christ has covered a lot of ground. It has addressed the entire Church Age and even expressed realities that span all human history. It is no wonder that God has routinely referred to himself as the First and the Last in this book. Now John's vision is moving into that transition between this age and the final state. We have seen the demise of and judgment of all earthly and demonic evil that opposes God. As Jesus has been revealed, so too have his faithful been revealed. John's visions turn from the eternal fate of the rebellious who reject Christ to that of the faithful who worship him.

The New Heaven and New Earth

These faithful enjoy the renewal of all creation. The process had already begun in their own personal renewal upon trusting Christ. Now that process is completed in their resurrection bodies, and it is also expressed in the entire cosmos, a new heaven and new earth:

> **Revelation 21:1–2**
> **1** Then I saw a new heaven and a new earth; for the first heaven and the first earth had passed away, and the sea was no more. **2** I also saw the holy city, the new Jerusalem, coming down out of heaven from God, prepared like a bride adorned for her husband.

Though we remain cautious of asserting chronological sequence, it does read like v.1 here picks up where 20:11 left off: "Earth and heaven fled from his presence, and no place was found for them." The judgments of seals, trumpets and bowls, and the cosmic effects of God's judging of evil have played out in descriptions of de-creation. The old cosmos corrupted by sin has passed away, and now a new one is brought into being.

A New Kind of Heaven and Earth

We have discussed that some take this transition as a complete annihilation of the old followed by utterly new creation while others take this to mean a complete renovation of the old. Either way, the clear understanding is that the "new" reality is qualitatively different from the old but with a continuity that carries over from it. "New" in this case is not merely Cosmos 2.0. It is a different *kind* of cosmos.

The qualitative difference of the new heaven and earth is emphasized by the tie of this chapter to Is 65-66 and Ezek 40-48. In particular, the language of Is 65:17 is nearly identical, and is closely mirrored in 66:22:

> **17** "For I will create new heavens and a new earth;
> the past events will not be remembered or come to mind.
> **22** "For just as the new heavens and the new earth,
> which I will make,
> will remain before me"—
> this is the LORD's declaration—
> "so your offspring and your name will remain."

The first qualitative difference in the new order is its eternality (cf. 22:5). This new universe will "remain" before God. Just as believers receive incorruptible resurrection bodies that last forever (1 Cor 15:50-54), so will the entire cosmos be renewed in an everlasting kind of heaven and earth. This new cosmos will be reminiscent of the old one described in Genesis (and in which we presently live) but will be escalated in not only its duration but in its excellence, as we will see in the ongoing depictions.

Paul wrote about the temporal nature of this present creation to contrast the way the glory of the eternal state will far surpass our temporary suffering "with Christ" (and for his sake):

> **Romans 8:18–21**
> **18** For I consider that the sufferings of this present time are not worth comparing with the glory that is going to be revealed to us. **19** For the creation eagerly waits with anticipation for God's sons to be revealed. **20** For the creation was subjected to futility—not willingly, but because of him who subjected it—in the hope **21** that the creation itself will also be set free from the bondage to decay into the glorious freedom of God's children.

How would and does the eternal nature of this new heaven and new earth encourage suffering saints to persevere?

No More Sea
Another key difference in this new eternal cosmos is found in the statement, "the sea was no more." This may or may not have anything to say about a literal sea, but it surely is meant to communicate something about the symbolic, metaphorical sea. The symbolic usage of this term in Revelation has presented five options: 1) the origin of cosmic evil (12:18; 13:1; 15:2 interpreted according to an ancient and OT background), 2) the mass of rebellious humanity who persecute the faithful (12:18; 13:1; 15:2), 3) the place of the dead (20:13), 4) the main locus of idolatrous trade (18:10-19) and 5) a part of the representative whole of creation (5:13; 7:1-3; 8:8-9; 10:2, 5-6, 8; 14:7; 16:3).

The New Heaven, the New Earth, and the New Jerusalem

John probably means to communicate all these ideas summarily as the forces that threaten humankind, and especially those that embody the threat of evil against God's faithful servants. In other words, in the eternal heaven and earth all threats have been removed forever. No more chaos, no more evil, no more attacks, nor more idolatry, and even death has been abolished! In fact, the sea is one of seven evils that John will write of as being no more (including "death," "grief," "crying" and "pain" in v.4, "curse" in 22:3, and "night" in v.5).

How does the future and permanent elimination of all these threats help the saint persevere?

No sooner does John write of the new heaven and earth than he sees the New Jerusalem. This new city will also be qualitatively different from the old. In fact, it may be taken to be a more in-depth description of the entire new cosmos as we shall see when John gives its description in vv.9ff. "New" and "holy" describe this qualitative difference, while "Jerusalem" anchors it in the present age to provide continuity. Jerusalem has been a big deal for millennia, frequently at the center of the world's attention. The New Jerusalem will be an even bigger deal, for it comes down out of heaven from God like a carefully prepared wedding gift. More on that in a bit.

God's Dwelling with Humankind

The New Jerusalem symbolizes another key distinctive of the new cosmos. It is defined by and totally permeated by *tabernacling*. This term – translated "dwelling" – communicates God's presence among his people. Christians have lived with the indwelling Spirit of Christ as his promise of enduring presence. In the new economy, this presence is direct and external as well as internal. This reality is announced from the heavenly throne:

> **3** Then I heard a loud voice from the throne: Look, God's dwelling is with humanity, and he will live with them. They will be his peoples, and God himself will be with them and will be their God. **4** He will wipe away every tear from their eyes. Death will be no more; grief, crying, and pain will be no more, because the previous things have passed away.

This is the last of twenty times John records hearing a "loud voice," and once again the message is big. The term "tabernacle" communicated God's presence and his glory. Here, then, John is being told that God's presence and glory will be with humanity.

God dwelt with mankind in the Garden. He dwelt among his chosen people in the OT tabernacle and temple. He dwells now within and among his chosen in the Church. This new eternal dwelling is far greater, for it is with ALL mankind. Only the faithful are present in this new and eternal heaven and earth, and so now it may be said that God dwells with all humans everywhere. This is an eternal and unrestricted cohabitation. God's presence – which has always been everywhere and at all times – will now be experienced always and in a more robust way by humans.

The Revelation of Jesus Christ

The emphasis is on the universal nature of this experience. The term "peoples" emphasizes the unity in diversity, that God has fulfilled his promise to bring blessing upon those from all the nations of the world. In John's first century context, this would especially communicate the sameness of the experience of all Jews and non-Jews as the people of God. Five independent phrases in v.3 emphasize this unified coexistence of God with his peoples. God has no other peoples, and these peoples have no other God. All humans, all peoples, have one God.

This eternal dwelling with God will bring every kind of blessing God has promised. These are expressed in v.4 in terms of things that have been robbing and corrupting God's blessings ever since the Garden. They will be summarized in the "curse" of 22:3, and they are seen together with "sea" and "night" as things that will be "no more" because they have "passed away."

How does this promise of eternally dwelling with God keep the suffering saint's future blessing in focus?

It Is Done!

Now, John records a statement directly from God:

> **5** Then the one seated on the throne said, "Look, I am making everything new." He also said, "Write, because these words are faithful and true." **6** Then he said to me, "It is done! I am the Alpha and the Omega, the beginning and the end. I will freely give to the thirsty from the spring of the water of life. **7** The one who conquers will inherit these things, and I will be his God, and he will be my son. **8** But the cowards, faithless, detestable, murderers, sexually immoral, sorcerers, idolaters, and all liars—their share will be in the lake that burns with fire and sulfur, which is the second death."

This statement comes not only directly from the heavenly throne but also is affirmed as "faithful and true." Notice that John is not only privileged to hear this message, but he is explicitly commanded to record it. This directly accords with the PFG, that John is to communicate these things to encourage and challenge the saints, so they may be qualified for this inheritance as "one who conquers."

God says he is "making everything new." This summarizes the ideas already mentioned in the first four verses: God's renewal of all the cosmos, the new economy where his dwelling is with mankind and his removal of all threats to his people. Stated in the present tense as it is, this truth also reaches back into our own time and all the way back to John's original audience to remind the believer that God's work of renewal is already happening in his faithful and he will bring it to completion (Php 1:6).

The New Heaven, the New Earth, and the New Jerusalem

When God declares, "I am the Alpha and the Omega, the beginning and the end," he asserts with absolute sovereignty the surety that he will bring his plan to completion. The only other place in Revelation where it is explicit that God is speaking is in 1:8, where he uses this same title. The placement of that title near the beginning and end of the book amplifies the truth being expressed.

The sentence, "It is done!" is actually one *plural* verb (Γέγοναν), that translates more literally, "*they* are done." The idea seems to be that all of God's plans to redeem and to bring judgment are completed. The same term that declared the completion of God's deconstructive wrath in the seventh bowl (16:17) now declares the completion of his reconstructive blessing in the renewed creation. The term echoes a similar statement of Jesus upon the cross, "It is finished" (Jn 19:30), but using a different term (Τετέλεσται). That term described the fulfillment of payment in satisfying a debt. That completed payment began the reality of new creation in Jesus' followers that is declared complete on a cosmic scale in Rv 21:6.

Notice the shift from the corporate focus to the personal. In v.3, "They will be his peoples and...God will be their God." Now, in v.7, "I will be his God, and he will be my son." The blessing of dwelling with God in a perfect world will be a universal human experience, but it will also be a personal and individual experience.

How does it impact you to know that renewal will one day become complete for you personally and also for the whole cosmos?

Right on the heels of these guarantees, the conqueror is contrasted again with the ungodly for the sake of warning (for this eternal bliss is still yet future). The unfaithful will not experience this eternal blessing, but instead will suffer eternal torment once again described as "the second death." Temporarily suffering for Christ yields eternal life, while temporarily compromising for oneself yields eternal death. Even in the midst of his description of final blessing, John is given a warning that reminds us of the PFG, **to reveal Jesus Christ so that his servants faithfully endure suffering in order to receive blessing.**

There is a particular focus here on apostasy and blasphemous worship that is firmly rooted in that first century struggle we covered in Lesson 1. The list in v.8 begins with "cowards" and ends with "liars." Literary conventions of John's day would elevate these terms as predominant in the list, and this would focus squarely upon those who caved to the pressures of compromise that corrupted true Christianity with false doctrine and ungodly living. A supposed Christ-follower who would minimize Christ in order to retain his economic stability in the trade guild or to appease the pressures of the Judaizers would show himself a "coward" and a "liar." The other terms in the list are probably intended as specifics of their corrupt religious practices ("murderers" could refer to child-sacrifice or perhaps betrayals of true believers to authorities for possible execution).

How does this stark contrast between "the one who conquers" and the "cowards and liars" challenge you today?

The New Jerusalem

John has already given an introductory description of the New Jerusalem as the "holy city...prepared like a bride adorned for her husband." Some take this city to be a central *place* in the new heaven/earth union, while others take it to be a symbolic description of the *entirety* of this new existence. The highly symbolic nature of this city seems to favor the latter option, but even if taking the first option, New Jerusalem is clearly telling us what the new economy is like. John goes into far more detail with rich symbolic images:

> **9** Then one of the seven angels, who had held the seven bowls filled with the seven last plagues, came and spoke with me: "Come, I will show you the bride, the wife of the Lamb." **10** He then carried me away in the Spirit to a great, high mountain and showed me the holy city, Jerusalem, coming down out of heaven from God, **11** arrayed with God's glory. Her radiance was like a precious jewel, like a jasper stone, clear as crystal.

The language of v.9 is nearly identical to 17:1, where one of the seven "bowl" angels (perhaps the same one) showed John the harlot Babylon. In both cases, John is carried away to get a clearer perspective. With the harlot, the remote desert helped John see through the façade of glory. With the bride, the high mountain helps him see her true glory more fully. Her glory is God's glory. The harlot's false glory was the deceptive attire of the dragon to dress up her appearance. The bride's glory is the true glory of God that is given to her like bedazzling clothes. God's glory in her is pure and radiant.

In contrast with gaudy Babylon, the symbol of false worship, the faithful are depicted as a heavenly Jerusalem coming down from God. This city is holy, as she reflects God's own holiness. The jasper stone reveals this close association, for God's own glory was described in terms of this same stone in 4:3, in the midst of the heavenly worship scene. The extremely costly nature of this stone conveys God's presence and his kingdom as the most prized and valuable possession, just as Jesus portrayed in his Kingdom Parables (Mt 13:44-45).

The New Heaven, the New Earth, and the New Jerusalem

The Wall, the Gates and the Measurements

After this initial description of New Jerusalem as radiating God's own glory, John continues to echo Ezek 40 and 48 as he records several other details that give symbolic understanding of the new eternal reality for the believer:

> **12** The city had a massive high wall, with twelve gates. Twelve angels were at the gates; the names of the twelve tribes of Israel's sons were inscribed on the gates. **13** There were three gates on the east, three gates on the north, three gates on the south, and three gates on the west. **14** The city wall had twelve foundations, and the twelve names of the twelve apostles of the Lamb were on the foundations.
>
> **15** The one who spoke with me had a golden measuring rod to measure the city, its gates, and its wall. **16** The city is laid out in a square; its length and width are the same. He measured the city with the rod at 12,000 *stadia*. Its length, width, and height are equal. **17** Then he measured its wall, 144 cubits according to human measurement, which the angel used.

Literal interpretations of the measurements present significant problems. The wall is said to be "massive and high" but if taken literally would only be about 216 feet high (144 cubits), which is not so impressive around a city 1500 miles high (12,000 stadia). Even if the wall's measurement is taken as the wall's thickness, it would be an impressive structural miracle at 1500 miles high (which God may well do), but it still would only qualify as "high" and not "massive." If 144 cubits is taken as its perimeter length, the picture is absurd, since the city's perimeter would be 48,000 stadia, placing it ridiculously far *outside* the wall. These are strong indications that we should concern ourselves with what John is conveying through the symbolism of this whole passage about the New Jerusalem, and so we will.

The massive wall certainly symbolizes the absolute security and inviolability of God's eternal kingdom. As with the phrase "no more sea," this communicates the removal of all threats to God's people. This city and its inhabitants are safe from attack and free from corruption. The angels at the gates reinforce these ideas of security and inviolability as angelic beings have served as watchmen and guards before (Gn 3:24) and may well be ascribed these roles in the end-time Jerusalem by Isaiah (62:6).

Why then measurements at all? Surely it is to communicate through the symbolism of the numbers. 144 is equal to twelve squared, and the cubit is a human measurement. In fact, v.17 specifies that the angel uses a "human" cubit. Remember, the phrase "number of a person" used about the beast in 13:18 emphasized the mere humanity of this antichrist. The same idea seems in play here. Together, the product of twelves expressed in cubits probably functions to represent the totality of God's people. This idea is reinforced by the imagery of the apostles in the foundation of this wall and the Jewish tribes in its gates. Paul used this language when describing the building of God:

Ephesians 2:19–22

19 So, then, you are no longer foreigners and strangers, but fellow citizens with the saints, and members of God's household, **20** built on the foundation of the apostles and prophets, with Christ Jesus himself as the cornerstone. **21** In him the whole building, being put together, grows into a holy temple in the Lord. **22** In him you are also being built together for God's dwelling in the Spirit.

Since this new city embodies the cohabitation of God with mankind, its wall embodies the unity of all faithful mankind as God's people. At first, it may seem backward for the ancient Israelite tribes to be pictured within the gates while the apostles, who came much later in the redemptive plan, are depicted in the foundations. This might be especially strange for those who emphasize the distinctions between believing (ethnic) Israel and the Church in the final state and or the Millennium.

However, the oddity dissolves if both gates and foundations are understood in terms of the *new* Israel, the Church, which includes all faithful believers from all time. In this case, the description may function the way that the 144,000 sealed of ch.7 may be taken. The Church gates hang upon the wall of the gospel, which is founded on the witness and teaching and miraculous works of the apostles with Christ as the Cornerstone (1 Cor 3:10-15; Eph 2:20; Heb 11:10). The truth about Christ defines insider versus outsider, and the testimony about Christ offered by all the tribes of this new Israel provides access (through the gates) to this eternal bliss.

The singularity of the wall would also communicate the unity characteristic within this kingdom in stark contrast to the multi-walled temple of the first century that was destroyed in AD 70. Beale provides that backdrop:

> "The Herodian temple had a court of the Gentiles, adjacent to the inner courts of women, of Israel, and of priests, respectively, while the Solomonic temple, the second temple before Herod, and the temple of Ezekiel 40–48 were divided by a wall into inner and outer courts (cf. Eph. 2:14; see further on 11:1–2). In contrast, there will be only one wall in the new Jerusalem, and it will surround the entire city, thus stressing the unity of the city's inhabitants with one another and with God."[65]

This idea would accord beautifully with Paul's assertion that spiritual unity is already a reality that demolishes the old Jew/Gentile wall in the Church:

---

[65] Beale, G. K. (1999). *The book of Revelation: a commentary on the Greek text* (p. 1078). Grand Rapids, MI; Carlisle, Cumbria: W.B. Eerdmans; Paternoster Press.

The New Heaven, the New Earth, and the New Jerusalem

Ephesians 2:11–14
11 So, then, remember that at one time you were Gentiles in the flesh—called "the uncircumcised" by those called "the circumcised," which is done in the flesh by human hands. **12** At that time you were without Christ, excluded from the citizenship of Israel, and foreigners to the covenants of promise, without hope and without God in the world. **13** But now in Christ Jesus, you who were far away have been brought near by the blood of Christ. **14** For he is our peace, who made both groups one and tore down the dividing wall of hostility.

Paul asserts that all believers in Christ are now "insiders" and John's singular wall would paint the same picture. This Ephesians 2 passage is especially relevant as Paul goes on to talk about the apostles as part of the foundation of the household of faith, symbolism we will see in greater detail in the next section of Rv 21.

The description of the twelve gates bearing the names of the twelve sons of Israel echoes Ezek 48:31-34, but in John's description the names are not listed. This would affirm that, as Morris puts it, "this heavenly city is the true fulfilment of Israel's high calling"[66] but would also de-emphasize the Jewish distinction in favor of the Jew/Gentile unity. (Remember the Jewish list in Rv 7 left out Dan while including Manasseh but not Ephraim, probably in that case to emphasize faithfulness.)

The grouping of the gates by compass directions echoes the Ezek 48 passage, but the order of those directions follows the pattern of Ezek 42:16-19, where the prophet is shown the temple complex. The function in Rv 21 seems to be to prioritize east, though it is not clear why. It may be worth noting that whenever the Lord would move the Israelite camps in their journey from Sinai to Paran, the eastern camp of Judah always headed out first (Nu 10:14-28).

Besides the wall, the city itself also bears significance in its measurements. If we take John literally, we are most impressed with a city 1500 miles square soaring well into what is outer space in this present world. This city is probably far greater than that, if we really grasp the symbolism. The twelve-times-twelve of the wall finds even greater amplification in the city. In this case, the twelve is ascribed threefold in length, width, and height. The twelve is multiplied by a thousand which is a threefold product of ten, the number of completion. That is further amplified by the unit of stadia versus the much smaller unit of cubits. Taken together, the dimensions of the city dramatically depict the totality of God's people.

This over-the-top numeric depiction is then fused with another symbol. These city measurements echo several series in Ezekiel's visions. In his case, whether measuring the wall and gates, the temple complex or the city, the pattern is length-and-width (Ezek 40; 45:1-5; 48:1-13). For John's vision there is an important escalation – the third dimension of height. This added detail ties

---

[66] Morris, L. (1987). *Revelation: an introduction and commentary* (Vol. 20, p. 238). Downers Grove, IL: InterVarsity Press.

directly to the Most Holy Place of the temple, for it was a perfect cube, twenty cubits in length, width and height (1 Kgs 6:20). Applied to this city, this ties together the totality of God's people with the "hotspot" of God's presence. If this city represents more broadly the character of the eternal state, then it depicts in the strongest terms that God's dwelling is among his people.

John may have another symbol in mind too. Ancient Babylon was described in ways that were similar to this New Jerusalem, including having a river flowing through its center (see Rv 22:1-2). If the three-dimensional measurements of the New Jerusalem are taken as a pyramid – like a Babylonian ziggurat – rather than a cube, then the point would be to contrast the false, arrogant and temporary Babylon with the true, glorious and eternal New Jerusalem.

Perhaps John is thinking in terms of both possibilities. The ancient tower of Babel's pride (Gn 11:4, cf. Rv 18:5) has given way to the eternal Holy of Holies. Mankind bent on self-exaltation has been cast out into the lake of fire, while mankind humbled in worship of God has been brought into his holy presence forever.

How do these dramatic symbols depict the overcomer's eternal blessing? How would these amazing images impact a struggling, persecuted Christian?

The Materials

While these descriptions may well be literal, the astounding truths in the symbolism continue to amaze. If L. Frank Baum could captivate the imagination with his Emerald City in Oz, then John's vision of the precious jewels and metals in the New Jerusalem takes things to entirely new heights!

> **18** The building material of its wall was jasper, and the city was pure gold clear as glass. **19** The foundations of the city wall were adorned with every kind of jewel: the first foundation is jasper, the second sapphire, the third chalcedony, the fourth emerald, **20** the fifth sardonyx, the sixth carnelian, the seventh chrysolite, the eighth beryl, the ninth topaz, the tenth chrysoprase, the eleventh jacinth, the twelfth amethyst. **21** The twelve gates are twelve pearls; each individual gate was made of a single pearl. The main street of the city was pure gold, transparent as glass.

As we noted regarding v.11, jasper stone carried the idea of radiating God's glory. There, it described the bride of the Lamb, which is the New Jerusalem. Here, it is the material of the wall itself and of its foundations. It is God's glory among and in his people that separates the insiders (the faithful) from the outsiders (the unholy who have been cast out into eternal punishment). The "adorning" of the foundations here echoes the "adorning" of the bride in v.2.

The New Heaven, the New Earth, and the New Jerusalem

Gold "clear as glass" symbolizes both purity and priceless value. In John's day, crystal-clear glass was rare and extraordinarily valuable, something fit for a king's court.[67] To live forever in the presence of God is the most valuable and glorious kind of dwelling.

How does the cost of enduring persecution compare to the worth of the New Jerusalem?

The foundations of the wall are almost certainly a reflection of the high priestly garment prescribed by God in the Exodus (see also 39:8-14):

> **Exodus 28:15–21**
> **15** "You are to make an embroidered breastpiece for making decisions. Make it with the same workmanship as the ephod; make it of gold, of blue, purple, and scarlet yarn, and of finely spun linen. **16** It must be square and folded double, nine inches long and nine inches wide. **17** Place a setting of gemstones on it, four rows of stones:
> The first row should be
> a row of carnelian, topaz, and emerald;
> **18** the second row,
> a turquoise, a lapis lazuli, and a diamond;
> **19** the third row,
> a jacinth, an agate, and an amethyst;
> **20** and the fourth row,
> a beryl, an onyx, and a jasper.
>
> They should be adorned with gold filigree in their settings. **21** The twelve stones are to correspond to the names of Israel's sons. Each stone must be engraved like a seal, with one of the names of the twelve tribes.

The stone names that are different are probably due to translations from the ancient Hebrew designations to the first century Greek ones. The changing of order does not seem significant. What does seem significant in John's mind is the connection to v.21 above, that *the stones represented the twelve tribes of Israel*. These tribes together embodied the collective of God's people under the Old Covenant. (Notice the stones were engraved like a seal, for that term has been important in Revelation.) The high priest wore these stones upon his garment to show that he represented all Israel in performing his ceremonial actions.

As John overlays the template of the high priest's breastplate onto the New Jerusalem wall, the twelve stones do not correspond to the names of Israel's tribes but rather to the twelve apostles.

---

[67] Morris, L. (1987). *Revelation: an introduction and commentary* (Vol. 20, p. 239). Downers Grove, IL: InterVarsity Press.

These twelve provided the apostolic witness and teaching that are the gospel foundation for the Church:

> **Ephesians 2:19–22**
> **19** So, then, you are no longer foreigners and strangers, but fellow citizens with the saints, and members of God's household, **20** built on the foundation of the apostles and prophets, with Christ Jesus himself as the cornerstone. **21** In him the whole building, being put together, grows into a holy temple in the Lord. **22** In him you are also being built together for God's dwelling in the Spirit.

Taken together, this means that the jewels of the New Jerusalem wall represent the totality of God's people embodied in the Church. Under the Old Covenant, only the high priest could come into God's nearest presence, the Most Holy Place. The rest came only by proxy of the breastplate. Under the New Covenant, Christ gained access for all God's people to draw near through his blood (Heb 10:10). Now, in the final state of the New Jerusalem, this theological truth is depicted as fully realized. All God's people from all the ages will forever enjoy the nearness of his presence.

The correlation of the wall jewels to the breastplate jewels ties in another aspect of symbolism already mentioned regarding the city's dimensions. Beale explains:

> "The logic in transferring the jewels of the breastpiece to the city-temple's wall and foundations lies partly in the fact that Aaron's garments in general were meant to be a small replica of the earthly tabernacle, which itself was modeled on the heavenly tabernacle. And even the bejewelled breastpiece was intended to be a scaled-down version of the holy of holies (where God's shekinah glory dwelt), which itself was to be a reflection of the heavenly holy of holies. The breastpiece was made of the same material and formed in the same square shape as the holy of holies."[68]

This reinforces the idea that the wall of the New Jerusalem, in reflecting the breastplate which reflected the Holy of Holies, is meant to communicate that all believers will forever have the priestly privilege of being in God's presence. Given Revelation's backdrop of persecution as a believer's offering, this makes good sense of Peter's comments in 1 Peter 2:4–5:

> **4** As you come to him, a living stone—rejected by people but chosen and honored by God—**5** you yourselves, as living stones, a spiritual house, are being built to be a holy priesthood to offer spiritual sacrifices acceptable to God through Jesus Christ.

John's vision in ch.21 is depicting the eternal blessing of the priesthood of the believer. We see our eternal privilege of serving God in his direct presence.

---

[68] Beale, G. K. (1999). _The book of Revelation: a commentary on the Greek text_ (p. 1081). Grand Rapids, MI; Carlisle, Cumbria: W.B. Eerdmans; Paternoster Press.

The New Heaven, the New Earth, and the New Jerusalem

The depictions of the twelve gates in the walls as being of pearls is another symbol of great value and beauty. Thomas wrote: "Among the ancients, pearls were ranked highest among precious stones, because their beauty derives entirely from nature, improvement by human workmanship being an impossibility..."[69] Besides this, there is probably an ancient Jewish expectation behind what John sees. Morris explains:

> "There is a rabbinic statement: 'The Holy One, blessed be He, will in time to come bring precious stones and pearls which are thirty (cubits) by thirty and will cut out from them (openings) ten (cubits) by twenty, and will set them up in the gates of Jerusalem' (Baba Bathra 75a)."[70]

If such expectations were in mind, then the New Jerusalem far exceeds them.

All of these connections to precious and beautiful jewels and stones further provides a contrast to the false beauty of the whore Babylon. Many see an ancient judgment against the king of Tyre as depicting the foil of Rv 21, for when God is rejected, beauty is lost. This prophecy against this king may be a possible back story for Satan himself:

Ezekiel 28:12–15
12 "Son of man, lament for the king of Tyre and say to him, 'This is what the Lord GOD says:

> You were the seal of perfection,
> full of wisdom and perfect in beauty.
> **13** You were in Eden, the garden of God.
> Every kind of precious stone covered you:
> carnelian, topaz, and diamond,
> beryl, onyx, and jasper,
> lapis lazuli, turquoise and emerald.
> Your mountings and settings were crafted in gold;
> they were prepared on the day you were created.
> **14** You were an anointed guardian cherub,
> for I had appointed you.
> You were on the holy mountain of God;
> you walked among the fiery stones.
> **15** From the day you were created
> you were blameless in your ways
> until wickedness was found in you.

---

[69] Constable, T. (2003). *Tom Constable's Expository Notes on the Bible* (Re 21:21). Galaxie Software.
[70] Morris, L. (1987). *Revelation: an introduction and commentary* (Vol. 20, p. 241). Downers Grove, IL: InterVarsity Press.

The Revelation of Jesus Christ

Remember that Revelation is given to spur the believer on to the prize that is true glory. To abandon faith is to lose out on these blessings, which is a tragedy on par with what Ezekiel prophesied above. How terrible to give up such a treasure as is depicted in this New Jerusalem!

Since the PFG calls the believer to serve faithfully in suffering, how would this promise of eternally serving in joy and glory be an encouragement?

The Temple and the Glory

If the correlation between the Most Holy Place and the New Jerusalem were not already clear enough, what John writes next is over the top:

> **Rev 21:22-27**
> **22** I did not see a temple in it, because the Lord God the Almighty and the Lamb are its temple. **23** The city does not need the sun or the moon to shine on it, because the glory of God illuminates it, and its lamp is the Lamb. **24** The nations will walk by its light, and the kings of the earth will bring their glory into it. **25** Its gates will never close by day because it will never be night there. **26** They will bring the glory and honor of the nations into it. **27** Nothing unclean will ever enter it, nor anyone who does what is detestable or false, but only those written in the Lamb's book of life.

All of the symbolism comes to a clear explicit statement. This new dwelling for the Christ-follower does not *have* a temple because it *is* the temple. God's presence and his light permeate the whole new creation, and the focus is the Lamb.

Beale shows how this new reality fulfills OT prophecies:

> "Hag. 2:9 prophesied that "the latter glory of this house will be greater than the former," and Jer. 3:16–17 predicted that "they will no longer say 'The ark of the covenant of the Lord.' And *it will not come to mind, nor will they remember it,* nor will they miss it, nor will it be made again. At that time they will call Jerusalem 'The throne of the Lord,' and all the nations will be gathered to it, to the name of the Lord in Jerusalem." The italicized words are repeated almost verbatim in Isa. 65:17 (which is alluded to in Rev. 21:1, 4)."[71]

Beale goes on to point out that this new temple reality encompassing the entirety of the new cosmos breaks out of a pre-Christian expectation of a physical temple in heaven:

---

[71] Beale, G. K. (1999). *The book of Revelation: a commentary on the Greek text* (pp. 1090–1091). Grand Rapids, MI; Carlisle, Cumbria: W.B. Eerdmans; Paternoster Press.

The New Heaven, the New Earth, and the New Jerusalem

"The primary reason that John throughout 21:9–22:5 excludes most of the detailed descriptions of the Ezekiel 40–48 temple and its ordinances is because he understands it as fulfilled in God and Christ's presence and not in a physical structure. This expectation of a nonliteral temple is, for the most part, a break with Judaism, which consistently affirmed the hope of a final, material temple structure on a scale greater than any before."[72]

The expectations of Judaism were grand, but not grand enough. Jesus had already begun to prepare believers to expect this shift from a mere physical temple to a better one. In Jn 2:19 he introduced the idea that he himself was the temple. That new truth finds full expression in this New Jerusalem.

The statements of vv.23-25 fulfill Isaiah's prophecy:

Isaiah 60:19–20
19 The sun will no longer be your light by day,
and the brightness of the moon will not shine on you.
The LORD will be your everlasting light,
and your God will be your splendor.
20 Your sun will no longer set,
and your moon will not fade;
for the LORD will be your everlasting light,
and the days of your sorrow will be over.

John has written much about light. It is a primary theme of the prologue to his Gospel. In these verses about the new heavens and new earth he uses light to communicate that God's glory utterly permeates everything. God's light is everywhere, and all men walk by it. This picture stands in stark contrast to the scenes of this present world, where God's glory filling the temple made it impossible for man to enter (Ex 40:35; 2 Chr 7:2). Now the temple is everywhere, and all mankind are in it, completely surrounded and illuminated by God's presence.

How does the statement of Rv 21:22 connect to the PFG?

When John writes that the kings of the earth will "bring their glory into" the city, he probably means that even the most glorious (and by extension all people) will give homage to God. No one can add to God's glory, but he has created mankind in his image to reflect that glory. This extends

---

[72] Beale, G. K. (1999). *The book of Revelation: a commentary on the Greek text* (p. 1091). Grand Rapids, MI; Carlisle, Cumbria: W.B. Eerdmans; Paternoster Press.

the idea that we are all servants to the king, offering ourselves in worship to reflect his glory, particularly Christ's glory as King of Kings.

This picture of worship pilgrimage is on a grand scale, for the temple of the new world will be served by all the nations (vv.24,26). It is characterized by total purity and security (v.27). It is also characterized by freedom, as the open gates show (v.25, cf. 2 Cor 3:17). Notice once again the emphasis that no one "who does what is detestable or false" will ever enter it. The purity of worship in this New Jerusalem serves as a warning against false worship in the present age.

How do these themes of purity and security relate to the PFG?

The River and the Tree: Life and Healing

If you have wondered if we are supposed to think that God is an urbanite, that he has abandoned the Garden project of Genesis in the new heavens and earth, then read on:

> **Revelation 22:1-3**
> **1** Then he showed me the river of the water of life, clear as crystal, flowing from the throne of God and of the Lamb **2** down the middle of the city's main street. The tree of life was on each side of the river, bearing twelve kinds of fruit, producing its fruit every month. The leaves of the tree are for healing the nations, **3** and there will no longer be any curse.

It is a common strategy in large metroplexes like our own New York City to offset the hard, cold bones of skyscrapers, streets, and sidewalks with the gentle, refreshing skin of city parks, green zones, water walks and trails. New Jerusalem does far more than that. This city has something far better than Central Park. It has the river of the water of life flowing down Main Street, and it has the tree of life producing its fruit all around. It seems God is bringing the Garden of Eden back forever, and on a grander scale, in his eternal City.

Remember, these descriptions may well be literal, but even assuming they are, they are communicating symbolically to tell us what the new cosmos and our eternal existence are like. These depictions fulfill what OT prophets saw (e.g., Zec 14:8), especially the description Ezekiel gave of a river flowing out from the temple and expanding as it went, bringing life everywhere (ch.47:1-9). In fact, the parallel language of Ezekiel's temple vision seems to be in John's mind when he records what he sees in his revelation of the New Jerusalem.

The language of life-giving water may draw from what Jesus said in Jn 7 about the Holy Spirit:

The New Heaven, the New Earth, and the New Jerusalem

John 7:37–39
37 On the last and most important day of the festival, Jesus stood up and cried out, "If anyone is thirsty, let him come to me and drink. **38** The one who believes in me, as the Scripture has said, will have streams of living water flow from deep within him." **39** He said this about the Spirit. Those who believed in Jesus were going to receive the Spirit, for the Spirit had not yet been given because Jesus had not yet been glorified.

If this metaphor is in mind, it would reflect a Christian doctrine that the Spirit proceeds from the Father and the Son.[73] Closely related is the truth that Jesus told the Samaritan woman at the well: "…whoever drinks from the water that I will give him will never get thirsty again. In fact, the water I will give him will become a well of water springing up in him for eternal life" (Jn 4:14). Whatever the case, this river of life clearly reflects upon the truth that true life comes eternally from and through fellowship with God.

The water metaphor, along with the statement of Rv 21:27, also echoes Is 35:6-10:

> **6** Then the lame will leap like a deer,
> and the tongue of the mute will sing for joy,
> for water will gush in the wilderness,
> and streams in the desert;
> **7** the parched ground will become a pool,
> and the thirsty land, springs.
> In the haunt of jackals, in their lairs,
> there will be grass, reeds, and papyrus.
> **8** A road will be there and a way;
> it will be called the Holy Way.
> The unclean will not travel on it,
> but it will be for the one who walks the path.
> Fools will not wander on it.
> **9** There will be no lion there,
> and no vicious beast will go up on it;
> they will not be found there.
> But the redeemed will walk on it,
> **10** and the ransomed of the LORD will return
> and come to Zion with singing,
> crowned with unending joy.
> Joy and gladness will overtake them,
> and sorrow and sighing will flee.

---

[73] Beale, G. K. (1999). *The book of Revelation: a commentary on the Greek text* (p. 1104). Grand Rapids, MI; Carlisle, Cumbria: W.B. Eerdmans; Paternoster Press.

Besides the water of life, the New Jerusalem also has the tree of life, and once again there is an amplification. The tree of life was present in the center of Eden's garden. Now it is multiple, and its fruit plentiful. According to Morris, the twelve "kinds of fruit" in the CSB are better understood as *twelve crops of fruit* (i.e. twelve crops in succession, not twelve kinds of fruit).[74] That this fruit brings "healing to the nations" may be interpreted as "health-giving" if the ongoing status of those in the city is that of well-being. Otherwise, the number twelve is key in understanding this effect to symbolize the complete healing of all the previous world's ills, as Beale states:

> "A total of twelve months of fruitbearing together with "twelve kinds [or "crops"] of fruits" in 22:2 reinforces the repeated multiples of twelve already used in the vision to highlight fullness of redemptive provision. Therefore, the best conclusion is that the healing effect of the fruit is figurative for the redemption accomplished by Christ, which will be consummated at his final parousia."[75]

As the descriptions pile on, it seems more and more likely that this New Jerusalem is intended as a metaphor for the entire new creation. Absolute purity and security; the pervading glory of God everywhere; the direct and immediate presence of God with man; eternal life and well-being – these certainly describe the totality of the final state for the believer, not simply a particular municipality in it.

The Throne and the Light

In all of this amazing splendor and blessing, the focus is especially on the Lamb:

> The throne of God and of the Lamb will be in the city, and his servants will worship him. **4** They will see his face, and his name will be on their foreheads. **5** Night will be no more; people will not need the light of a lamp or the light of the sun, because the Lord God will give them light, and they will reign forever and ever.

This is the second time already in ch.22 where John mentions "the throne of God and of the Lamb" (the other is in v.1). This is one throne and one rule by one God, though both Father and Son occupy the throne (3:21; 7:17).

That there is no more curse (v.3) would speak to the removal of both physical and spiritual evils, including the very challenges facing the Church in John's day and thereafter. God's servants are healed and sustained by relating with him face to face in a way Moses could only imagine (v.5).

The images of Eden reflected in this eternal paradise may come together to explain what is meant that God's faithful will "reign forever and ever." If we are all servants to the Lord in eternal worship, over whom or what might we be reigning? We do know that we will stand with Christ in

---

[74] Morris, L. (1987). *Revelation: an introduction and commentary* (Vol. 20, p. 243). Downers Grove, IL: InterVarsity Press.
[75] Beale, G. K. (1999). *The book of Revelation: a commentary on the Greek text* (p. 1108). Grand Rapids, MI; Carlisle, Cumbria: W.B. Eerdmans; Paternoster Press.

The New Heaven, the New Earth, and the New Jerusalem

judgment over the ungodly and the angels (1 Cor 6:3), but that seems to occur before the eternal state, though the punishment for rebellion will extend forever. A simple answer may be that this phrase merely communicates our exalted status in sharing in royalty as adopted children.

Beale presents another reasonable possibility. This reigning by the saints may well be a restoration of Adam's original mandate to rule over the earth. In support of this, it seems that the Garden of Eden was the first "temple" where God dwelled with man. Apart from the Fall, man's representative rule would have extended to the whole world, and thus would have extended God's representative presence as well. This seems to be what we find described here in the new eternal economy. "What Adam failed to do, Revelation pictures Christ as finally having done. The Edenic imagery beginning in Rev. 22:1 reflects an intention to show that the building of the temple, which began in Genesis 2, will be completed in Christ and his people and will encompass the whole new creation."[76]

What an amazing picture! The whole universe the temple of God, and redeemed saints with full access. Every action everywhere a worship service. Purity and unity. Life and light and joy. Exercising our unique gifts in reigning with Christ as we were created to do.

Commentator William Newell reminds us that while this amazing city symbolizes Revelation's goal, its function is to keep our eyes free from distraction along the way:

> "We do well to return again and again to Revelation 21 and 22, for it is the end of the pilgrim path. The more distinct the vision to the pilgrim of the beauty and glory of the city to which he journeys, the less the immediate environments of his journey attract him."[77]

Beale affirms this same idea, pointing even more clearly to the PFG:

> *This final vision of the book concerning these same five themes—new covenant, new temple, new Israel, new Jerusalem, and new creation—is also the climax and the expression of the main point of the Apocalypse thus far. But it is not the main point of the whole book. Why is this vision placed at the end of the book? It is here to underscore the ultimate basis for John's final goal and purpose in writing: to exhort God's people to remain faithful.*[78]

---

[76] Beale, G. K. (1999). *The book of Revelation: a commentary on the Greek text* (p. 1111). Grand Rapids, MI; Carlisle, Cumbria: W.B. Eerdmans; Paternoster Press.
[77] Constable, T. (2003). *Tom Constable's Expository Notes on the Bible* (Re 22:5). Galaxie Software.
[78] Beale, G. K. (1999). *The book of Revelation: a commentary on the Greek text* (pp. 1119–1120). Grand Rapids, MI; Carlisle, Cumbria: W.B. Eerdmans; Paternoster Press.

The Revelation of Jesus Christ

Reflecting on the new heavens and earth and New Jerusalem, what ways has Jesus Christ been revealed in this vision?

In this lesson, what reminders have we seen that the Christian must hold fast to faith in Christ?

Which descriptions of the eternal blessing for the believer had the greatest impact on you?

Lesson 18: Testimony, Blessing, Warning, and Invitation (Ch.22, Vv.6-21)

Reaffirming the PFG

We have worked so hard to stay anchored to the PFG that by now you may feel like rolling your eyes at the mention of it. But as John brings this testimony to its conclusion by neatly tying up the strands of its themes, he restates the purpose, function and goal throughout this last chapter:

> **Revelation 22:6–7**
> **6** Then he said to me, "These words are faithful and true. The Lord, the God of the spirits of the prophets, has sent his angel to show his servants what must soon take place."
>
> **7** "Look, I am coming soon! Blessed is the one who keeps the words of the prophecy of this book."

There are a remarkable number of statements in ch.21 about the authority of this testimony, and the angel's affirmation in v.6 reflects the authority and surety of Christ himself in borrowing from that title of the Rider in 19:11. Jesus is the Faithful and True One (see also 3:14), and these words from and about him are faithful and true. Once again, the testimony of Jesus is expressed as the spirit of all prophecy (19:10).

How do vv.6-7 above express each of the three elements of the PFG?

Testimony, Blessing and Warning

From John
Now that the PFG has been reaffirmed, John ties back to the prologue in terms of reverse engineering the chain of transmission of this testimony. He starts with his own apostolic authority:

> **8** I, John, am the one who heard and saw these things.

From the Angel
Then John moves to the authoritative angel through whom God has mediated this Revelation. This angel is so closely associated with the Lord that John seems to mistake him for God himself:

The Revelation of Jesus Christ

> When I heard and saw them, I fell down to worship at the feet of the angel who had shown them to me. **9** But he said to me, "Don't do that! I am a fellow servant with you, your brothers the prophets, and those who keep the words of this book. Worship God!"

This is the second time John makes this mistake, and the wording is very similar to the other occasion in 19:10. In both cases the angel puts off John's worship on the basis that he is "a fellow servant" with John. Likewise, in both cases the angel asserts the importance of prophetic witness – specifically the witness of Jesus in this book – in protecting John (and all other believers) from misplaced worship.

How does this situation show the humility of both John and the angel? How does this humility contrast with the beast and those who worship him?

Revelation echoes the OT prophets, and none of them more remarkably than Daniel. When Daniel was given visions of the end of the age, he was told to seal up those visions:

> **Daniel 8:26**
> **26** The vision of the evenings and the mornings
> that has been told is true.
> Now you are to seal up the vision
> because it refers to many days in the future."

> **Daniel 12:4**
> **4** "But you, Daniel, keep these words secret and seal the book until the time of the end. Many will roam about, and knowledge will increase."

John was told NOT to seal up his vision.

> **Rv 22:10** Then he said to me, "Don't seal up the words of the prophecy of this book, because the time is near. **11** Let the unrighteous go on in unrighteousness; let the filthy still be filthy; let the righteous go on in righteousness; let the holy still be holy."

What seems to be the reason why Daniel's visions were to be sealed while John's were to remain unsealed? How might that relate to the breaking of the seven seals by the Lamb in this book (5:1-8:5)?

Testimony, Blessing, Warning, and Invitation

In Daniel's time, no one was yet authorized to unseal the prophecies. In Revelation, Jesus has been shown to be worthy to break the seals of God's ancient plan. The difference is the time. Now that Christ has ascended to his throne, the seals may be opened. The fact that John is told to leave his prophecy *unsealed* indicates that he was (and we are) living in the "time of the end."

As the angel goes on, we are reminded that the testimony about Jesus is the basis for sorting out the faithful from the unrighteous. Those who are inclined to false worship will gravitate toward the deception of the dragon, beast, and false prophet. They will be lured by the corruption of the prostitute Babylon. The true believers will emerge in their faithfulness and show themselves holy.

From Jesus

John completes the chain now to show that the testimony of this letter has not only come to him through the angel but that it comes from God as the testimony of Christ himself, who now speaks directly once again:

> **12** "Look, I am coming soon, and my reward is with me to repay each person according to his work. **13** I am the Alpha and the Omega, the first and the last, the beginning and the end.
> **14** "Blessed are those who wash their robes, so that they may have the right to the tree of life and may enter the city by the gates. **15** Outside are the dogs, the sorcerers, the sexually immoral, the murderers, the idolaters, and everyone who loves and practices falsehood.
> **16** "I, Jesus, have sent my angel to attest these things to you for the churches. I am the root and descendant of David, the bright morning star."

The Greek term translated "reward" can carry negative or positive meaning. This ties strongly to the White Throne Judgment of the end of ch.20. Christians are saved by faith in Christ alone. The verb "wash" (v.14) is a present active, literally "those who are washing their robes." Still, their righteous work based on that washing – their faithful deeds – this work is rewarded. The unbelievers are "rewarded" for their work in light of their rejection of Christ. The righteous live by faith, but the unrighteous pay for their faithless work forever.

Notice again in vv.14-15 the absolute purity and security of the "city" where the blessed live forever with God. Insider and outsider are defined by trust in or rejection of Christ, the Alpha and Omega (v.13). The titles of vv.13 and 16 echo those throughout the book, and particularly those given in Jesus' addresses to the churches in chs.2-3. This connection is strengthened as Jesus affirms that this Revelation is to be circulated to all churches.

How do these verses again assert the PFG? How do they encourage YOU to remain faithful?

The Revelation of Jesus Christ

Invitation from the Spirit and the Bride

In the next verse it seems that the text shifts back from the voice of Jesus to that of John, but it is to issue an invitation that comes from more than only him:

> **17** Both the Spirit and the bride say, "Come!" Let anyone who hears, say, "Come!" Let the one who is thirsty come. Let the one who desires take the water of life freely.

This invitation is said first to come from two entities, the Spirit and the bride. We already understand that the bride represents the faithful saints of all the ages, who now make up the Church. The voice of this invitation is one. The Spirit-inspired Church breathes it out. The next description seems to also describe the Church but with a focus on individual believers, "anyone who hears." Only true believers truly "hear," and anyone of them says, "Come!" So, the invitation comes from the Spirit-filled Church collectively and from Spirit-filled Christians individually.

This invitation goes out to those who will show themselves to be true believers. Only true believers will thirst after Christ (Jn 4:14; 6:35; 7:37; Rv 21:6). Only true Christians will desire the water of life. Does the invitation go out to all, or only to all who will believe? That question has been around for the entire Church Age, and the answers always have to do with how one explains the mysterious inter-relationship between God's sovereignty and man's free will. The greater biblical witness seems to indicate that all are invited to repentance, but certainly many do not heed that invitation. Understanding this invitation may seem even more challenging in light of earlier statements in this chapter.

Fatalistic Determination, or Free Invitation?

In vv.10-11 it sounds like the categories are set. Those destined for righteousness will trust and obey Christ, and those destined for destruction will continue to rebel. Then in v.17 it sounds like the categories are *not* set. Why would there be an invitation to come take of the water of life (which is now only accessible to the righteous), if it were not possible to repent and believe?

This apparent paradox reaches back to the question we asked in the beginning of the study. *In what sense is something new being revealed about Jesus?* It also connects once again to the PFG of the book: **to reveal Jesus Christ so that his servants faithfully endure suffering in order to receive blessing.** How so?

If Jesus is being revealed in this book, it is to the Christians but not only to them. He is also revealed *through* them. We have seen that the primary function of the book is to encourage Christians to remain faithful in spite of temptations to hide, corrupt or even reject their faith. Still, there are several indications – and this invitation so late in the book in 22:17 is the strongest – that Jesus Christ is also being revealed to the entire cosmos with at least the possibility of engaging a similar function, that of repentance.

Testimony, Blessing, Warning, and Invitation

How many generations already have had access to this text? For each one, the hearer has had the opportunity to *keep* these words. Anyone who approaches this revelation *without* faith has had opportunity to see Christ revealed, to hear the invitation to faith and to respond with repentance and belief. The urgency to do so is heightened by "soon" (vv.6,7,12,20) and "near" (v.10). John echoes Paul's urgent plea for the Corinthians to heed the gospel invitation: "Now is the acceptable time; now is the day of salvation!" (2 Cor 6:1-3).

It is the responsibility of the Church and of individual Christians to broadcast this invitation, for we are not yet to that moment of Christ's return. It is still "soon" to come. We still have daylight to work before the night comes (Jn 9:4). We do not know who will turn out to be thirsty for Christ, the Water of Life. Like John we issue the invitation to all, so the truly thirsty will come.

Has this Revelation challenged you to faithfully issue this invitation to Christ? If so, how?

Testimony of Warning Against Loss of Blessing

Having voiced this invitation, John circles back once again to PFG themes, but this time the function of keeping the words of this prophecy is expressed in a stern warning:

> **18** I testify to everyone who hears the words of the prophecy of this book: If anyone adds to them, God will add to him the plagues that are written in this book. **19** And if anyone takes away from the words of the book of this prophecy, God will take away his share of the tree of life and the holy city, which are written about in this book.

With the term "plagues" in v.18 John makes a strong connection back to the plague judgments of the seals (6:8), trumpets (9:18,20), and especially the bowls (15:1,6,8; 16:9,21). There is also a direct connection to the plagues that come upon the harlot Babylon as judgment for her deception and violence (18:4,8). This connection heightens the likelihood that all those realities are in play to some degree throughout the church age and not only the very end of it.

The twofold curse of vv.18-19 (adding to or taking away from) here correlates to faithfulness regarding the words of this book. The "anyone" of v.19 makes it clear that these plagues will come upon those who mishandle the truth from John's day forward. The cursed will have plagues piled on and blessings lost, and they may be found both inside and outside the church.

Adding to or taking away from Scripture is accursed because it is a crime of the highest order. This is affirmed even in OT Wisdom literature:

The Revelation of Jesus Christ

Proverbs 30:4–6
4 Who has gone up to heaven and come down?
Who has gathered the wind in his hands?
Who has bound up the waters in a cloak?
Who has established all the ends of the earth?
What is his name,
and what is the name of his son—
if you know?
5 Every word of God is pure;
he is a shield to those who take refuge in him.
6 Don't add to his words,
or he will rebuke you, and you will be proved a liar.

The penalty for mishandling God's word is the very reason that James warns that those who teach it will be judged for how they did so (Jas 3:1). There is no mistaking the severity of John's warning in Rv 22. The corruption of the truth about Jesus results in the loss of eternal life!

How does this warning affect how you go about witnessing to invite others to trust in Christ?

Testimony, Longing, and Blessing
In vv.18-19, John is emphasizing the prophetic nature of this Revelation by warning the reader/listener to heed and keep its words. Now, in the last two verses, he shifts his focus:

20 He who testifies about these things says, "Yes, I am coming soon."
Amen! Come, Lord Jesus!

21 The grace of the Lord Jesus be with everyone. Amen.

We are reminded of the unique genre blend of Revelation, that while it is full of apocalyptic images and symbols and prophetic warnings, it is also a letter meant to be circulated among all the churches to bless them. It is appropriate, then, that John again affirms the highest authority by which he writes – that of Christ himself (v.20). This bookends neatly with the prologue, where John testified that God gave this Revelation to John by an angel (1:1); that it comes with the very authority of the Father "who is, who was, and who is to come" and of the Son, "Jesus Christ, who is the faithful witness, the firstborn from the dead and the ruler of the kings of the earth" (1:4-5).

Then John offers his own personal closing. He affirms the totality of this Revelation that has come to him with a simple but solemn apostolic "Amen!" To this he adds the statement of his own personal longing for his Savior: "Come quickly, Lord Jesus."

Testimony, Blessing, Warning, and Invitation

To feel the weight of this longing, recall that John was a close friend to Jesus during his earthly ministry, and that he was charged by Jesus *from the cross* to take in his mother, Mary, as his own. John was one of the three who got a glimpse of the glorified Christ upon the mountain. He is in exile at the time of this letter because of his testimony about this same Jesus. And now he has been given this Revelation of the glories that await him when his Lord, his Savior, his Friend comes back to judge the wicked and renew the whole world. Can you imagine the eagerness behind John's words after all he has seen? *Yes! Bring it on! I'm ready!*

Has this Revelation impacted your own longing for Christ's return? If so, how?

But John, more than any other of the apostles, is aware that these things come in God's timing and that the Christ-follower can only wait in readiness. It is for this very reason he is writing now, to help others do that very thing. So, he bookends the letter not only with his apostolic authority but with his pronouncement of blessing. He does so with a customary farewell: "The grace of our Lord Jesus be with everyone."

Since John's own blessing concludes this letter, and since blessing is its goal, it is worth recapping how blessing has been a major theme. John records seven blessings in this book:

Revelation 1:3
3 Blessed is the one who reads aloud the words of this prophecy, and blessed are those who hear the words of this prophecy and keep what is written in it, because the time is near.

Revelation 14:13
13 Then I heard a voice from heaven saying, "Write: Blessed are the dead who die in the Lord from now on."
"Yes," says the Spirit, "so they will rest from their labors, since their works follow them."

Revelation 16:15
15 "Look, I am coming like a thief. Blessed is the one who is alert and remains clothed so that he may not go around naked and people see his shame."

The Revelation of Jesus Christ

Revelation 19:9
9 Then he said to me, "Write: Blessed are those invited to the marriage feast of the Lamb!" He also said to me, "These words of God are true."

Revelation 20:6
6 Blessed and holy is the one who shares in the first resurrection! The second death has no power over them, but they will be priests of God and of Christ, and they will reign with him for a thousand years.

Revelation 22:7
7 "Look, I am coming soon! Blessed is the one who keeps the words of the prophecy of this book."

Revelation 22:14
14 "Blessed are those who wash their robes, so that they may have the right to the tree of life and may enter the city by the gates.

What brings blessing in each case, and what is symbolized by the fact there are seven of them?

Conclusion

This Revelation of Jesus Christ is now complete, though we wait for many of its events to unfold completely. The Scriptures have not only revealed Jesus as the Suffering Servant, but now as the glorious King of Kings and Lord of Lords who is coming soon to extend his reign to all creation. In his absolute sovereignty, God has already inaugurated Christ as ruler over all, raising him to his heavenly throne. He is restraining the deceptive and oppressive work of Satan until the last believer has heard and kept the words about Jesus, offering himself or herself as a living sacrifice even to the point of physical martyrdom.

Jesus is coming soon. Until that day, he has given us this Revelation of himself so that we may understand that his coming is sure and that he will judge everyone and then will bring his faithful into the blessing of eternal life in his presence. We will live together in worship of and service for our God, in incorruptible resurrection bodies. If we will cling to Christ through John's true testimony, if we will faithfully endure whatever suffering the enemy brings upon us, we will enjoy all the blessings of Eden in the greater Eden of the New Jerusalem.

Union, fellowship, comfort, peace, rest, security and eternal life. May this Revelation accomplish its purpose to deepen our commitment to endure whatever temporary suffering we must, so that we come to our final goal and enjoy these eternal blessings in and with the One who calls us!

Testimony, Blessing, Warning, and Invitation

O Courts

O courts of earth and heaven above
I testify of grace and love
My one defense, my only plea
Is Jesus Christ who died for me

I was a wretch, a child of wrath
A slave to sin and bound for death
By nature, spoiled, by choice the same
I stumbled on in sin and shame
Then came a Light I had not known
In dead of night was glory shown
I was exposed, my soul laid bare
Before the Source who met me there

This glorious Light established all
These are His courts, His love is law
He is the Judge, His standard sure
His Lasting Life forever pure
The sentence rang, my soul despaired
Alone as death hung in the air
Then at the last, my one escape
In perfect love He took my place!

All rise, all rise before the Honorable Jesus Christ!

I cannot know to full extent
The depths of love my Savior spent
But what I know I will proclaim
My life is bound to Jesus' Name
In Him I rise to join the song
Of those redeemed from heaven's throng
No more alone, we cry as one:
"All glory be to God alone!"

I'll rise, I'll rise before the Honorable Jesus Christ!

O courts of earth and heaven above
I testify of grace and love
My one defense, my only plea
Is Jesus Christ who set me free

About the Author

Benjamin Gum holds a Master of Theological Studies degree from Midwestern Baptist Theological Seminary (MBTS). He blogs at bengum.blogspot.com. He is also a musician and songwriter. Gum has been in vocational ministry for over 25 years, serving as pastor, teacher, worship leader, music teacher, and small group leader. He currently serves as a pastor in the western suburbs of Kansas City and continues to write worship songs for the church. At this writing, Benjamin and his wife, Dawna, have four adult children and twelve grandchildren. They have also fostered nearly ninety boys.

Other works by this author include similar workbook studies titled **Job: The Cry of the Righteous Sufferer** and **Hebrews: The Superior Son and the Exhortation to Endure**. Gum has also written **Making Disciples**, a basic discipleship tool, as well as **Skinny Jeans Fat Shoes**, a challenge aimed primarily at worship leaders. (See back cover.)

www.ingramcontent.com/pod-product-compliance
Lightning Source LLC
LaVergne TN
LVHW061253060426
835507LV00020B/2307